Equity and Difference in Physical Education, Youth Sport and Health: A Narrative Approach

Equity remains an essential theme throughout the study and practice of physical education (PE), youth sport and health. This important new book confronts and illuminates issues of equity and difference through the innovative use of narrative method, telling stories of difference that enable students, academics and professionals alike to engage both emotionally and cognitively with the subject.

The book is arranged into three sections. The first provides an overview of current theory and research on difference and inequality in PE, youth sport and health, together with an introduction to narrative forms of knowing. The second section includes short narratives about difference that bring to life the key themes and issues in a range of physical activity contexts. The third section draws upon a selection of narratives to offer detailed, practical suggestions for how they might be used in, or inform, teaching sessions.

This is the first book to explore issues of equity through narrative, and the first to examine the pedagogical value of a narrative approach within PE, youth sport and health. With contributions from many of the world's leading equity specialists, it will be invaluable reading for all students, scholars and professionals working in PE, youth sport, health, sports development, gender studies and mainstream education programmes.

Fiona Dowling is Associate Professor at the Norwegian School of Sports Sciences. She has worked with teacher education at both undergraduate and postgraduate level for many years, after teaching in schools in England and Norway. Her research interests include teacher professionalism, gender in PE and sport, and qualitative research methodology.

Hayley Fitzgerald is Senior Lecturer at Leeds Metropolitan University, UK. Prior to this she was a researcher at Loughborough University, UK and managed a range of projects supporting young disabled people in PE and youth sport. Hayley has also worked for a number of disability sports organizations in England.

Anne Flintoff is Professor of Physical Education and Sport at Leeds Metropolitan University, UK. Her teaching, research and consultancy centre on issues of equity and social inclusion, particularly gender, in PE and sport. Her recent work has focused on the experiences of black and minority ethnic students in PE teacher education.

Routledge studies in physical education and youth sport

Series Editor: David Kirk, University of Bedfordshire, UK

The *Routledge studies in physical education and youth sport* series is a forum for the discussion of the latest and most important ideas and issues in physical education, sport and active leisure for young people across school, club and recreational settings. The series presents the work of the best well-established and emerging scholars from around the world, offering a truly international perspective on policy and practice. It aims to enhance our understanding of key challenges, to inform academic debate, and to have a high impact on both policy and practice, and is thus an essential resource for all serious students of physical education and youth sport.

Also available in this series:

Children, Obesity and Exercise
A practical approach to prevention, treatment and management of childhood and adolescent obesity
Edited by Andrew P. Hills, Neil A. King and Nuala M. Byrne

Disability and Youth Sport
Edited by Hayley Fitzgerald

Rethinking Gender and Youth Sport
Edited by Ian Wellard

Pedagogy and Human Movement
Richard Tinning

Positive Youth Development Through Sport
Edited by Nicholas Holt

Young People's Voices in PE and Youth Sport
Edited by Mary O'Sullivan and Ann Macphail

Physical Literacy
Throughout the lifecourse
Edited by Margaret Whitehead

Physical Education Futures
David Kirk

Young People, Physical Activity and the Everyday
Living physical activity
Edited by Jan Wright and Doune Macdonald

Muslim Women and Sport
Edited by Tansin Benn, Gertrud Pfister and Haifaa Jawad

Inclusion and Exclusion Through Youth Sport
Edited by Symeon Dagkas and Kathleen Armour

Sport Education
International perspectives
Edited by Peter Hastie

Cooperative Learning in Physical Education
An international perspective
Edited by Ben Dyson and Ashley Casey

Equity and Difference in Physical Education, Youth Sport and Health:
A Narrative Approach
Edited by Fiona Dowling, Hayley Fitzgerald and Anne Flintoff

Equity and Difference in Physical Education, Youth Sport and Health: A Narrative Approach

Edited by
Fiona Dowling, Hayley Fitzgerald
and Anne Flintoff

LONDON AND NEW YORK

First published 2012
by Routledge
2 Park Square, Milton Park, Abingdon, Oxon OX14 4RN

Simultaneously published in the USA and Canada
by Routledge
711 Third Avenue, New York, NY 10017

Routledge is an imprint of the Taylor & Francis Group, an informa business

British Library Cataloguing in Publication Data
A catalogue record for this book is available from the British Library

Library of Congress Cataloging in Publication Data
Equity and difference in physical education, youth sport and health :
a narrative approach / edited by Fiona Dowling, Hayley Fitzgerald and
Anne Flintoff.
p. cm. – (Routledge studies in physical education and youth sport)
Includes bibliographical references and index.
1. Sports for children–Social aspects. 2. Physical education for children–
Social aspects. 3. Discrimination in sports. 4. Sports–Sex differences.
5. Sports for children with disabilities. I. Dowling, Fiona. II. Fitzgerald,
Hayley. III. Flintoff, Anne
GV709.2.E69 2012
372.86–dc23
2011048403

ISBN: 978-0-415-60149-8 (hbk)
ISBN: 978-0-203-13288-3 (ebk)

GV
709.2
.E69
2012

Typeset in Times
by Taylor & Francis Books

Contents

Contributors

Lisette Burrows is an Associate Professor in Physical Education Pedagogy at the School of Physical Education, University of Otago, New Zealand where she has taught for 20 years. Her research is primarily focused on understanding the place and meaning of health and physical culture in young people's lives.

David Carless is a Reader at Leeds Metropolitan University, UK. His interdisciplinary research – which lies at an intersection of psychology, sociology and the arts – uses a variety of narrative and arts-based methods to explore identity and mental health in sport and physical activity contexts.

Kitrina Douglas is a Visiting Fellow at the University of Bristol, UK. Her work communicates a desire to illuminate, explore and understand ethical dilemmas that practitioners face in a variety of physical activity contexts. She is committed to making her research accessible to diverse audiences and to this end uses narrative, creative and performative methodologies.

Fiona Dowling is an Associate Professor in Physical Education at the Norwegian School of Sports Sciences. She has worked with teacher education at both undergraduate and postgraduate level for many years, after teaching in schools in England and Norway. Her research interests include teacher professionalism, gender in physical education and sport, and qualitative research methodology.

Hayley Fitzgerald is a Senior Lecturer at Leeds Metropolitan University, UK. Prior to this she was a researcher at Loughborough University, UK and managed a range of projects supporting young disabled people in physical education and youth sport. Hayley has also worked for a number of disability sports organizations in England.

Anne Flintoff is Professor of Physical Education and Sport at Leeds Metropolitan University, UK. Her teaching, research and consultancy centre on issues of equity and social inclusion, particularly gender, in physical education and sport. Her recent work has focused on the experiences of black and minority ethnic students in physical education teacher education.

Satoko Itani is a doctoral student in the Department of Curriculum, Teaching and Learning at OISE, University of Toronto, Canada. She uses queer and postcolonial theories alongside qualitative narrative research methods. Her research analyzes the construction of, and resistance against, normative and respectable bodies and identities produced through sports and physical education.

Kelly Knez holds a research position with the Qatar Orthopaedic and Sports Medicine Hospital, Doha. Her current research is informed by post-structural and postcolonial theory with a particular focus on the intersections between Islam, Qatari culture, health, physical activity and the body. Kelly is also an Adjunct Lecturer with the University of Queensland, Australia.

lisahunter is a Senior Lecturer/Researcher in the Department of Sport and Leisure at the University of Waikato, New Zealand. Her research focus includes embodied subjectivities and young people, middle years of schooling and cultural analysis of boardsports. Her work is developing around visual ethnographies and narrative.

Doune Macdonald is Professor of Health and Physical Education (HPE) and Head of the School of Human Movement Studies at the University of Queensland, Australia. Her research has built on initial interests in HPE curriculum and teachers' work to look at broader issues of young people, physical activity and culture.

Nate McCaughtry is Director of the Center for School Health and Associate Professor in the Department of Kinesiology, Health and Sport Studies at Wayne State University in Detroit, Michigan, USA. His research focuses on teacher development, critical and socio-cultural issues, and curriculum theory and development.

Catherine Morrison is a Senior Lecturer in Health and Physical Education at the College of Education, University of Otago, New Zealand. Her research involves the examination of culture, social and gender influences on young males with Developmental Coordination Disorder (DCD) and their engagement in physical education and sport.

Kimberly Oliver is Professor of Physical Education Teacher Education in the Department of Human Performance, Dance and Recreation at New Mexico State University in Las Cruces, New Mexico, where she directs the Physical Education Teacher Education Program. Her research focuses on adolescent girls, curriculum and instruction, and student-centred/inquiry-based teacher education.

Dawn Penney is Professor of Physical Education and Sport Pedagogy in the Faculty of Education at the University of Waikato, New Zealand. Dawn has led research projects in the UK and Australia focusing on curriculum development, pedagogy and assessment in physical education. Equity and inclusion remain key agendas for her research.

Emma Rich is a Senior Lecturer in the Department of Education, University of Bath, UK. Her research draws upon the sociology of education, pedagogy, the body and physical culture. Her key publications include *The Medicalization of Cyberspace*; *Education, Disordered Eating and Obesity Discourse: Fat Fabrications*; and *Debating Obesity: Critical Perspectives*.

Antony Rossi is Senior Lecturer with the School of Human Movement Studies at the University of Queensland, Australia. His current interests are in work-based learning in kinesiological and allied health professions and in sport interventions for marginalized groups. He is currently working on a project looking at surfing programmes and Indigenous communities along the eastern seaboard of Australia.

Sheila Scraton is Emeritus Professor at Leeds Metropolitan University, UK, where she taught at both undergraduate and postgraduate levels. Prior to this she taught in secondary schools and in tertiary colleges in England. Her main research interests have been in gender and physical education, sport and leisure; feminist theories; and 'race', ethnicity and racism.

Heather Sykes is an Associate Professor in the Department of Curriculum, Teaching and Learning at OISE, University of Toronto, Canada. Heather teaches courses in queer theory, curriculum theory and qualitative research. Her research uses queer-feminist poststructuralism and psychoanalytic theories to explore issues of social exclusion in physical education, schooling and sport.

Foreword

Richard Tinning

This book makes a long-overdue contribution to our field. In terms of dee-pening our understandings of (in)equity and difference in physical education, youth sport and health, *Equity and Difference in Physical Education, Youth Sport and Health: A Narrative Approach* provides us with both intellectual and emotional understandings. Further, it explores pedagogical possibilities for developing more sensitive and reflective attitudes towards enduring oppressive, marginalizing or inappropriate practice.

A feature of the book is that it takes a stance on knowledge and the way it is represented. There is little doubt that Human Movement Studies (HMS) (Exercise and Sports Science or Kinesiology) as an academic and professional field has long been dominated by bio-physical science knowledge of physical activity, the body and health (Tinning 1996). Significantly, these science dis-ciplines, like all disciplines, are not just content knowledge, they are also ways of thinking about the world. They represent particular ways of knowing. The ways of thinking that science fosters have a privileged place in shaping the attitudes and dispositions of future professionals in our field. On the other hand, socio-cultural knowledge has been relatively marginalized and accordingly less influential.

However, both science and socio-cultural disciplines privilege intellectual, cognitive ways of knowing. They both privilege the rational and the empiri-cal. Other ways of knowing that are somatic, embodied or affective are typi-cally marginalized within these disciplines. Moreover, the ways in which knowledge is represented in journals, books and conference presentations are also a product of certain 'disciplined' ways of thinking. *Equity and Difference in Physical Education, Youth Sport and Health: A Narrative Approach* dis-rupts this privilege in regard to thinking about issues of (in)equity and dif-ference in physical education, youth sport and health. Consequently this collection is both important and innovative.

The narrative and rhetorical devices that we use to tell our stories (repre-sent our work) clearly vary across the disciplines. To some in the field of exercise and sports science/Human Movement Studies, the APA (American Psychological Association) Manual is the gold standard for authorship style. We can understand this as a particular rhetorical style. Of course for many who locate their work in positivist science, there is no rhetoric in the way they write their stories. They are simply reporting in an objective manner, a manner free from the subjectivism of rhetoric. But of course as work in the philosophy of science (see Gross 2006), the sociology of science (see Gilbert and Mulkay 1984), feminist epistemology (see Harding 1991) and our own field of Human Movement Studies (see Sparkes 2002) has revealed, even the best science is reported (represented) using rhetorical devices. There is no escape from this in the act of communication.

So what is going on here? Put simply, there are different perspectives on 'truth telling'. In regard to issues of (in)equity and difference in physical education, health and youth sport we can ask what forms of truth telling are dominant? Whose *voices* are heard in the reporting of issues of (in)equity and difference, and what rhetorical styles are in the storytelling? To pursue this question I want to connect to an article by Dennis Carlson (1998) titled 'Finding a voice, and losing our way?' According to Carlson, finding a voice is not a simple process since we must find three things simultaneously: something to say; a rhetorical style in which to speak and write; and a conversation or 'truth game' to join. Indeed, as he argues, 'there are so many truth games and conversations, each talking about different things, each adhering to its own rules and rhetorical styles, each associated with its own politics' (Carlson 1998: 541). A 'truth game' is a Foucauldian concept referring to a discursive practice that establishes norms regarding who can speak, what they can speak about and the form in which they must speak. Different truth games produce different truths.

Carlson claims that there have been different rhetorical styles in use since the days of ancient Greece. Indeed, Plato's dialogues 'may be read as an attempt to distinguish among different rhetorical styles, and to privilege some over others' (Carlson 1998: 543). The three rhetorical styles or ways of speaking distinguished by Plato include: *logos*, an analytic voice of critique associated with the 'truth games' science and philosophy; *thymos*, a voice of rage at injustice from the perspective and position of the disempowered, the disenfranchised, and the marginalized; and *mythos*, a personal voice of storytelling, cultural mythology, autobiography and literature (Carlson 1998: 543). Of course the exact translation of these terms into modern-day English involves a little 'slippage', but nevertheless the distinction between their main purposes is, I suggest, useful in thinking about which 'truth tales' are dominant in our field.

Importantly, according to Carlson (1998), a major mission of much of Western philosophy, science and education in the modern era has been to privilege the voice of *logos* and accordingly subordinate other ways of speaking that are considered 'less truthful', and which 'can lead us away from the truth' (p. 543). This dominance of *logos* not only has the effect of subordinating other voices but it also renders them less believable. However, we are now in a postmodern context and the postmodern project 'involves the resurfacing and revalorizing of aspects of the human voice that have been suppressed and marginalized in the modern academy' (p. 543).

This book can be thought of as a wonderful example of a postmodern project. The authors represent the new postmodern academic voice. This is

> a hybrid voice that crosses borders, one that interweaves voices of logos, thymos, and mythos and that shifts back and forth from analysis to anecdote, from theory to personal story-telling, from principled talk of social justice to personal and positioned expressions of outrage at injustice.
>
> (Carlson 1998: 543)

There are three distinct parts of this collection: Part I: Theoretical perspectives; Part II: Stories of difference and (in)equity; Part III: Engaging with narratives. Part I sets up the theoretical case for a narrative approach to physical education, youth sport and health. The chapter by Anne Flintoff and Hayley Fitzgerald titled 'Theorizing difference and (in)equality in physical education, youth sport and health' uses the voice of *logos* to make a case for the importance of theorizing. It is a case well made. Fiona Dowling's chapter, 'A narrative approach to research in physical education, youth sport and health', also uses the voice of *logos*, but it does so specifically to advocate for narrative forms that privilege *thymos* and *mythos*. Again the case is well made.

Thymos and *mythos* are the privileged voices of Part II. The fifteen narratives in this section range from what might be classified as realist tales to fictional tales, auto-ethnographic tales, poetic tales and ethno-drama tales (Sparkes 2002). Certainly writing evocative narratives, poems or ethno-dramas is not an easy task. It takes practice and is typically not a voice that sits comfortably with a background in intellectual/academic training. However, it is obvious that the authors of these narratives have managed to do so with competence and flair. They are highly readable stories.

As the editors say, 'narratives [such as these] recognize the role emotions play in how we come to understand our worlds, in addition to cognitive ways of knowing' (p. 3). Each of the authors of the narratives in this section would like their stories to evoke feelings. Feelings are personal, and the extent to which these narratives are successful in this endeavour is something that only the reader can answer.

Part III includes three chapters. In the chapter titled 'Professional development and narrative inquiry', Fiona Dowling uses the voice of *logos* to present a persuasive case that a narrative approach can contribute to, and enhance, professional development. She writes, 'we believe that a narrative approach, including both autobiographical reflection and engagement with Others' stories in education, can contribute to, and enhance, such professional critical reflection and inquiry' (p. 155). Carlson (1998: 553) adds another dimension when he claims that those who argue with what he calls the 'progressive voice' must also be self-reflexive. By this he is referring to the need for them to be 'continuously engaged in critiquing how they speak as much as what they have to say about education and schooling'. Such reflexivity requires an openness to multiple 'truth games', research paradigms and ways of representation.

The remaining two chapters in Part III provide exemplars for how narratives can be interrogated to provide a pedagogical encounter with issues of (in)equity and difference in physical education, youth sport and health. Each exemplar focuses attention on two different narratives from Part II. They do so by means of a deconstructive process that owes much to *logos* and to *thymos*. The deconstruction is a part of what we might call a poststructuralist 'truth game' and it presents a useful pedagogical tool to foster critical reflection and to evoke questions such as 'How could the story be otherwise?' In other words, how could we (the readers) re-script the story as a pedagogical device that enables us to articulate more inclusive practices (see Hickey and Fitzclarence 1999)?

In regard to the new postmodern academic voice, Carlson offers the caution that, in the process of interweaving voices, we may lead to the marginalization of the voice of *logos*, even as the voice of *logos* once marginalized other voices. This is a risk that the authors take. Indeed, this is a risk that must be taken if the marginalized voices *thymos* and *mythos* are to be heard in the discourse of (in)equity and difference in physical education, youth sport and health. The spirited rage against the injustice of certain practices in physical education, youth sport and health is expressed in the voice of *thymos*. Moreover, as Carlson argues,

> Storytelling, autobiography, the use of literary references, and other expressions of a *mythos* voice have enriched progressive discourse, and they have helped make theory much more accessible to a public audience. They also are more honest and truthful rhetorical styles, since they acknowledge the personal that looms behind our theoretical pronouncements.
>
> (Carlson 1998: 553)

Since our field has long been dominated by *logos*, this collection offers an entrée into rhetorical styles not often used. In connecting with the voice of *thymos* the authors engage with ethical claims which, as Carlson points out, 'rarely stand above or totally apart from our own personal experiences, hopes, and fears, for that is the position where rage at injustice and the voice of *thymos* begins' (p. 550). In this regard I would have been interested to know something of where the editors' rage against injustice 'comes from'. While recognizing the constraints of page limits in collections such as this, I still would have liked to read something of their own personal biographies.

In this collection there is a spirited interweaving of voices. However, we are not left with 'merely' personal tales of inequity, injustice or difference. Rather, through the thoughtful exemplars, we are given a powerful pedagogical tool to interrogate the narratives by engaging certain sociological 'truth games'. In addition to the emotional power of the narratives, this is a strength of the collection.

Inside the dust cover of Julie Myerson's wonderful little book, *Not a Games Person* (2005), the publisher's note asserts that 'PE is one of life's great levellers, a uniquely ruthless aspect of school experience which shapes us all and leaves its traces in unexpected and lingering ways'. In my view this collection provides powerful insights into some of these traces, or at least how they develop. These stories have the potential to create empathy in the reader which, in turn, might lead to more thoughtful pedagogical practice. As I have argued elsewhere (see Tinning 2010), the stories we tell of pedagogy in health and physical education (HPE) and youth sport all do pedagogical work by virtue of their substance (what they are about) and the genre used to tell the story. This book puts considerable 'flesh' around this claim. Pedagogical work is not only done through the content, it is also done through the voice or rhetorical style used to convey the content. Such pedagogical work cannot be predicted with any certainty; however, like the editors and contributing authors to this collection, I believe that the chances of genuine praxis (informed, committed action) will be enhanced by such engagement. In terms of deepening our understandings of issues of (in)equity and difference in physical education, youth sport and health, *Equity and Difference in Physical Education, Youth Sport and Health: A Narrative Approach* is indeed both timely and important.

References

Carlson, D. (1998) 'Finding a voice, and losing our way?', *Educational Theory*, 48(4): 541–54.

Gilbert, G. and Mulkay, M. (1984) *Opening Pandora's Box: A Sociological Analysis of Scientists' Discourse*, Cambridge: Cambridge University Press.

Gross, A. (2006) *Starring The Text: The Place of Rhetoric in Science Studies*, Carbondale: Southern Illinois University.

Harding, S. (1991) *Whose Science? Whose Knowledge?* Ithaca, NY: Cornell University Press.

Hickey, C. and Fitzclarence, L. (1999) 'Educating boys: Using narrative methods to develop pedagogies of responsibility', *Sport, Education and Society*, 4(1): 51–62.

Myerson, J. (2005) *Not a Games Person*, London: Yellow Jersey Press.

Sparkes, A. (2002) *Telling Tales in Sport and Physical Activity: A Qualitative Journey*, Champaign, IL: Human Kinetics.

Tinning, R. (1996) 'Orienting discourses in the field of human movement and the problem of professional training' (in Spanish), *Revista de Educación*, 311: 123–34.

——(2010) *Pedagogy and Human Movement: Theory, Practice, Research*, London: Routledge.

Acknowledgements

We would like to thank all those who have made this project possible, from the participants in the many research studies represented in the narratives and the authors of the tales, to colleagues around the globe whose insights and encouragement have been invaluable.

Abbreviations

American Psychological Association (APA)
Australian and New Zealand Army Corps (ANZAC)
Black and minority ethnic (BME)
Body mass index (BMI)
British Broadcasting Corporation (BBC)
Diagnostic and Statistical Manual of Mental Disorders (DSM)
Gender identity disorder (GID)
Health and physical education (HPE)
Maximal oxygen consumption (VO2 max)
Office for Standards in Education, Children's Services and Skills (OFSTED)
Personal, social and health education (PSHE)
Physical education (PE)
Physical education teacher education (PETE)
United Kingdom (UK)
United States (US)
United States of America (USA)

Introduction

This book aims to enliven our professional and research conversations about difference and inequalities in physical education (PE), youth sport and health. Ultimately it has a modest aim to help teachers and coaches to create more inclusive learning environments for young people in physical activity and health contexts, although we are abundantly aware that education for social justice and democracy is a complex project which requires widespread political support from far beyond the boundaries of our field. The book was conceived on account of our sense of frustration at the ways in which issues of difference and inequality seem to be increasingly marginalized in the field of PE and sports science, as well as an acknowledgement about how difficult it is to gain broad acceptance for 'different' ways of knowing.

All three of us have experienced the mechanisms of being silenced in an academy which is once again becoming saturated with 'male', neo-liberal notions of 'what counts' (Hekman 1995). We have felt the professional melancholy described by Evans and Davies (2008), as the discourses of professional flagellation and the pedagogy of despair engulf us during our work with teachers, coaches, students and young people, when we recognize the persistence of inequities despite rhetorical claims to the contrary. We do not concede the view that 'what works' for 'effective' PE teaching or sports coaching can best be gleaned from the physical, biological and behavioural sciences, although we are fully aware that knowledge from these fields has long held a hegemonic place in sports science (Evans and Davies 1986; Tinning 2004, 2010). We respect, of course, these disciplines' contribution to the field of knowledge about the body and human movement, but we believe, like Tinning (2004), that this has regrettably been, and continues to be, at the cost of a focus upon social theory. Young people entering a school gymnasium or a community sports hall are not objects or machines waiting to be tuned, as the commonly used metaphor in the bio-behavioural sciences implies, but they are subjects and their identities need to be acknowledged as central to their learning experience. Teachers and coaches participate in social interaction with their learners, and their actions have social consequences (both intended and unintended); they, therefore, require knowledge about the *social* body, as well as the bio-behavioural body. Teachers and learners are enfleshed, emotional and intellectual beings, and they are inevitably located in social matrixes of power in society within and beyond the arena of physical activity. Despite the way in which slogans such as 'Sport for All' and 'Every Child Matters' readily slip off the tongue, and the long-established idea in the taken-for-granted public consciousness that sport, with its level playing fields, is a social equalizer, statistics and individual experience tell a different story. PE and health classes, and sport, are sites of struggle about competing definitions of what and who counts as worthwhile, where some young people benefit and others lose out because they have the 'wrong' body or lack 'ability' in relation to the dominant values within a given time and context. Ultimately, what goes on in physical activity contexts is 'implicated in social and cultural reproduction and the distribution of power and principles of control' in society at large (Evans and Davies 2004: 4).

During the last three decades a considerable body of knowledge has been developed which can help us to better understand these aspects of 'learning' in PE, health and sport, yet we are concerned that too many important insights into the complexities of 'schooling the body' remain largely within the domain of theoreticians and only fragmentarily filter down into practice. By making this observation we have no intention to apportion any sense of blame; to do so would deny the 'social base of the pedagogic relation, its various contingent realisations, the agents and the agencies of its enactments' (Bernstein 2001: 364, cited in Evans and Davies 2004: 4). Nor do we wish to imply that professionals in the field intend to create inequitable learning environments, because clearly this is preposterous. Moreover, we are complicit in these observations. However, at the same time, we would argue that failure to systematically engage in critical reflection about the values which underpin PE and sport and, in particular, ideas about social difference, can lead to unintended inequitable outcomes. We hope therefore that this book may help to nurture such critical reflection, and via its use of narrative also expand the profession's 'toolkit' for getting to know and better understand 'difference'.

Interest in narrative ways of knowing has grown dramatically in recent times, across the range of subject disciplines, but in spite of its promise as a way of knowing the social world, it has to date remained a relatively little used research approach within the field of PE and sport. We think this is a pity given that narratives can help to illuminate individual experiences located within broader social and cultural structures, and their potential to facilitate professional self-reflection (Barone 1995; Butt *et al.* 1992; Clandinin and Connelly 2000; Day 1999a, 1999b; Goodson 1995; Polkinghorne 1995). Research on teachers, and indeed our many years of experience as teachers, tells us that teaching is always very personal. Our teacher selves cannot be separated from self-identities (Goodson 1995). Who we are, as individual subjects and as teachers, is in fact the story (or stories) we tell to ourselves, and to others, about our lives. In other words, the art of storytelling is something we do on a daily basis in the process of making sense of who we are and what we experience. These self-stories are also a reflection of cultural narratives: about the social spaces we inhabit. Whilst many of us take this aspect of our life for granted – it is just something we do – we suggest we might capitalize upon our skills as storytellers and analysts; it may represent an approach to knowledge which is close to our actual worlds. Like genuine critical reflection in teacher professional development (Day 1999a), a narrative approach to difference in PE and sport is about the past, the present and the future, and it is about 'problem posing', as well as 'problem solving'. It demands a *critique* of practice and the values implicit in that practice, as described above. Importantly, narratives recognize the role emotions play in how we come to understand our worlds, in addition to cognitive ways of knowing. Few would deny that their enthusiasm, or indeed loathing, for physical activity or sport is linked to strong feelings, yet surprisingly little attention has been paid to how these emotions structure embodied experience in the field of PE, health and sport. By engaging in educational storysharing (Barone 1995), both teachers and students can co-construct knowledge about their social worlds, which can counteract the current tendency to marginalize their voices in the neo-liberal 'market place of education' dominated by the discourses of achievement, assessment and accountability.

Like Hargreaves (2003), Hargreaves and Shirley (2009), Lingard (2007) and Sachs (2003), we envisage professionals as people engaged with a broad project of education for social justice and democracy. In a global world increasingly characterized by diversity, mobility and uncertainty, with a rise of xenophobic political climates (e.g. the 'war on terror', 'cracking down' on illegal immigrants) and world economic crisis, the need to recognize and understand difference has perhaps never been as necessary as in the current moment. This need appears to be accentuated in the case of physical educators in the developed world, who persistently comprise a homogeneous, mainly white group of able-bodied people, unlike the increasing social diversity to be found among their students. The gap between the rich and the poor widens in many countries and discrimination on account of gender, sexuality, 'race', religion and/or disability persists despite the passing of many laws of equality. The neo-liberal project of 'meritocracy' has gained global purchase, disguising 'failure' as the result of the individual rather than the effects of inequitable social structures. When the profession is asked by governments, for example, to increase activity levels or improve eating habits for the purposes of combating the so-called 'obesity crisis', or they are requested to teach competitive sport in order to promote the right 'values' for increasing the nation's competitiveness in world markets or for the purposes of re-engaging disaffected youth, inequitable relations will more than likely prevail if educators confine their professional knowledge to simply that of the 'objective' performing body. Health behaviours, physical activity patterns and experiences in PE lessons are inevitably linked to structural factors and circulating discourses, and professionals need, therefore, to take account of such factors when making pedagogical decisions about what, and how, and, not least, why they teach what they do. The same is true if certain activities are prioritized in new legislation, such as dance or outdoor activity was in Norway in recent years. PE teachers need to ask, for example, 'Why is a focus on dance in PE important, who benefits, who loses out, what and how should it be taught?' Although it is possible, of course, to limit reflection to the 'hows' of technique and 'effective' teaching methods, we argue that physical educators need to pitch their critical analytical gaze within a broader socio-political framework; what types of citizens do we want to educate for tomorrow's society?

In Part I of the book, we discuss theoretical debates about difference and inequality, and provide an overview of narrative research. These chapters aim to discern the contours of the major developments during the past 40 years within these fields so that professionals working in PE, youth sport and health can access ideas about difference and narrative, and moreover use them actively as tools for reflection in their working lives. We hope that the theoretical lenses which we describe can be applied in everyday teaching and learning situations. Clearly it is impossible to explore in depth the many theoretical perspectives that have sought to explain difference and inequality between individuals, such as theory about social class, gender or disability, or to describe in depth the many theoretical discussions about the field of narrative inquiry. By providing illustrative examples, and by referencing some of the major research in the respective areas, we hope of course that readers will be encouraged to pursue in more detail the range of themes we raise.

In Part II of the book, we deliberately suspend explicit theoretical debate, although this is an illusion since we cannot write from 'nowhere' and theoretical concepts implicitly inform the texts (Richardson 2000). The section comprises 15 narratives written by leading scholars in the field of PE, youth sport and health about difference and (in)equalities in a range of physical activity contexts. The tales capture lifelike experiences which are partial, ambiguous, sometimes contradictory fragments of what 'really' has occurred in the characters' lives. By adopting a range of literary styles, the researchers wish to invite you into their informants' social worlds, to reveal the emotions with which these worlds are imbued and, in the process, they hope to 'touch' you. Based upon a view that knowledge about difference and (in)equality involves both emotional and cognitive understanding, the authors want the narratives to evoke *feelings*. To inspire you to cognitively engage with the tales, they provide a short list of recommended reading at the end of each narrative which, in addition to the theories described in Part I, provide a variety of theoretical lenses for interpreting, 'What's the story about?' It is important to realize that theoretical lenses recommended by one scholar may, of course, be relevant for other tales. Due to individuals' multiple identities, and the inter-subjective process of interpretation, multiple ways of knowing the social worlds of a single tale are possible. The 'quality' of any interpretation can only be judged via dialogue (Smith and Deemer 2000), and we hope therefore that the stories provoke much discussion, both in relation to personal and professional experience, and in relation to the application of different theoretical lenses. By sharing different interpretations, professional learning communities may develop (Day 1999a). It is probably useful to read, interpret and discuss several of the tales at the same time; often we gain new insights through the process of comparing and contrasting experiences. Similarly, when appropriate, it can be a useful learning strategy to read aloud or act out the narratives, not least with regard to the dramatic and poetic representations.

Given that a narrative approach is uncommon in sports sciences, in Part III of the book we provide some exemplars about how theories of difference and inequality may be used to help unpack and interpret the narratives. We locate these within a short discussion about critical reflection and professional development (Apple 2006; Carr and Kemmis 1986; Day 1999a). We envisage that readers have acquainted themselves with the specific tales and the recommended literature (or at least some of the suggested texts) which are discussed in each exemplar, prior to reading our interpretations of the narratives. In this way, we hope readers will be able to have an ongoing dialogue with our viewpoints, as they evolve. At the end of each exemplar we have also included a number of exercises relating to the themes of difference and (in)equality, which we perceive as central to the particular narratives, and these are intended to facilitate ongoing engagement with stories of difference. We aim, among other things, to draw the reader's attention to the prevalence of storytelling and story-analysis which occurs in our daily lives, and to encourage her/him to be more conscious of this way of knowing and to adapt it for the purposes of continuing professional development. There are exercises which relate to 'naturally' occurring stories of difference in our work environments and the organizational structures in which our work is located, and exercises which aim to activate or generate stories, in order to analyse them and better understand how difference and (in)equality pervades teaching and learning.

Difference does matter and inequalities persist in societies, despite public rhetoric constructing images of equality. Research shows that many young people, through no fault of their own, remain on the margins of sport and PE lessons, and that some of them are more likely than others to experience poor health. Although we paint a somewhat bleak picture in this regard, we nevertheless genuinely believe that the reader can *make a difference*, albeit in relatively modest ways in local contexts. Being a professional educator in today's society not only means having to develop sound subject knowledge, but it also depends upon acknowledging a moral duty to do what is 'right' for the individual and society (Arendt 1958). To this end, we see both narratives and theories of social difference as the professional's 'friend', in that they can provide tools for unravelling the many complexities of inequitable relations. In order to create narratives of equality, we need first of all to recognize and understand narratives of injustice. This book is intended as a small, but nonetheless important, contribution to this major, ongoing project.

Fiona Dowling, Hayley Fitzgerald and Anne Flintoff

References

Apple, M. (2006) *Educating the 'Right' Way. Markets, Standards, God and Inequality*, 2nd edn, London: Routledge.

Arendt, H. (1958) *The Human Condition*, Chicago: University of Chicago Press.

Barone, T. (1995) 'Persuasive writings, vigilant readings, and reconstructed characters: The paradox of trust in educational storysharing', in J. Amos Hatch and R. Wisniewski (eds) *Life History and Narrative*, London: Falmer Press, pp. 63–74.

Butt, R., Raymond, D., McCue, G. and Yamagishi, L. (1992) 'Collaborative autobiography and the teacher's voice', in I. Goodson (ed.) *Studying Teachers' Lives*, London: Routledge, pp. 51–98.

Carr, W. and Kemmis, S. (1986) *Becoming Critical: Education, Knowledge and Action Research*, London: Falmer Press.

Clandinin, D. J. and Connelly, F. M. (2000) *Narrative Inquiry. Experience and Story in Qualitative Research*, San Francisco: Jossey-Bass.

Day, C. (1999a) 'Professional development and reflective practice: Purposes, processes and partnerships', *Pedagogy, Culture and Society*, 7(2): 221–33.

——(1999b) *Developing Teachers. The Challenge of Lifelong Learning*, London: Routledge/Falmer Press.

Evans, J. and Davies, B. (1986) 'Sociology, schooling and physical education', in J. Evans (ed.) *Physical Education, Sport and Schooling. Studies in the Sociology of Physical Education*, London: Falmer Press, pp. 11–37.

——(2004) 'Pedagogy, symbolic control, identity and health', in J. Evans, B. Davies and J. Wright (eds) *Body Knowledge and Control. Studies in the Sociology of Physical Education and Health*, London: Routledge, pp. 3–18.

——(2008) 'The poverty of theory: Class configurations in the discourse of physical education and health (PEH)', *Physical Education and Sport Pedagogy*, 13(2): 199–213.

Goodson, I. (1995) 'The story so far: Personal knowledge and the political', in J. Amos and R. Wisniewski (eds) *Life History and Narrative*, London: Falmer Press, pp. 89–98.

Hargreaves, A. (2003) *Teaching in the Knowledge Society. Education in the Age of Insecurity*, Maidenhead: Open University Press.

Hargreaves, A. and Shirley, D. (2009) *The Fourth Way. The Inspiring Future for Educational Change*, Thousand Oaks, CA: Corwin.

Hekman, S. (1995) *Moral Voices, Moral Selves. Carol Gilligan and Feminist Moral Theory*, Cambridge: Polity Press.

Lingard, B. (2007) 'Pedagogies of indifference', *International Journal of Inclusive Education*, 11(3): 245–66.

Polkinghorne, D. (1995) 'Narrative configuration in qualitative analysis', in J. Amos Hatch and R. Wisniewski (eds) *Life History and Narrative*, London: Falmer Press, pp. 5–23.

Richardson, L. (2000) 'Writing: a method of inquiry', in N. Denzin and Y. Lincoln (eds) *Handbook of Qualitative Research*, 2nd edn, London, and Thousand Oaks, CA: Sage Publications, pp. 923–48.

Sachs, J. (2003) *The Activist Teaching Profession*, Buckingham: Open University Press.

Smith, J. K. and Deemer, D. (2000) 'The problem of criteria in the age of relativism', in N. Denzin and Y. Lincoln (eds) *Handbook of Qualitative Research*, 2nd edn, London, and Thousand Oaks, CA: Sage Publications, pp. 877–96.

Tinning, R. (2004) 'Conclusion: Ruminations on body knowledge and control and the spaces for hope and happening', in J. Evans, B. Davies and J. Wright (eds) *Body Knowledge and Control. Studies in the Sociology of Physical Education and Health*, London: Routledge, pp. 218–38.

——(2010) *Pedagogy and Human Movement: Theory, Practice, Research*, London: Routledge.

Part I
Theoretical perspectives

1 Theorizing difference and (in)equality in physical education, youth sport and health

Anne Flintoff and Hayley Fitzgerald

Introduction

On a daily basis we are bombarded with messages and stories about difference and inequality. A TV news report highlights increased levels of poverty endured by people living in an unfamiliar, third world country; a radio interview on International Women's Day features the continuing pay gap between women's and men's salaries; a national billboard campaign urges us to rethink our views and prejudices towards disabled people in society; or an article in a local newspaper reports on the rise in unemployment for immigrant young men. Differences and inequalities are felt locally and globally; they are all around us, although we may not always be aware of them. This chapter is about difference and inequality and specifically why they matter for understanding young people's experiences of physical education (PE), youth sport and health. As teachers, coaches or others working with young people, we are involved in hundreds of decisions and interactions, some made on a moment-by-moment basis, that will determine who gets made to feel different, who learns and experiences success and, conversely, those who don't. Whilst everyone should have an equal right to achieve educational or sporting merits, or to be healthy, the reality we know is somewhat different.

Think about some of the young people with whom you have worked and reflect upon how you relate to them in 'different' ways. Are they, for example, like James? He is growing up in an urban, working-class suburb, has a dual-heritage background, and lives with his mum and two older brothers. James loves playing one-on-one basketball and has even constructed an improvised basketball net onto a nearby telegraph pole so he can play with his friends. Or do you perhaps more easily recognize Anna? She has used a wheelchair since an early age and lives with both parents in a wealthy, rural green-belt area. After being collected from school by her mum, she is often ferried to an assortment of clubs and activities. Or does Matt remind you of a young person you've known? He lives in a working-class part of a large city with his dad and three sisters. For them, space is tight; they only have two bedrooms and Matt sleeps in the lounge. When Matt's dad is at work he often has to look after his sisters. Even though these three young people have different kinds of lives, this shouldn't matter to their learning and everyday experiences of PE and sport.

Young people like James, Anna and Matt live in an increasingly differentiated world, where socio-economic, and other inequalities associated with disability, gender, ethnicity or religion, structure their experiences. In democratic societies, education and sports systems have developed with the political goal of seeking to contribute to a more equal distribution of wealth and knowledge. Specific policies abound seeking to promote equality, drawing on well-known mottoes such as 'Sport for All'. More recently, the discourse has turned to 'inclusion' and 'inclusive education', reflected, for example, in the *Every Child Matters* agenda in the UK and *No Child Left Behind* in the USA. However, whilst there is much talk of inclusion in policy and practice, how much actual change is there? Armstrong and Barton (2007: 5) contend that much of the discourse has become 'an empty signifier' – there may be a lot of talk, but with little change in practice. After all, how often do we actually reflect on what inclusion in youth sport or education means? How do we include James, Anna, Matt and all the other pupils in PE when we know that their social backgrounds and health behaviours can be so diverse? Is it possible to counteract such differences? This book aims to shake up the 'taken-for-grantedness' of this policy rhetoric, and help you to see the complexities behind the realities of striving towards providing positive educational experiences in PE, sport and health, irrespective of social and cultural background.

In this first chapter, we map how difference and inequality can be understood by drawing upon social theory in general and, more specifically, social research in the field of PE, youth sport and health, and we explore the implications of these understandings for practice. In doing so, we aim to show how social theory is *useful* to our everyday practices working with young people, rather than something abstract or merely something that researchers do in their dusty, university offices! In focusing on social theory, we are not forgetting that differences have also been the focus of bio-behavioural scientific theories too; for example, physiologists explain differences in men's and women's 100-metres times as a result of differences in males' and females' physiological makeup. However, in this chapter, we are concerned with social thought, and specifically the relationships between differences and *inequalities*. Some time ago, Willis (1974: 3) questioned 'Why is it that *some* differences and not others, are taken as so important, become so exaggerated, [and] are used to buttress social attitudes or prejudice?' Willis was talking here about sex/gender difference in sport, and how the very small, physiological differences between men's and women's bodies have, nevertheless, been used to support discriminatory practices against women. However, ethnicity, sexuality, disability, age and religion are other categories of identity that can also result in individuals being treated inequitably.

We are particularly interested in this chapter in embodied difference – the ways in which individuals and groups get constituted and constructed as different, and unequal, on the basis of their bodies; how particular bodies become valued and celebrated, whilst others are marginalized or ignored, and how these inequalities are taken up and reproduced in everyday and institutional practices. As a teacher, sports coach or health personnel (and as researchers too), we have a professional responsibility to work positively with difference, to celebrate difference and promote positive learning environments that enable all young people to learn, to develop skills and to flourish. Yet, in practice, this is far from easy. Whilst many PE teachers claim that their main priority is for their students to have fun, which we can assume they see as a prerequisite for good learning (see Dismore and Bailey 2010; Green 2000), research shows that, for a good many children, they fail in this quest. For these young people, physical activity becomes something to be avoided rather than embraced, with many looking back negatively on their time in school PE (Beltrán-Carrillo *et al.* 2010; Ennis 1996; Sykes 2010). As Evans and his colleagues note:

> the most that many [young people] ... learn is that they have neither the ability, status nor value, and that the most judicious course of action to be taken in protection of their fragile educational physical identities is to adopt a plague-like avoidance of its damaging activities.
>
> (Evans, Davies and Penney 1996: 167)

How is it that some young people come to develop such 'fragile physical identities', learning that their bodies are not valued in PE? What is the role of PE and sport in the development of such identities? How do these identities impact on young people's choices to participate (or not) in youth sport and physical activity in out-of-school settings? What part do these identities play in young people's adoption or rejection of particular health behaviours, in their very sense of who they are and feelings of self-worth? And importantly, what is *our* role as teachers, coaches and academics involved in the delivery of sport, health and PE programmes? This book aims to help you to reflect on these questions, and this chapter focuses in particular on the role of social theory for helping with this task.

What's the use of theory?

The vast array of social theories in PE, youth sport and health may, at first, seem somewhat daunting, yet if we think of theories simply as explanations – explanations that serve to help understand the world as it currently is (and, importantly, provide pointers for how it might be improved in the future) – we can appreciate theory's central and important role in our practice as professionals working with young people. As Evans and Davies (2004) argue, theories help us 'unpack' the taken-for-granted, accepted ways of doing things. The role of theory is, they suggest, to make [practices] *less* self-evident and ... to open up spaces for the invention of *new* forms of experience and pedagogy ... the message is clear, in PE ... we should make research and teaching more, not less complex, and 'theory', ideas and innovation, not our enemies but our friends [our emphasis].

(Evans and Davies 2004: 11)

Like Evans and Davies, our task here is to help you to see theoretical complexity as your friend, and as a useful tool for reflecting upon and improving professional practice. Engaging critically in theoretical explanations of difference and equity might seem a long way from the everyday practices of teachers, coaches and health professionals for some of you. However, we suggest the opposite is true. As Evans and Davies (2006a: 111) note, 'all forms of practice are theory laden; rarely, if ever, is our thinking "theory-free"'. For example, think for a moment about how you would divide a class of 30 children into groups of four. As the teacher or leader, would you divide them to ensure a careful mix of abilities, and/or genders in each group? Or let the children choose, enabling them to work with friends? Or do you select some children to be 'captains', who then choose their groups? Each of these methods gets used regularly in PE or sports sessions, and each is underpinned by different kinds of assumptions about the nature of learning, behaviour management, pedagogy and so on. Each choice will also have significant consequences for the subsequent learning experiences of different children. So, when practitioners make assumptions, they are making attempts to *explain* things, or predict what might happen next – using what Evans and Davies (2006a) called 'first order' theorizing. Following Evans and Davies, our challenge in this chapter is to show the connections between this kind of theory – that helps individuals make sense of their worlds – and what might be called 'second order' theories, those that seek to explain the nature of power, order and control in schools, communities and society. As we will explore in more detail below and in the next chapter too, our individual experiences are always linked into macro contexts, and wider social relations. Social theories are, then, attempts to explain the relationships between individuals and social structures and relations. This is sometimes called the agency/structure debate – to what extent are we 'free' agents to choose the way we live our lives, or are our experiences 'structured' by institutions (such as schools) and social relations (such as class or gender relations)? Different theories attempt to explain this relationship in different ways.

An important part of our discussion will be a consideration of the language and concepts used to 'talk about' differences and inequalities. As Penney (2002a) notes, concepts such as equal opportunities, equality, equity, inclusion and difference are all commonly used in contemporary discussions about PE, sport and health, often interchangeably, and yet their meanings are contested and vary across different contexts and over time. As our theoretical understandings develop and become more sophisticated, so too do our conceptual frameworks. We will say more about different concepts below, and also discuss the importance of language in more detail in the next chapter.

In Part II of this book, we present different experiences across a variety of PE, youth sport or health settings through the use of narratives or stories. Whilst at first glance these might be viewed simply as individual accounts, we argue instead that they illuminate links between subjective experience and social structures; how individual identities are based upon the 'choices' available to us in the social and cultural contexts in which we live. So, if you have read this far, we urge you not to skip this chapter and move onto what might be viewed as the more interesting 'stories' that follow in Part II. By reading to the end of this chapter, we hope you will appreciate the various ways in which difference and inequalities have been explored in social research in PE, youth sport and health and be able to reflect upon how these competing ways of knowing have influenced your values and practice. Rather than thinking that theory is something to be avoided, we hope you will see its importance and use in critically assessing your, and others', practice, and for providing pointers towards better, more equitable practice in the future. If professionals do not confront their value-laden practice they may unwittingly produce and reproduce inequalities.

'Waves' of theory: theorizing difference in PE, youth sport and health

We have organized the chapter under what we have called three 'theoretical trajectories' or 'waves' of social thought: categorical, relational and postmodern/poststructural. Like Macdonald (2006), we recognize that the terms used to describe different strands of social thought are numerous and somewhat 'slippery'. For example, 'theories', 'perspectives' or 'paradigms' all say something about our preferred view of the world, the nature of reality and how we should go about our research practice. We have chosen to use 'theoretical trajectories' here specifically to suggest a broad 'direction of travel' that acknowledges the 'fuzziness' at the boundary edges, and to encapsulate the idea that theories are always fluid and changing. Flintoff and Scraton (2006) have suggested it might be useful to think of theories as 'waves', where new ones do not totally replace existing ones but, like waves in the sea, grow out of and contain aspects of the wave that started further out from the shoreline. Whilst different explanations and concepts have developed to address new and emerging questions, nevertheless, these do not totally replace existing ones, and many of the 'old' questions remain equally relevant to contemporary life. It is impossible to do justice in this chapter, or indeed this book, to the extensive theoretical and empirical work that has addressed issues of difference and inequality in PE, youth sport and health (e.g. see Benn *et al.* 2011; Evans *et al.* 2004; Houlihan and Green 2011; Kirk *et al.* 2006; Penney 2002b; Wright and Harwood 2009). Instead, in the next section, we map out some of the defining features of the three theoretical trajectories, identify what they offer to our understanding of difference and equity, and explore their use in practice. Ultimately we hope, of course, that your profes-sional curiosity will be sufficiently aroused such that you will be motivated to read the increasingly available literature on social class, age, ethnicity/'race', disability, gender and religion in PE, youth sport and health.

Difference, what difference?

It is not surprising that debates about how best to research, theorize and write about 'difference' in social life have been complex. At issue is not just the development of 'better' theory but, as we have argued above, the implications for 'better' practice that emerge from this different engagement. This chapter and the following ones explore some of these complexities. As Penney (2002a) and Figueroa (1993), amongst others, have noted, how differences are con-ceived and which differences get noted, and why some, and not others, are viewed as significant or relevant, and by whom, are all important questions for those wishing to *make* a difference in education. A few preliminary observations are worth highlighting here.

First, we should note that researchers in PE and sport/health science com-munities are not well renowned for their sensitivity to difference and inequalities. Perhaps this is not surprising, given that PE teachers are a remarkably homogeneous group – mostly white, young and non-disabled – and, with a history of successful involvement in physical activity themselves, they often struggle to empathize with others less talented or motivated in their subject area, and are often resistant to equity issues (Armour and Jones 1998; Flintoff *et al.* 2008a; Macdonald and Tinning 1995). University scho-lars and researchers working in the same area share many of these same char-acteristics too. For example, many of those involved in PE teacher education appear to be at best apathetic, and at worst hostile, to issues of social justice and equity (Dowling 2006, 2008; Flintoff 1993). The dominance of the bio-behavioural theories of the body (e.g. physiology/psychology) over the social sciences within school, university and teacher/coach preparation courses does little to disrupt these positions or practices (Macdonald *et al.* 1999; Tinning 2010). Research indicates that PE teachers and coaches often seem ill-equipped to acknowledge, celebrate and plan for difference amongst the groups with whom they work. They may, often unwittingly, struggle to deliver inclusive sessions, and find altering or 'targeting' provision to suit the needs of parti-cular groups of children difficult or unfair (Flintoff 2008; Fitzgerald *et al.* 2004; Morely *et al.* 2005; Penney and Harris 1997). Where do you position yourself in relation to these issues? Thinking about your own professional development for a moment – which kind of theoretical work do you currently find most useful to you? You may gravitate towards bio-behavioural theories, not least because they seem to have such straightforward applicability to your practice. For example, biomechanical theory about the body's centre of grav-ity seems highly appropriate knowledge if we are teaching the high jump. But very different kinds of theories are necessary to help us understand and work with different youngsters' responses to the learning task itself. To understand, for example, why it is that some are interested and engaged, whereas others seem disruptive or disinterested? Or how we might work to ensure positive and empowering relationships and interactions between group members during the lesson? Social theory can help to understand that we need to move beyond the immediacy of these micro-level interactions and see them as inevitably linked to bigger macro stories or discourses.

Second, we should acknowledge that this is very much a developing field. For example, as we will explore below, poststructural analyses are still relatively underdeveloped within our field, particularly in PE (Wright 2006), and there remain significant gaps in our understanding of specific differences, particularly those linked to ethnicity, religion, social class and disability. In addition, existing research has tended to be 'single issue' (Penney 2002a), underplaying the interrelations between forms of social difference such as social class, gender and disability. In this way, the field could be characterized as being 'one step behind' the wider critical debates in education, sport and health more broadly that have addressed the complexity of differences and individuals' multiple identities (e.g. Archer *et al.* 2001; Hargreaves 2000; Mac an Ghaill 1994; Mirza 2009). We should note at this point that gender has been the dominant 'lens' of difference in research on PE, youth sport and health in each of the three theoretical trajectories outlined below. We might ponder why this might be the case and why other aspects, such as social class, or disability, have been less dominant in our research questions. It might be to do with the final point we make here about the positionality of researchers themselves. To what extent do research questions reflect (and are therefore limited by) the biographies, identities and interests of the researchers themselves?

Lastly, our personal biographies are very much a part of the way in which we have approached and written this book. Inevitably, the literature on which we draw is a particular selection, reflecting those biographies and our individual career histories as white, middle-class and non-disabled women in the UK. For this chapter, our position as English speakers has limited the range of research and ideas accessible to us, too. Having these caveats in mind, the next section turns to explore what the different theoretical trajectories to explaining difference and equality might offer.

Categorical research

One of the most accepted and commonly used theoretical explanations of difference and inequalities in PE and youth sport has drawn on categories. In categorical research, differences between categories – for example, between girls and boys – are emphasized, and the 'distributive' research that results seeks to identify inequalities through reviewing patterns of opportunity, access and distributions of resources. To use the example of groups again, think for a minute of a typical PE lesson, or a sports coaching session. What groups would you see? How does the teacher or coach organize groups and for what purposes? What categories are used, and how do the resulting groups affect what happens next? Which groups seem to be least well included? For researchers using this theorization of difference, *access* and *equal opportunity* are key concepts; they are keen to identify how an aspect of difference has resulted in a lack of opportunity for one particular group. For example, early research on gender and PE questioned the ways in which particular curricular activities were offered to girls and others to boys, based on their so-called 'different' capabilities. Sex differences were used to categorize boys and girls as two different groups, each requiring different kinds of PE. Feminists argued that this differential treatment was unfair, and served to limit girls' and boys' opportunities to develop a full range of physical skills and abilities. Rather than there being natural differences in capability, they argued that the PE curriculum itself contributed to the development of these differences (Leaman 1984). Inequalities were explained as resulting from a lack of access to the same opportunities.

Research that uses categorical theorizing of difference more often than not uses quantitative, survey methodologies, where individuals are grouped as different by drawing on one aspect (or sometimes more) of identity, such as age or sex. These are then treated as 'variables' in the research. In doing so, patterns of differences between the groups can be highlighted (such as those between girls and boys), but only at the expense of suppressing those within groups (for example, those between girls as a group, resulting from, for example, age, social class or ethnic differences). Surveys of youth sport participation across the Western world consistently show girls' lower participation rates, overall, compared to boys' (e.g. Sabo and Veliz 2008; Sport England 2003, 2011). In relation to health, epidemiological studies drawing on this conception of difference reveal significant gaps in the health status of Indigenous and non-indigenous groups in many of the world's developed countries, particularly in Australia, where the gaps are increasing (Nelson *et al.* 2010). Both of these examples show how such research provides important information on differences in relation to sports participation and health status; however, it cannot tell us *which* girls or boys take part or not, and *why*, or *how* such health disparities are experienced in the everyday lives of different Indigenous populations. Girls and Indigenous populations are clearly not homogeneous groups, and yet this kind of theorizing underplays the differences found *within* categories. It is also important to note, too, that data from quantitative surveys like this can tell us little about the often very different meanings and place of physical activity, or health practices, in young people's lives (Wright *et al.* 2003). However, whilst weak on explanation, distributive analyses are useful for describing and highlighting patterns of inequality, and point to the need for action. It is for this reason that they remain significant, and it is very often these kinds of analyses that are the ones used by politicians and policy makers. If one group is shown to be under-represented or under-performing, then changes can be made to address this, through 'targeting' special provision aimed at the needs of this group.

This kind of theorizing focuses on examining inequalities in relation to access to particular opportunities, but rarely questions whether the opportunities themselves are ones that different groups might value or recognize in the first place (Penney 2002a). For example, many youth sports opportunities focus on competitive team sports where young people are expected to commit themselves to training and competing regularly if they become members. This kind of involvement requires not just valuing these kinds of activities, but also a commitment in time and resources (travelling to venues, buying the appropriate kit, and so on). It is not surprising, then, to learn that young people from middle-class or more affluent backgrounds are more likely to see this as a worthwhile investment, and 'choose' to participate, since they have access to exactly the kinds of social and economic 'capital' to support such an involvement compared to other groups (Evans and Davies 2010; Kay 2000, 2006; Wright and Macdonald 2010).

As well as not questioning the status quo of the opportunities on offer, distributive accounts are also not explanatory in nature. They can show us who takes part, but not why, and therefore they open up the possibility of specific groups of young people becoming 'labelled' as 'underachievers', or as 'problems', and measured as 'deficient' against a so-called 'norm' or 'target' (usually non-disabled, white, middle-class males). So, for example, South Asian pupils' under-representation in participation figures in PE and youth sport in the UK have been explained as a result of their 'problem' culture or religion (e.g. Carroll and Hollinshead 1993), or low self-esteem, or motivation. By constructing boundaries around one aspect of identity, such as ethnicity or age, such research can operate to essentialize and in fact reproduce differences. The differences *within* groups get hidden in the quest to emphasize the differences *between* groups.

Another issue with categorical research is that the categories themselves are not always straightforward or easy to use in practice. Even what is commonly assumed to be the unproblematic category of sex does not automatically adequately account for everyone. Sykes' (2006) research, for example, shows how transsexuals struggle to be included in professional sport, which is underpinned by rigid, bipolar concepts of sex. The narrative by her and Itani in Part II explores the impact of this in more detail. Attempts to categorize ethnicity or disability are equally contentious (Carrington and Skelton 2003; Pfeiffer 1998). The ways in which different countries categorize people on the basis of ethnicity differ significantly and, as populations change, so too is there a need to change and adapt the categories. For example, we have both recently received our latest census form, which the UK government requires us to complete. This includes new ethnic categories of 'Arab' and 'Irish Gypsy or Traveller' in addition to those from the previous census of 2001 (Lupton and Power 2004). How our ethnicity is categorized in the UK is very different to those in use in other countries, reflecting the historical and cultural variations in 'race' relations. Ethnic categories are always more than simply tick boxes on a piece of paper; they are significant mechanisms for the classification and ordering of different people. Whilst they may be used positively to inform policy change, there are plenty of examples (such as in apartheid South Africa) where they have been used to deny or restrict opportunities. We should perhaps not be surprised to learn that a key limitation of categorical research is that the data on which it relies are not always complete or accurate. If individuals do not identify themselves in the predetermined categories, or are uneasy about how the data might subsequently be used, they are clearly less likely to proffer information. Categorical accounts of difference, then, are not as straightforwardly unproblematic and useful as they might at first seem when we draw upon them in our taken-for-granted practice in PE and sport.

Relational research

In contrast to distributive analyses of difference, relational analyses focus on the social relations *within* and *between* different groups, and how these are historically and culturally variable (Kirk 1999). In this kind of theorizing, difference is seen as fundamentally about hierarchy and value – about relations between different groups, rather than simple characteristics held by different groups. Using this theoretical 'lens', we might ask questions about how it is that particular behaviours and attributes get to be valued, and others denigrated. How is it that particular discourses (or ways of seeing and being) become dominant understandings and accepted practice? For example, Western governments encourage us to eat more fruit and vegetables, and to take part in regular physical activity to ensure good health. We are encouraged to take care of our bodies and to 'work' on them for their own sake. Yet this kind of orientation to the body is more likely to be one held by those from middle rather than working-class backgrounds (Turner 2008). As a result, particular (working-)class-based orientations to the body become defined as a 'problem' waiting to be 'fixed', through government policy initiatives, education programmes, and so on. As Evans and Davies (2006b: 797–98) suggest, 'The label social class ... implies not just a categorization or classification of some people with reference to some "quality" ... but an invidious, hierarchical ranking of people which is inherently value laden'. Similar practices occur in PE lessons or sports environments when one message is seen to fit all.

Relational analyses of difference centralize the concept of *power*, and seek to understand how inequalities are produced and reproduced through everyday practices and institutions across different contexts, including PE, youth sport and health. Power here is conceived as structural, and it is produced, reproduced and resisted through institutions and social practices. Research that adopts this trajectory draws on the concepts of *equity* and *social justice*, and shows the link between PE, sport and health arenas to wider structures of

inequalities in society; as a result, researchers argue for more of a fundamental change to unjust societies. Relational analyses seek to highlight the
socially constructed nature of behaviours and characteristics, and challenge
the essentialism of biology-based theories (where everything is explained in
relation to one, true, 'essence' – in this example, biology). So, for example,
research on 'race' and ethnicity in sport has sought to challenge the ways in
which black or Aboriginal athletes have been subject to stereotyping and discrimination on the basis of their so-called 'natural', biological, athletic talent
(Long *et al.* 2009; Nelson *et al.* 2010). They show how such stereotyping
works to prevent particular athletes from being selected to play in key positions or taking up powerful decision-making positions in sport, such as the
coach or manager. The stereotypical view that black athletes 'are naturally
fast, but don't have the decision making to play a central role or become a
coach' is one that is often heard in sporting arenas. Instead, relational theory
would seek to show how sport contributes to or challenges wider 'race' relations in society. Similarly, relational theorizing about disability centralizes the
social and historical construction of disability and challenges the focus on
impairment adopted by those who advocate a medical model (Barnes *et al.*
1999). This kind of research asks how our everyday actions 'construct' exclusionary practices for different groups, and does so by emphasizing the
separation of the biological body from the social. Differences, and the
inequalities that result from these, are explained as socially constructed rather
than inherent and therefore can be challenged and changed.

Research adopting a relational analysis more usually draws on qualitative
methodologies, and centralizes specific groups' lived experiences as the starting point from which macro, social structures and processes can be referenced
and foregrounded. Theorizing around difference as social relations moves
beyond the 'static', homogeneous conceptions of difference used in categorical
research and recognizes the complexities of lived experience. Relational
accounts of difference acknowledge the intersection of different aspects of
identity, and that individuals' identities are best seen as multiple and dynamic.
For example, the commonsense view that boys are interested in PE and sport,
and girls are not, is clearly problematic and fails to recognize the different
ways in which 'doing boy' or 'doing girl' are possible (Bramham 2003; Hickey
2008; Paechter 2003; Paechter and Clark 2007), and that it is important to
talk about and recognize femininities and masculinities, rather than a singular
femininity and masculinity (Connell 1985, 2008). Scraton's (1992) research
remains highly significant as one of the first studies that began to problematize universal conceptions of femininity, and explored girls' different
experiences of PE. Her work showed the significance of social class differences between girls for their experiences of PE and sport. Socio-economic
resources are important factors in girls' and young women's participation in
sport, with opportunities to join sports clubs, travel to venues, afford equipment, and so on all having an impact on young people's chances to develop
physical 'capital' or skills (Kirk 2005). Scraton also highlighted the centrality

of heterosexuality within notions of 'acceptable' femininity. We might therefore ask what kinds of 'doing girl' are closed down or viewed as 'unacceptable' in contemporary PE practices, and how these work to exclude some girls and young women.

Although gender clearly impacts on boys' experiences of PE and sport just as much as girls', it is important to note that there has been much less research focusing on boys and masculinity (Dowling Næss 2001; Gard 2006; Gard and Meyenn 2000; Hickey 2008; Hickey and Fitzclarence 1999). This is despite sustained concern with boys' so-called 'underachievement' in schooling generally (e.g. Epstein *et al.* 1998; Martino and Pallotta-Chiarolli 2003; Skelton 2001). Agreeing with Messner (1996), we need much more 'studying up' in the power structures if we are to fully understand how power relations operate to privilege particular groups. In order to understand how power works, we need to explore the experiences of the powerful, as well as the powerless. So, for example, how do class relations, whiteness and heterosexuality work to maintain the privileges of the middle classes, white people and those who identify as heterosexual? (Azzarito 2009; Clarke 2004; Evans and Davies 2010; Oliver and Lalik 2004; Squires and Sparkes 1996; Sykes 1998).

All too often, relational research, particularly in PE and youth sport, has foregrounded gender and paid insufficient attention to other identity markers, or their intersections (see Flintoff *et al.* 2008b). Until recently, there has been a marked absence of research centralizing black and minority ethnic (BME) young people's experiences of PE, sport and health (Atencio 2010; Benn and Dagkas 2006; Benn *et al.* 2011; Kay 2006; Nelson *et al.* 2010). Benn's work (1996, 2002; Benn and Dagkas 2006) made a key early contribution, highlighting the struggles of Muslim women to access PE as part of their primary initial teacher education course, and showing the complex interplay of gender, 'race' and religion. Others have developed this work by going on to explore Muslim girls' and young women's experiences of Western models of PE and sport (Kay 2006; Knez 2007). However, there remain significant gaps in our understanding and theorizing of 'race' and ethnicity, leaving the enduring effects of racism largely unexplored within mainstream theorizing in PE, youth sport and health.

In addition to 'race' and ethnicity, disability, too, has been absent as a key 'lens' of difference in relational accounts. Bio-behavioural research, drawing on categorical theorizing, and underpinned by medical model understandings of disability, predominates (e.g. Broadhead and Burton 1996). There are a small number of notable exceptions in PE and youth sport, including the work of Brittain (2004a, 2004b), which provides some valuable insights through elite disabled athletes' reflective accounts of PE; Goodwin and Watkinson's (2000) work; and Fitzgerald's research on disabled young people's experiences of PE (Fitzgerald 2005, 2009). These few accounts of research on disability serve to illustrate the many gaps in our understandings around *particular* kinds of difference. In part, we would suggest this is compounded by data-generation methods that preclude or are exclusionary in their design; if we are to be more attentive to difference, arguably we need to pay serious attention to the use of different methodologies (see Fitzgerald 2007, 2011).

Despite these limitations, relational accounts are important for recognizing the complex nature of identities and their relationship with structural power relations. However, because they are sophisticated analyses of difference, centralizing complex power relations of patriarchy, capitalism and racism, they are also more challenging to use to identify frameworks for action, not least for the PE classroom or a health-promotion session. As discussed above, categorical accounts of difference point clearly to action; if a group is doing less well than others, then resources and action can be targeted towards that group. For relational analyses, the link between theory and action is less straightforward and less clear. By highlighting the differences *within* groups, the basis for mobilizing around *shared* characteristics of a group becomes more problematic. Should we, for example, talk about changing our practice around the needs of 'girls' as a group, or 'working-class' youngsters, when we recognize the qualitatively different lived experiences of individuals within these groups? Postmodern and poststructural analyses seek to problematize such structural accounts of inequality, arguing that these theories are no longer useful in what is an increasingly fragmented and changing world. These analyses of difference are the focus of our next section.

Postmodern/poststructural research

Although relatively new in this field, for those working within postmodernism and poststructuralism,[1] a key task has been to deconstruct and problematize the categorical thinking and the binaries central to modernist research on difference, reviewed above. Although much less evident in research in PE, youth sport and health, we also briefly mention postcolonial and queer theorizing here in this section too (see below), since it could be argued that, as with postmodern/poststructural thought, they also contest the idea that there is one 'truth' or a single explanation for a particular issue. As Wright (2006: 59) notes, '"post" in this way signifies a disjuncture, a disruption, a critical engagement with an existing "set of ideas"'. Thinking based on categorical notions of difference – boy/girl; able/disabled; heterosexual/homosexual; black/white, and so on – are questioned for being too static and simplistic. The ideas expressed above in the previous sections, suggesting that a lack of opportunity or access, or social relations of power (patriarchy, racism, capitalism) can be used to explain inequalities, are rejected for being overdeterministic and monolithic.

In contrast, in postmodern and poststructural thought, there is a focus on difference and diversity and recognition of diverse identities, such as sexualities, femininities, masculinities, or a hybridity of ethnic identities. Essentialist notions of identity/self are rejected (where identity/self is seen as having an essential, stable, unchanging core) and there is a concern instead about our shifting, multiple subjectivities (sense of being). This kind of theorizing seeks to show how young people's experiences of PE or sport cannot be neatly explained through a particular category such as 'middle class' or 'gay', for example. Instead it argues that we may experience different aspects of our identity as more or less significant within different spaces or contexts. Think about yourself for a moment, and try and identify particular contexts where a particular aspect of your identity becomes more important or significant. In Flintoff *et al.*'s (2008a) study, for example, BME student teachers experienced their ethnicity in quite different ways within the 'white' spaces of the university compared to the multi-ethnic spaces of some of their teaching practice schools. One Asian Muslim woman described how her ethnicity and religion were viewed as valuable pedagogical 'resources' within one multi-ethnic school, but as 'problems' within the university swimming class, where her request for modesty had to be 'accommodated'.

In conjunction with seeing identities as fluid and shifting, power in 'post'-theorizing is conceptualized differently, as plural and productive, rather than as top down and repressive as in relational analysis. This theorizing of power allows more readily for resistance and struggle, and therefore is seen as a more optimistic understanding of difference. There is a focus on understanding *how* relations of power operate through discourse to privilege particular practices and meanings in particular contexts, and what that means for different individuals. Poststructural theorizing seeks to question the taken-for-granted 'truths' and accepted practices in PE, youth sport and health. In so doing, it aims to open up possibilities for new ways of knowing and new ways of being (subjectivities).

A key concept in poststructural theorizing is *discourse*, drawing on the work of Foucault (1980, 1983). Paechter (2001) describes a discourse as a

> way of speaking, thinking or writing that presents particular relationships as self-evidently true. Because such 'truths' are presented as unchallenge-able, this means that within a particular discourse, only certain things can be said or thought … . Discourses are important for they structure the way in which we can think about things. Because they are treated as, and appear to be, self-evidently a reflection of 'reality', they remain unchal-lenged, prescribing for us what is 'normal' or 'natural' behaviour, and penalizing those who attempt to challenge or step outside them.
>
> (Paechter 2001: 42)

Because of the centrality of discourse in poststructural theorizing, language is deemed to be important for the ways in which it constructs meanings and people. Poststructural theorizing, however, goes beyond an interest in lan-guage in a purely linguistic sense and considers how individuals are posi-tioned within discourses, and how these affect actions and behaviours. Discourses literally become embodied or inscribed on the body. The ways in which the body is used reflect the discourses in which that use takes place. Paechter and Clark (2007), for example, argue that the discourse of the 'good, quiet girl' serves to constrain the ways in which girls are able to use their bodies, and the description of a 'tomboy' serves to position girls who are active as 'abnormal'. Although not all girls are positioned in the same way within them, discourses of femininity act on girls' bodies so that they are literally 'shaped' to become less active and strong. poststructuralists interested in gender difference and inequality focus on exploring the nature of discourses of femininity and masculinity in particular contexts (such as the PE class, or sports club) and how young men and women take up, position themselves relative to, and are positioned within these, and to what effect.

Since discourses constrain what can be regarded as 'true', then discourses are always tied up with power. Dominant discourses present particular ways of thinking that become accepted as the 'norm' or the 'truth', and are therefore powerful forms of knowledge. A genealogical approach to PE, for example, has explored how particular constructions of the subject have existed throughout historical texts (e.g. Kirk 1992, 2002, 2010). More recently, scholars have focused on analysing more contemporary practice and pedagogy, drawing on Bernstein's more recent conceptualization of discourse (e.g. Penney and Evans 1999). For example, in Penney and Evans's (1999) study of the first national curriculum in PE in England they identified sport to be a dominant discourse, exploring the implications of this for the everyday experiences of different pupils and teachers in PE. With sport as a dominant discourse within PE (as well as outside PE, within physical culture more broadly), they argue that it becomes almost impossible to think about the subject in any other way; certainly many politicians in the UK talk about PE as if it were sport, making little or no distinction between the two. However, for poststructuralists, the structural notions of power (top down, repressive) are rejected, and power is regarded instead as productive and plural, and located in a multiplicity of sites and networks. This means that, wherever there is power, there is resistance. Individual teachers, school departments, parent groups and young people themselves can actively challenge or sustain particular discourses through their everyday actions. In relation to the PE curriculum, this means that there is always more than one discourse, and therefore always the potential for different discourses (for example, around dance, or outdoor education) to find expression in alternative readings – for 'slippage' between the intended and actual outcomes of a policy text. Despite these possibilities, Penney and Evans (1999) concluded that the consistency between the dominant discourses promoted in the new curriculum and those of existing practice meant that a shift away from competitive, sport-based PE towards a more equitable form of practice seemed extremely unlikely. Later research suggests that their predictions were accurate (Curtner-Smith 1999; Penney 2001, 2006).

As well as exploring the nature of discourse in formal policy texts, a further strand of poststructural accounts of difference is interested in the role of discourse in constituting particular subjectivities in and out of PE. The use of the term *subjectivity* here reflects a poststructural view of the 'self' – that is, not as a unified, rational and consistent entity, but as shifting, fragmented and always in process. Research from this trajectory more usually draws on qualitative methods, such as interviews and observations of teacher–pupil interactions, and aims to show how young men and women from different class, ethnic and religious backgrounds experience their subjectivities in different ways. For example, Western views of Muslim women who wear the veil as being oppressed have been questioned by recent research adopting this approach. Knez's (2010) research shows that, although the subjectivities of the young women in her study were clearly shaped by dominant feminine discourses of both Islam and popular culture, the ways in which these discourses were taken up, negotiated and resisted varied.

Burrows's (2010a, 2010b) research is one of a number of recent studies exploring physical activity and health from this perspective (see also e.g. Cliff and Wright 2010; Evans *et al.* 2004; Garrett 2004a, 2004b; Lee and Macdonald 2010; Rich *et al.* 2004). These studies are interested in the role that schools play in addressing the so-called 'obesity epidemic'. What physical activity and health discourses do they re(produce) and how do different young people take up and act on these? Burrows (2010a, 2010b), for example, shows how even very young children are cognizant of, and respond to, some of the government's key health discourses, albeit in different ways. She used focus group interviews with primary-aged children and analysed their interview texts not as the 'truth' of how they were experiencing physical activity and health but rather as illustrations of the kinds of discursive resources they have available to draw on, and how they position themselves as 'healthy' subjects (or not) in relation to these. What is interesting, she notes, are the signs of children rejecting and negotiating some of the dominant messages about health. However, equally interesting (and concerning) is the way in which some of the more affluent young children are able to 'other' pupils who do not/are not able to recognize their 'self' within government discourses of health.

As mentioned above, queer theory and postcolonial theory are two strands of scholarship that are virtually absent from PE, youth sport and health research to date. There are almost no examples of postcolonial analyses within PE and youth sport, although these are more evident in the related area of sports studies (e.g. Bale and Cronin 2003). Postcolonialism seeks to destabilize notions of national identity and engages with diaspora, the transnational and new identities (Macdonald *et al.* 2009; Pheonix 2009). Queer theory has developed from poststructuralist theory with a particular focus on gender and sexuality, bringing a deconstructionist approach to sexual identity and heteronormative discourse. As Caudwell (2006: 2) notes, queer theory shifts the debate from 'a lesbian and gay politics of identity to a politics of difference, resistance and challenge'. In PE, the work of Larsson *et al.* (2009), Sykes (1998, 2010), and Wellard (2007) are important examples.

What these different aspects of 'post'-theorizing have in common is recognition of individual experiences as complex, diverse and changing; individuals resist and negotiate their positions within dominant discourses, rather than simply accept them. However, people are differently positioned to be able to draw upon, and benefit from, dominant and/or resistant discourses. 'Post'-theorizing is interested in exploring how young people are differently positioned in relation to gender, 'race', class, sexuality, disability or religion to benefit from particular 'truths' within PE, sport and health. Within PE and youth sport, as with the previous two trajectories, gender has been a central focus of studies adopting this perspective (e.g. Azzarito *et al.* 2006; Garrett 2004a, 2004b; Hills 2006, 2007; Paechter 2003; Webb and Macdonald 2007a, 2007b; Wright 1996, 1997). Studies in physical activity and health have better acknowledged individuals' complex identity positions in relation to gender, social class and ethnicity (e.g. *Sport, Education and Society*, Special Issue 2010; Wright and Macdonald 2010); in highlighting discourse, culture and identity/self, these studies seek to rebalance the tendency to overplay the impact of structural inequalities within relational analyses. However, not all agree that such analyses are helpful, warning that an overemphasis on difference and diversity should not be at the expense of ignoring enduring, material inequalities that remain evident (Francis 1999, 2006; Flintoff and Scraton 2001). For example, some feminists have expressed concerns that, in seeking to deconstruct discourses of femininity, women's *shared* experiences in relation to gender become lost. Without some sense of a shared notion of experience (whether that comes from individuals' shared class, ethnicity, religion, etc.), then it becomes difficult to argue for political action to change practice. In this sense, the social categories or groupings of people discussed in the previous sections may well remain useful politically and strategically. As a result, some authors have argued for what they have called 'middle-ground' or 'middle-way' theorizing between relational analysis and poststructuralism. Middle-ground theorizing recognizes identities as 'situated accomplishments' (Valentine 2007) – heterogeneous, fluid and actively produced across and within different social contexts – and yet acknowledges, too, the ways in which 'race', gender, sexuality and so on continue to be implicated in patterns of very real inequalities. This means, in relation to practice, that there may still be the need to draw 'temporary boundaries' around particular identities.

So, is theory useful? Some concluding comments

So, what can we conclude from this chapter? We hope we have convinced you of the usefulness of theory as a tool to help understand the complexities of difference and inequality, and for reflecting on practice. As we indicated at the beginning of this chapter, everyone's practice is underpinned by theory, whether they explicitly state this or not. As professionals involved in working with children and young people, we do have a responsibility to be able to provide coherent rationales for the choices we make and the actions we take. This means that engaging in good practice necessarily involves adopting a theoretical position; we can't choose to leave theory 'on the shelf' for someone else to deal with. How we respond to differences and inequalities in our work with young people will reflect particular theoretical positions, whether we are conscious of these or not. But, as we have seen, engaging in theory is complex. However, remembering Evans's earlier plea for us to make theory our friend, we urge you to see it as an essential tool to developing and refining your practice. Ball (2006) argues that we should see different theories like tools in a tool-box; for certain jobs we might need a hammer but, for others, a screwdriver. In the same way, different theories are useful in addressing *different* questions. As we have seen above, if we are interested in exploring the sports participation rates of different groups of young people, categorical research could be useful. Using survey data, we can explore groups' participation rates by, for example, social class, or disability or gender, enabling us to identify the groups that are less active. Alternatively, if we are more interested in how young people's sports provision contributes to or challenges class relations, a relational approach would be useful. We can ask questions about how young people's sporting opportunities are structured and organized, and who benefits and who loses out from these particular constructions. To explore the meaning and place of sport within young people's lives, a post-structural analysis could identify the kinds of discursive resources available to draw on, and how young people position themselves as 'sporty' subjects (or not) in relation to these. We are, therefore, certainly not suggesting that you have to choose between one or other of the broad trajectories we have outlined here, or indeed see each as uniform sets of ideas and mutually exclusive. Rather, we would urge you to appreciate what each of them has to offer our understandings, to be aware of their advantages but also of their limitations.

We have presented an overview of the theoretical work on difference and inequality in PE, youth sport and health as falling into three key trajectories; however, we do so only for heuristic reasons to attempt to provide some order to what is a vast field of knowledge. In practice, theoretical ideas are not always so neatly divided, and are constantly changing and developing. As social life changes, so too do theories, generating new questions that require answers. Although very different, social theories are, in essence, explanations that can help us to understand social life and to identify and promote changes that aim to improve it. Think back to James, Anna and Matt, introduced at the beginning of this chapter. How can the different theoretical trajectories explored in this chapter help us to understand and improve their individual experiences? We agree with Macdonald *et al.* (2002: 151) in that theory is indispensable to conducting quality research, and for helping us to reflect on practice, but our choice of theory 'should not obscure the need to ask good questions, seek well-considered ways of coming to know, and communicate in ways that are inclusive'. By exploring different individuals' stories and seeing them within wider macro contexts, social relations and discourses, we are better able to understand and challenge the inequities that continue to structure and limit young people's lives and their learning experiences within PE, youth sport and health. In Chapter 2 the potential of narrative inquiry is explored with this purpose in mind.

Note

1 Postmodernism and poststructuralism are terms that are often used interchangeably, with the former used more in North America (and also across different disciplinary areas, e.g. in arts and architecture), the latter in Europe. Whilst they share the same concerns with problematizing structural accounts of power and fixed notions of identity, they do have different roots and emphases, of which space prevents a full exploration here. For the purposes of our discussions we will use the term poststructuralism throughout this chapter.

References

Archer, L., Hutchings, M. and Leathwood, C. (2001) 'Engaging in commonality and difference: Theoretical tensions in the analysis of working class women's educational discourses', *International Journal of Sociology of Education*, 11(1): 41–62.

Armour, K. M. and Jones, R. L. (1998) *Physical Education: Teachers' Lives and Careers*, London: Falmer.

Armstrong, F. and Barton, L. (2007) 'Policy, experience and change and the challenges of inclusion', in L. Barton and F. Armstrong (eds) *Policy, Experience and Change: Cross Cultural Reflections on Inclusive Education*, Dordrecht: Springer, pp. 5–18.

Atencio, M. (2010) '"I don't wanna die too early". Young people's use of urban neighbourhood spaces in the United States', in J. Wright and D. Macdonald (eds) *Young People, Physical Activity and the Everyday*, London: Routledge, pp. 29–41.

Azzarito, L. (2009) 'The panopticon of physical education: Pretty, active and ideally white', *Physical Education and Sport Pedagogy*, 14(1): 19–40.

Azzarito, L., Solmon, M. A. and Harrison, L., Jr. (2006) '"If I had a choice I would … ". A feminist post-structuralist perspective on girls in physical education classes', *Research Quarterly for Exercise and Sport*, 77(22): 222–39.

Bale, J. and Cronin, M. (eds) (2003) *Sport and Postcolonialism*, Oxford: Berg.

Ball, S. J. (2006) *Educational Policy and Social Class: The Selected Works of Stephen J. Ball*, Abingdon: Routledge.

Barnes, C., Mercer, G. and Shakespeare, T. (eds) (1999) *Exploring Disability: A Sociological Introduction*, Cambridge: Polity Press.

Beltrán-Carrillo, V., Devís-Devís, J., Peiró-Velert, C. and Brown, D. (2010) *Youth and Society*, DOI: 10.1177/0044118X10388262.

Benn, T. (1996) 'Muslim women and physical education in initial teacher training', *Sport, Education and Society*, 1(1): 5–21.

——(2002) 'Muslim women in teacher training: Issues of gender, "race" and religion', in D. Penney (ed.) *Gender and Physical Education: Contemporary Issues and Future Directions*, London: Routledge, pp. 57–79.

Benn, T. and Dagkas, S. (2006) 'Incompatible? Compulsory mixed-sex physical education initial teacher training (PEITT) and the inclusion of Muslim women: A case-study on seeking solutions', *European Physical Education Review*, 12(2): 181–200.

Benn, T., Dagkas, S. and Jawad, H. (2011) 'Embodied faith: Islam, religious freedom and educational practices in education', *Sport, Education and Society*, 16(1): 17–34.

Benn, T., Pfister, G. and Jawad, H. (eds) (2011) *Muslim Women in Sport*, London: Routledge.

Bramham, P. (2003) 'Boys, masculinity and PE', *Sport, Education and Society*, 8(1): 57–71.

Brittain, I. (2004a) 'Perceptions of disability and their impact upon involvement in sport for people with disabilities at all levels', *Journal of Sport and Social Issues*, 28 (4): 429–52.

——(2004b) 'The role of schools in constructing self-perceptions of sport and physical education in relation to people with disabilities', *Sport, Education and Society*, 9(1): 75–94.

Broadhead, G. D. and Burton, A. W. (1996) 'The legacy of early adapted physical activity research', *Adapted Physical Activity Quarterly*, 13(2): 116–26.

Burrows, L. (2010a) '"Kiwi kids are Weet-Bix kids" – body matters in childhood', *Sport Education and Society*, 15(2): 235–51.

——(2010b) 'Push play every day: New Zealand children's constructions of health and physical activity', in M. O'Sullivan and A. MacPhail (eds) *Young People's Voices in Physical Education and Youth Sport*, London: Routledge, pp. 145–62.

Carrington, B. and Skelton, C. (2003) 'Re-thinking "role models": Equal opportunities in teacher recruitment in England and Wales', *Journal of Education Policy*, 18(3): 253–65.

Carroll, B. and Hollinshead, G. (1993) 'Equal opportunities: Race and gender in physical education: A case study', in J. Evans (ed.) *Equality, Education and Physical Education*, London: Falmer, pp. 154–69.

Caudwell, J. (ed.) (2006) *Sport, Sexualities and Queer/Theory*, London: Routledge.

Clarke, G. (2004) 'Threatening space: (Physical) education and homophobic body work', in J. Evans, B. Davies and J. Wright (eds) *Body Knowledge and Control: Studies in the Sociology of Physical Education and Health*, London: Routledge, pp. 191–203.

Cliff, K. and Wright, J. (2010) 'Confusing and contradictory: Considering obesity discourse and eating disorders as they shape body pedagogies in HPE', *Sport, Education and Society*, 15(2): 221–33.

Connell, R. (2008) 'Masculinity construction and sports in boys' education: A framework for thinking about the issue', *Sport, Education and Society*, 13(2): 131–45.

Connell, R. W. (1995) *Masculinities*, London: Polity Press.

Curtner-Smith, M. D. (1999) 'The more things change the more they stay the same: Factors influencing teachers' interpretations and delivery of national curriculum physical education', *Sport Education and Society*, 4(1): 75–97.

Dismore, H. and Bailey, R. (2010) 'Fun and enjoyment in physical education: Young people's attitudes', *Research Papers in Education*, DOI: 10.1080/02671522.2010.484866.

Dowling, F. (2006) 'Physical education teacher educators' professional identities, continuing professional development and the issue of gender equality', *Physical Education and Sport Pedagogy*, 11(3): 247–63.

——(2008) 'Getting in touch with our feelings: The emotional geographies of gender relations in PETE', *Sport, Education and Society*, 13(3): 247–66.

Dowling Naess, F. (2001) 'Narratives about young men and masculinities in organised sport in Norway', *Sport, Education and Society*, 6(2): 125–42.

Ennis, C.D. (1996) 'Student experiences in sport-based physical education: [More than] apologies are necessary', *Quest*, 48: 454–57.

Epstein, D. and Johnson, R. (eds) (1998) *Schooling Sexualities*, Buckingham: Open University Press.

Epstein, D., Elwood, J., Hey, V. and Maw, J. (1998) *Failing Boys? Issues of Gender and Achievement*, Buckingham: Open University Press.

Evans, J. (2004) 'Making a difference? Education and "ability" in physical education', *European Physical Education Review*, 10(1): 95–108.

Evans, J. and Davies, B. (2004) 'Pedagogy, symbolic control, identity and health', in J. Evans, B. Davies and J. Wright (eds) *Body Knowledge and Control: Studies in the Sociology of Physical Education and Health*, London: Routledge, pp. 3–18.

——(2006a) 'The sociology of physical education', in D. Kirk, D. Macdonald and M. O'Sullivan (eds) *The Handbook of Physical Education*, London: Sage, pp. 109–22.

——(2006b) 'Social class and physical education', in D. Kirk, D. Macdonald and M. O'Sullivan (eds) *The Handbook of Physical Education*, London: Sage, pp. 796–808.

——(2010) 'Family, class and embodiment: Why school physical education makes so little difference to post-school participation patterns in physical activity', *International Journal of Qualitative Studies in Education*, 23(7): 765–84.

Evans, J., Davies, B. and Penney, D. (1996) 'Teachers, teaching and the social construction of gender relations', *Sport, Education and Society*, 1(2): 165–83.

Evans, J., Davies, B. and Wright, J. (eds) (2004) *Body Knowledge and Control: Studies in the Sociology of Physical Education and Health*, London: Routledge.

Evans, J., Rich, E. J. and Holroyd, R. (2004) 'Disordered eating and disordered schooling: What schools do to middle class girls', *British Journal of Sociology of Education*, 25(2): 123–42.

Figueroa, P. (1993) 'Equality, multiculturalism, antiracism and physical education in the national curriculum', in J. Evans (ed.) *Equality, Education and Physical Education*, London: Falmer, pp. 90–102.

Fitzgerald, H. (2005) 'Still feeling like a spare piece of luggage? Embodied experiences of (dis)ability in physical education and school sport', *Physical Education and Sport Pedagogy*, 10(1): 41–59.

——(2007) 'Dramatizing physical education: Using drama in research', *British Journal of Learning Disabilities*, 35(4): 253–60.

——(ed.) (2009) *Disability and Youth Sport*, London: Routledge.

——(2011) '"Drawing" on disabled students' experiences of physical education and stakeholder responses', *Sport, Education and Society*, DOI: 10.1080/13573322.2011. 609290.

Fitzgerald, H., Stevenson, P. and Botterill, M. (2004) 'Including disabled pupils in PE and school sport: Teachers' CPD experiences', *British Journal of Teaching Physical Education*, 35(4): 43–48.

Flintoff, A. (1993) 'Gender, physical education and teacher education', in J. Evans (ed.) *Equality, Education and Physical Education*, London: Falmer, pp. 184–204.

——(2008) 'Targeting Mr Average: Participation, gender equity, and school sport partnerships', *Sport, Education and Society*, 13(4): 413–31.

Flintoff, A. and Scraton, S. (2001) 'Stepping into active leisure? Young women's perceptions of active lifestyles and their experiences of school physical education', *Sport Education and Society*, 6(1): 5–22.

——(2006) 'Girls and PE', in D. Kirk, D. Macdonald and M. O'Sullivan (eds) *The Handbook of Physical Education*, London: Sage, pp. 767–83.

Flintoff, A., with Chappell, A., Gower, C., Keyworth, S., Lawrence, J., Money, J., Squires, S. L. and Webb, L. (2008a) *Black and Minority Ethnic Trainees' Experiences of Physical Education Initial Teacher Training*. Unpublished Report for the Training and Development Agency, Carnegie Research Institute: Leeds Metropolitan University. Available from: <www.leedsmet.ac.uk/carnegie/F7DDB88DA13 F477E9E57 8A028E96FDB4.htm> (accessed 3 October 2011).

Flintoff, A., Fitzgerald, H. and Scraton, S. (2008b) 'The challenges of intersectionality: Researching difference in physical education', *International Studies in Sociology of Education*, 18(2): 73–85.

Foucault, M. (1980) *Power/Knowledge*, New York: Pantheon.

——(1983) 'The subject and power', in H. Dreyfus and P. Rabinow (eds) *Michel Foucault: Beyond Structuralism and Hermeneutics*, Chicago: Chicago University Press, pp. 208–26.

Francis, B. (1999) 'Modernist reductionism or post-structural relativism: Can we move on? An evaluation of the arguments in relation to feminist educational research', *Gender and Education*, 11: 381–93.

——(2006) 'The nature of gender', in C. Skelton, B. Francis and L. Smulyan (eds) *The Sage Handbook of Gender and Education*, London: Sage, pp. 7–17.

Gard, M. (2006) 'More art than science? Boys, masculinity and physical education', in D. Kirk, D.Macdonald and M. O'Sullivan (eds) *The Handbook of Physical Education*, London: Sage, pp. 784–95.

Gard, M. and Meyenn, R. (2000) 'Boys, bodies, pleasure and pain: Interrogating contact sports in schools', *Sport Education and Society*, 5(1): 19–34.

Garrett, R. (2004a) 'Gendered bodies and physical identities', in J. Evans, B. Davies and J. Wright (eds) *Body Knowledge and Control: Studies in the Sociology of Physical Education and Health*, London: Routledge, pp. 140–56.

——(2004b) 'Negotiating a physical identity: Girls, bodies and physical education', *Sport, Education and Society*, 9(2): 223–37.

Goodwin, D. L. and Watkinson, E. J. (2000) 'Inclusive physical education from the perspectives of students with physical disabilities', *Adapted Physical Activity Quarterly*, 17(2): 144–60.

Green, K. (2000) 'Exploring the everyday "philosophies" of physical education teachers from a sociological perspective', *Sport Education and Society*, 5(2): 109–30.

Hargreaves, J. (2000) *Heroines of Sport: The Politics of Difference and Identity*, New York: Routledge.

Hickey, C. (2008) 'Physical education, sport and hyper-masculinity in schools', *Sport, Education and Society*, 13(2): 147–61.

Hickey, C. and Fitzclarence, L. (1999) 'Educating boys in sport and physical education: Using narrative methods to develop pedagogies of responsibility', *Sport Education and Society*, 4(1): 51–62.

Hills, L. (2006) 'Playing the field(s): An exploration of change, conformity and conflict in girls' understandings of gendered physicality in physical education', *Gender and Education*, 18(5): 539–56.

——(2007) 'Friendship, physicality and physical education: An exploration of the social and embodied dynamics of girls' physical education experiences', *Sport Education and Society*, 12(3): 317–36.

Houlihan, B. and Green, M. (eds) (2011) *The Routledge Handbook of Sports Development*, London: Routledge.

Kay, T. (2000) 'Sporting excellence: The impact on family life', *European Physical Education Review*, 6(2): 151–70.

——(2006) 'Daughters of Islam: Family influences on Muslim young women's participation in sport', *International Review for the Sociology of Sport*, 41(3): 357–73.

Kirk, D. (1992) *Defining Physical Education: The Social Construction of a Subject in Postwar Britain*, Basingstoke: Falmer.

——(1999) 'Physical culture, physical education and relational analysis', *Sport Education and Society*, 4(1): 63–74.

——(2002) 'Physical education: A gendered history', in D. Penney (ed.) *Gender and Physical Education: Contemporary Issues and Future Directions*, London: Routledge, pp. 24–37.

——(2005) 'Physical education, youth sport and lifelong participation: The importance of early learning experiences', *European Physical Education Review*, 11(3): 239–55.

Kirk, D., Macdonald, D. and O'Sullivan, M. (eds) (2006) *The Handbook of Physical Education*, London: Sage.

Knez, K. (2007) *The Meaning and Place of Physical Activity in the Lives of Young Muslim Women*. Unpublished thesis, University of Queensland, Australia.

——(2010) 'Being Muslim and being female: Negotiating physical activity and a gendered body', in J. Wright and D. Macdonald (eds) *Young People, Physical Activity and the Everyday*, London: Routledge, pp. 104–17.

Larsson, H., Birgitta, F. and Redelius, K. (2009) 'Queering physical education. Between benevolence towards girls and a tribute to masculinity', *Physical Education and Sport Pedagogy*, 14(1): 1–17.

Leaman, O. (1984) *Sit on the Sidelines and Watch the Boys Play: Sex Differentiation in Physical Education*, London: Longman for Schools Council.

Lee, J. and Macdonald, D. (2010) '"Are they just checking our obesity or what?" The healthism discourse and rural young women', *Sport Education and Society*, 15(2): 203–19.

Long, J., Hylton, K., Sparklen, K., Ratna, A. and Bailey, S. (2009) *Systematic Review of Literature on Black and Minority Ethnic Communities in Sport and Physical Recreation*, Leeds: Carnegie Research Institute, Leeds Metropolitan University, for The UK Sports Councils and Sporting Equals.

Lupton, R. and Power, A. (2004) *Minority Ethnic Groups in Britain* [Internet], Case-Brookings Census Briefs, London School of Economics. Available from <www.sticerd.lse.ac.uk/dps/case> (accessed 2 October 2008).

Mac an Ghaill, M. (1994) *The Making of Men: Masculinities, Sexualities and Schooling*, Buckingham: Open University Press.

Macdonald, D. (2006) 'Theoretical perspectives in physical education research', in D. Kirk, D. Macdonald and M. O'Sullivan (eds) *The Handbook of Physical Education*, London: Sage, pp. 1–2.

Macdonald, D. and Tinning, R. (1995) 'Physical education teacher education and the trend to proletarianization: A case study', *Journal of Teaching in Physical Education*, 15(1): 98–118.

Macdonald, D., Kirk, D. and Braiuka, S. (1999) 'The social construction of the physical activity field at the school/university interface', *European Journal of Physical Education*, 5(1): 17–38.

Macdonald, D., Abbott, R., Knez, K. and Nelson, K. (2009) 'Taking exercise: Cultural diversity and physically active lifestyles', *Sport, Education and Society*, 14(1): 1–19.

Macdonald, D., Kirk, D., Metzler, M., Nilges, L. M., Schempp, P. and Wright, J. (2002) 'It's all very well, in theory. Theoretical perspectives and their applications in contemporary pedagogical research', *Quest*, 54(2): 133–56.

Martino, W. and Pallotta-Chiarolli, M. (2003) *So What's a Boy? Addressing Issues of Masculinity and Schooling*, Maidenhead: Open University Press.

Messner, M. (1996) 'Studying up on sex', *Sociology of Sport Journal*, 13(3): 221–37.

Mirza, H. S. (2009) *Race, Gender and Educational Desire: Why Black Women Succeed and Fail*, London: Routledge.

Morely, D., Bailey, R., Tan, J. and Cooke, B. (2005) 'Inclusive physical education: Teachers' views of including pupils with special educational needs and/or disabilities in physical education', *European Journal of Physical Education*, 11(1): 84–107.

Nelson, A., Macdonald, D. and Abbott, R. (2010) 'The cultural interface: Theoretical and "real" spaces for urban Indigenous young people and physical activity', in J. Wright and D. Macdonald (eds) *Young People, Physical Activity and the Everyday*, London: Routledge, pp. 75–92.

Oliver, K. and Lalik, R. (2004) '"The beauty walk": Interrogating whiteness as the norm for beauty within one school's hidden curriculum', in J. Evans, B. Davis and J. Wright (eds) *Body Knowledge and Control: Studies in the Sociology of Physical Education and Health*, London: Routledge, pp. 115–29.

Paechter, C. (2001) 'Using poststructuralist ideas in gender theory and research', in B. Francis and C. Skelton (eds) *Investigating Gender: Contemporary Perspectives in Education*, Buckingham: Open University Press, pp. 41–51.

——(2003) 'Power, bodies and identity: How different forms of physical education construct varying masculinities and femininities in secondary school', *Sex Education*, 3(1): 47–59.

Paechter, C. and Clark, S. (2007) 'Who are tomboys and how do we recognise them?', *Women's Studies International Forum*, 30(4): 342–54.

Penney, D. (2001) 'The revision and initial implementation of the national curriculum for physical education in England', *Bulletin of Physical Education*, 37(2): 93–135.

——(2002a) 'Equality, equity and inclusion in physical education', in A. Laker (ed.) *The Sociology of Sport and Physical Education*, London: Routledge, pp. 110–28.

——(2002b) *Gender and Physical Education: Contemporary Issues and Future Directions*, New York: Routledge.

——(2006) 'Curriculum construction and change', in D. Kirk, D. Macdonald and M. O'Sullivan (eds) *The Handbook of Physical Education*, London: Sage, pp. 565–79.

Penney, D. and Evans, J. (1999) *Politics, Policy and Practice in Physical Education*, London: E & FN Spon.

Penney, D. and Harris, J. (1997) 'Extra-curricular physical education: More of the same for the more able', *Sport Education and Society*, 2(1): 41–54.

Pfeiffer, D. (1998) 'The ICIDH and the need for its revision', *Disability and Society*, 13(4): 503–23.

Pheonix, A. (2009) 'De-colonising practices: Negotiating narratives from racialised and gendered experiences of education', *Race Ethnicity and Education*, 12(1): 101–14.

Rich, E., Holroyd, R. and Evans, J. (2004) '"Hungry to be noticed": Young women, anorexia and schooling', in J. Evans., B. Davies and J. Wright (eds) *Body Knowledge and Control: Studies in the Sociology of Physical Education and Health*, London: Routledge, pp. 173–90.

Sabo, D. and Veliz, P. (2008) *Go Out and Play: Youth Sports in America*, New York: Women's Sports Foundation.

Scraton, S. (1992) *Shaping up to Womanhood: Gender and Girls' Physical Education*, Buckingham: Open University Press.

Skelton, C. (2001) *Schooling the Boys: Masculinities and Primary Education*, Buckingham: Open University Press.

Sport, Education and Society, Special Issue (2010) Body Pedagogies, Education and Health, 15(2): 147–259.

Sport England (2003) *Young People and Sport in England: Trends in Participation 1994–2002*, London: Sport England.

——(2011) *Active People Survey* [Internet]. Available from <www.sportengland.org/research/active_people_survey.aspx> (accessed 4 September 2011).

Squires, S. L. and Sparkes, A. (1996) 'Circles of silence: Sexual identity in physical education and sport', *Sport, Education and Society*, 1(1): 71–101.

Sykes, H. (1998) 'Turning the closets inside/out: Towards a queer-feminist theory in women's physical education', *Sociology of Sport Journal*, 15: 154–73.

——(2006) 'Transsexual and transgender policies in sport', *Women in Sport and Physical Activity Journal*, 15(1): 3–13.

——(2010) 'Looking back, looking sideways: Adult perspectives about student experiences of queerness in Canadian physical education', in M. O'Sullivan and A. MacPhail (eds) *Young People's Voices in Physical Education and Youth Sport*, London: Routledge, pp. 123–41.

Tinning, R. (2010) *Pedagogy and Human Movement: Theory, Practice, Research*, London: Routledge.

Turner, B. (2008) *The Body and Society: Explorations in Social Theory*, London: Sage.

Valentine, G. (2007) 'Theorizing and researching intersectionality: A challenge for feminist geography', *The Professional Geographer*, 59(1): 10–21.

Webb, L. and Macdonald, D. (2007a) 'Dualing with gender: Teachers' work, careers and leadership in physical education', *Gender and Education*, 19(4): 491–512.

——(2007b) 'Techniques of power in physical education and the under-representation of women in leadership', *Journal of Teaching in Physical Education*, 26(3): 279–97.

Wellard, I. (2007) 'Inflexible bodies and minds: Exploring the gendered limits in contemporary sport, physical education and dance', in I. Wellard (ed.) *Rethinking Gender and Sport*, London: Routledge, pp. 84–98.

Willis, P. (1974) *Performance and Meaning: A Socio-cultural View of Women in Sport*, Birmingham: Centre for Contemporary Cultural Studies.

Wright, J. (1996) 'The construction of complementarity in physical education', *Gender and Education*, 8(1): 61–79.

——(1997) 'The construction of gender contexts in single sex and co-educational physical education lessons', *Sport, Education and Society*, 2(1): 55–72.

——(2006) 'Physical education research from postmodern, poststructural and postcolonial perspectives', in D. Kirk, D. Macdonald and M. O'Sullivan (eds) *The Handbook of Physical Education*, London: Sage, pp. 59–75.

Wright, J. and Harwood, V. (eds) (2009) *Biopolitics and the 'Obesity Epidemic': Governing Bodies*, London: Routledge.

Wright, J. and Macdonald, D. (eds) (2010) *Young People, Physical Activity and the Everyday*, London: Routledge.

Wright, J., Macdonald, D. and Groom, L. (2003) 'Physical activity and young people: Beyond participation', *Sport Education and Society*, 8(1): 17–34.

2 A narrative approach to research in physical education, youth sport and health

Fiona Dowling

What's in a story?

If I were to ask you to reflect upon some well-known storylines from physical education (PE) classes, you might well conjure up one of the following scenes: an image of a strict PE teacher, who seemingly wallows in his pupils' miseries; a mortally embarrassed pupil struggling to jump over an oversized gymnastics horse in front of her cajoling peers; or a self-satisfied group of pupils skiving off from the running circuit in order to have a cigarette without getting caught. The reason why these images easily spring to mind is, in part, due to their status in popular culture. Books have been written, and films have been produced, which reconstruct these particular narratives and they have accordingly become a part of the public discourse about the subject of PE. Divorced from specific people or settings they represent stereotypical or mythical tales, and it is easy to dismiss them as harmless and entertaining. Yet, as this chapter will illustrate, such tales should not easily be dismissed, but rather embraced as a means with which to better understand the professional worlds we have chosen to inhabit. Indeed, when such stories reflect the lived worlds of named persons they can be anything but innocent, representing instead incidents of social injustice and inequity. An analysis of them can provide invaluable insights into the mechanisms of power within such settings. Research in PE, youth sport and health has on the whole ignored this useful tool for understanding social action for reasons which will be outlined below, but I will argue that such an approach can no longer be marginalized within the field when we live in a society permeated by narrative.

Generally speaking, we can say that we all live our lives by stories or narratives. As the literary theorist and philosopher Roland Barthes (1977) observed,

> narrative is present in every age, in every place, in every society; it begins with the very history of mankind and there is nowhere, nor has been, a people without narrative ... . All classes, all human groups, have their narratives ... narrative is international, transhistorical, transcultural: it is simply there, like life itself.

> (Barthes 1977: 79)

We make sense of who we are, and the experiences we have, via storytelling. Stories are a linguistic form in which human experience can be expressed (Polkinghorne 1995). They provide a structure and a sense of order to 'the multitude of fragmentary experiences that constitute our lives' (Plummer 2001: 185). Our narratives may take the form of 'talking to oneself' or alternatively telling tales about ourselves in communication with others and, in so doing, we are in fact constructing our identities (Riessman 2008). This is not to say that our identities are fixed but, on the contrary, the stories we produce about ourselves are fluid; they are about becoming and being, as well as longing to become. New experiences or simply finding oneself in a different context can lead to our lives being re-storied. As Clandinin and Connelly (2000) remind us, our experience is temporal and we therefore need to see our experiences on a continuum, in addition to as part of a much wider encompassing socio-historical narrative; we are inevitably a part of both local and national cultures, and our past and imagined futures.

Just dwell a minute upon the way you present, or 'story', yourself in the context of your chosen programme of study and professional development. A love of sport and memorable experiences from PE lessons, positive experiences from coaching others or, alternatively, a desire to help others, are frequently mentioned reasons for choosing a career in PE, sport and health (Armour and Jones 1998; Dowling Næss 1996, 1998, 2001b) and perhaps a storyline not unlike your own? In all likelihood you provide a variety of reasons for your choice and organize them in what we might call a 'plotted form' – i.e. you provide the listener with a sense of coherence between the various reasons and some causality about when, and why, you chose your particular education. Such personal narratives provide us with meaning and they guide our action. If you are nearing the end of your course, you have no doubt modified your professional-identity narrative many times during the past few years in response to significant experiences both within the sphere of your education and from your life beyond. The tales you tell about yourself are also strongly influenced by the intended listener(s): quite clearly the story you tell to a close friend assumes more than likely a different form than the one you might tell a mentor during a work placement. It is particularly important to note the latter and to understand that stories are not simply social products (i.e. they are not merely reifications of lived realities) but they must be conceptualized as forms of social action. As Gubrium and Holstein (2009: xvi) remind us, 'storytellers not only tell stories, but they *do* things with them.' Narratives can serve a range of functions and their communication can have many consequences (Gubrium and Holstein 2009; Riessman 2008). With regard to a personal narrative about one's choice of professional education, the tale might be told, for example, for the purposes of justification, of persuasion, or perhaps simply to do some memory work. Via such storytelling we claim not only identities for ourselves, but inevitably designate roles to others. In constructing narratives about others (including assigning motive and reason to events), we are necessarily positioning them in relation to our own perceptions of the world. This is a theme I discuss further below.

Something else which is important to keep in mind about narratives is the fact that we are not simply free to choose 'our story', but the way we script our lives is most often a reflection of the socio-cultural locations we inhabit (Czarniawska 2004; Goodson 1995; Gubrium and Holstein 2009; Phoenix 2008; Riessman 2008; Squire 2008; Squire *et al.* 2008). In the context of this book, the way we present ourselves as gendered, classed and a member of a particular ethnic group will depend upon the available storylines for being girl and/or boy in our family and local community; storylines about what it means to be working, middle or upper class; and storylines about the values of different ethnic traditions. Similarly, socio-historical views about sexuality, disability, religion or age will influence the way in which we 'choose' to narrate our self-stories, and our stories of others. In this way our individual stories say something not only about us as individuals but equally something about the context in which we live and work; micro stories about individual lives are therefore also stories about macro societal relations, which is a theme addressed in Chapter 1. Tales from the locker room or the playing field are inextricably linked to local, national and global narratives. Nor are we, of course, free to 'hear' all forms of narratives; socio-economic and cultural norms affect the ways in which stories are consumed and this is an aspect of narrative inquiry which deserves further examination later on in the chapter.

The 'narrative turn' in social science and its significance for research in PE and sport

The increased interest in narrative ways of knowing, which is commonly referred to as the 'narrative turn', has occurred across the range of social science disciplines, including education, sociology, psychology, anthropology, history and the humanities (Plummer 2001). It is linked to the so-called 'postmodern turn', or what the sociologist Giddens (1991) terms the 'late-modern' turn, which indicates a shift 'in many social forms – from architecture and literature, through social theory and analysis, and on to culture in general, and society in particular' (Plummer 2001: 12). As Plummer (2001) explains further,

> At the heart of all this is the breakdown of a traditional form of society, one which was usually authoritarian with strong religious commitments to an overarching belief system. Bit by bit we see the arrival of a more provisional world, one where there is an increased sensitivity to diversities, differences, differentiations – to what has been called the 'pluralization ethos' (Connolly 1995). In this view the world becomes less dominated by generalities and 'master narratives', and there is a turn towards 'local cultures' and their 'multiplicity of stories'.
>
> (Plummer 2001: 12)

In relation to social research, including research on PE and sport, these conditions of postmodernity lead us to distrust universal truth claims, favouring instead the notion of multiple, local, contextual 'truths', which tend to be in flux and disorder (Plummer 2001; Sparkes 2002). In other words, our understandings about the nature of knowledge and how we can best understand our social conditions are once again being challenged. Chapter 1 shows clearly how competing ideas about social difference and inequality have evolved in a series of waves over the past few decades, reflecting shifts in paradigms, which Flintoff and Fitzgerald refer to as different theoretical trajectories. Although scholars describe the current status of social science research as 'unsettling' (Sparkes 2002), it is nevertheless important to remember that the ways in which we perceive the physical and social worlds of PE and sport, and how best we can come to know them, have always been a matter of judgement based upon competing philosophical assumptions. It is impossible for us to simply 'know'; we must make plausible and informed choices about our knowledge claims. Clearly the intricacies of the philosophy of science are well beyond the scope of this chapter but, for the purposes of contextualizing narrative ways of knowing, I think it is, however, important to distinguish between the paradigms that are most prevalent in our field.

When I talk about a paradigm, I refer to a set of 'hidden' assumptions which guide the research process and our ways of knowing: for example, about how we understand the concepts of gender or disability. These assumptions regard the nature of reality, what constitutes 'truth', and the guidelines for seeking and judging evidence about the 'truth'. In 1992, Sparkes identified three major paradigms in sports science and these continue to operate today. The dominant paradigm is that of 'positivism', and the competing paradigms are called the 'interpretive' and the 'critical interpretive' paradigms. Whilst the latter is concerned with criticism and emancipation, such as a recognition of social inequalities in sport and a desire to create more equitable arenas, it nevertheless shares many common elements with the interpretive paradigm, whereas positivist values are in strong contrast to them (for a more detailed discussion see Sparkes 1992). At the risk of being superficial, 'positivism' purports the existence of an objective social world, which awaits discovery as long as we find the right methods for the task of 'measuring' the many variables of which it is constituted. It claims that the social world can be investigated in much the same way as the physical or natural world, and hence methods in the natural sciences are employed to unveil the structures which exist independently of our appreciation of them. A process of deductive reasoning and the use of experimental methods enable researchers in their quests and, in keeping with scientific rigour, results are presented as mathematical relations, distancing the knower from the known. Categorical research on difference and inequality is carried out within this paradigm.

'Interpretive' and 'critical interpretive' assumptions rest on the other hand upon a world view which claims that reality, as we know it, is intimately connected to our subjective cognitive and emotional understandings of it.

Hence appropriate research methods are inductive, hermeneutical (inter-pretive) and dialectic: the knower and the known are inseparable, and knowledge is subjective, multiple, ambiguous, value laden, local and con-textual. Relational and postmodern research on difference and inequality is carried out within these paradigms. What is crucial to understand here is the explicit recognition of the active role of the researcher, and of those who are researched, in the co-production of knowledge about PE and sport and, accordingly, the recognition that the *language* used to describe and interpret social action in PE and sport is integral to our understanding, and indeed the very construction of these social worlds. It is not possible to have direct access to someone's experience and instead we are faced with ambiguous repre-sentations of it (Richardson 2000; Riessman 1993, 2008). When we endea-vour, for example, to enhance our professional knowledge about disability in the field of PE or sport we draw upon *narrated interpretations* of actors who have experience either directly, or indirectly, from the phenomenon. The lan-guage chosen to describe these experiences is not a 'transparent medium, unambiguously reflecting stable, singular meanings' (Riessman 1993: 4) about disability; rather it is chosen by the subject as a means for conveying emo-tional lived experience (a subjective, value laden interpretation). This medi-ated understanding of disability can then, in turn, be interpreted by a listener in the throes of daily life (the double hermeneutic) or by the explicit use of a particular theoretical lens or construct (the triple hermeneutic). Of course, the teller may also be in a position to interpret her/his experiences by the use of theoretical perspectives, and will inevitably draw upon disability discourses in society at large. In other words, the 'postmodern turn' has brought new vitality to the belief that individuals make sense of experience and award it some kind of value by casting it in narrative form, and when these narratives are communicated to fellow humans they provide a potential to share mean-ings and to understand our social worlds. Moreover, it celebrates the embo-diment of knowing, emphasizing the role that emotions and the senses play in how we come to understand our social worlds.

As I indicated above, the PE and sports science research communities have seemed loath to embrace the 'narrative turn', notwithstanding a few notable exceptions of narrative research within the field (e.g. Armour and Jones 1998; Brown and Rich 2002; Denison 1996; Denison and Markula 2002; Dowling Næss 1996, 1998, 2001a, 2001b; Garrett 2006; Groves and Laws 2003; Krogh Christensen 2007; Oliver 1998; Smith 2010; Smith and Sparkes 2005, 2008b; Sparkes 1994, 1996, 1997; Sparkes and Silvennoinen 1999; Templin *et al.* 1991; Tinning 1997). No doubt this hesitance reflects the multidisciplinary nature of sports sciences and the way in which the biological sciences (e.g. exercise physiology, biomechanics), with their clear links to the natural sciences, have historically dominated preferred 'ways of knowing' even in the social sciences in sport and PE research (Evans and Davies 1986, 2004; Sparkes 1992; Tinning 2004). Qualitative inquiry in PE, health and sport has nevertheless become more commonplace in the course of the past 20 years, and I hope that the remainder of the chapter, as indeed this book, will encourage you to think about 'interpretive' and 'critical interpretive' narrative inquiry, and to enable you to appreciate the untapped potential of this way of knowing.

Defining narrative

I must, however, disappoint you if you seek a clear definition of narrative inquiry because, due to its multidisciplinary nature, and indeed its range of epistemological foundations, there are multiple ways of discerning narrative research. According to Riessman the field of narrative inquiry in the human sciences can be likened to 'a veritable garden of cross-disciplinary hybrids' (Riessman 2008: 14), whereas Squire *et al.* (2008) characterize it as being 'incoherent' in part 'due to its divergent beginnings, and partly from the theoretical fault lines that traverse it' (Squire *et al.* 2008: 3). The problem of how to define narrative also arises because of its widespread use in popular culture. As many scholars observe, it is almost as if any text can be called a narrative in postmodern society.

Within the field of interpretive inquiry, Polkinghorne (1995) offers nonetheless a useful distinction between what he terms 'narrative as prosaic discourse' and 'narrative as story'. Narrative as prosaic discourse refers to 'any text that consists of complete sentences linked to a coherent and integrated statement' (Polkinghorne 1995: 6), which is therefore distinct from text with metre and rhyme. Interview transcriptions or field notes in qualitative research projects can fall into this category, and narrative, in this sense, draws attention to the emphasis that qualitative researchers pay to everyday linguistic expressions. Narrative as story refers, on the other hand, to a particular type of discourse, the story, which he defines as

> a special type of discourse production. In a story, events and actions are drawn together into an organized whole by means of a plot. A plot is a type of conceptual scheme by which a contextual meaning of individual events can be displayed.
>
> (Polkinghorne 1995: 7)

Narrative as story therefore also draws attention to linguistic expressions of human experience, but it focuses explicitly upon the ways in which particular incidents are linked together in, for example, an interview or a case study to form a unified episode. 'Stories are concerned with human attempts to progress to a solution, clarification, or unravelling of an incomplete situation' (Polkinghorne 1995: 7), and provide a means for studying the connectedness of life which is unique to human experience.

In a similar vein, Riessman (2008) citing Salmon (2008) purports that all narratives, whatever the subject discipline, work with the notion of contingency: 'Whatever the content, stories demand the consequential linking of events or ideas. Narrative shaping entails imposing a meaningful pattern on what otherwise would be random and disconnected' (Salmon 2008 cited in Riessman 2008: 5). Let me illustrate this through a very simple story. In the absence of a plot, two observations from a PE lesson remain as two independent happenings: the PE teacher shouted; the pupil burst into tears. By providing a contingent link between these two episodes, a story can provide a possible explanation for the events: the PE teacher shouted loudly across the gymnasium because there was a group of pupils misbehaving, at which point one of the pupils burst into tears as he felt unjustly treated both by his bullying fellow pupils and the teacher. Although plots are often taken for granted in everyday life, they provide us with the means for structuring the ways in which we understand and describe the relationship between the events and choices we make in human interaction, for example, in a PE lesson or during a health promotion activity. Plummer (2001: 187) likens plots to the dynamos of human narratives: they 'turn them on'. Plots provide a story with momentum and make them more interesting, as well as providing coherence between discrete events. This coherence may at the same time be illusory because many stories, like our experiences, are fragmentary and messy, and stories cannot always fulfil the listener's desire for closure (Riessman 2008). Plots also provide a temporal framework for the story, which can range from as long as a lifetime to daily or hourly episodes (e.g. a training session at the local sports club or doing homework). In Western cultures, stories tend to be organized around linear time with a beginning, middle and end, and the notion of 'and then what happened?', but post-modern sensibilities highlight the need to be open for episodic plots which are structured around themes as opposed to time (Plummer 2001; Riessman 1993, 2008).

Characters are another characteristic of stories, usually with one, or a few, main characters, supported by a cast of individuals. Drawing upon literary theory, it is possible to analyse the characters according to 'storytypes', such as a protagonist (chief person in a story), an antagonist (opponent) and a witness of some kind (Plummer 2001). Alternatively it is possible to see characters as 'archetypes', such as the Wise Old Man, the Perfect Child or the Hero. Within the stereotypical portrayals of PE and sports settings described in the introduction, such types might, for example, be the Sergeant Major PE teacher or the Clumsy Pupil. Indeed, Bruner (1990 cited in Phoenix 2008) draws our attention to the important distinction between 'canonical narratives', which are tales about how life *ought* to be lived according to normative, cultural expectations, and 'personal narratives', which are stories about how life is actually lived, and how the latter are inevitably linked to the available cultural stock of plots in the former. Biblical parables like 'The Good Samaritan' or fables, such as Aesop's 'The Tortoise and the Hare', are well-known examples of canonical narratives in Christian, Western societies. They have clear moral messages for the listener, which we all from time to time have perhaps had reason to draw upon (or tales like them) in the course of our own storytelling. Of course these stories function very differently from personal narratives of experience.

Another feature of narratives is the style in which they are told. Again, drawing upon literary theory, we can talk about the 'genre' of a story or a plot. Following White (1973), Czarniawska (2004) informs us that stories are often emplotted with the help of classical figures of speech (the tropes of metaphor, metonymy, synecdoche and irony), and they are organized according to certain dramaturgical conventions, such as romance, tragedy, comedy and satire. Due to our interest in the language used to describe lived experience in PE, health and sport, it is useful therefore to keep in mind the purpose of such figures of speech. Metaphor is the concept of understanding one thing in relation to another. A descriptive term or a name is used in relation to something, or someone else, to which it is imaginatively, but not literally, applicable. A PE teacher might, for example, ask her pupils to 'clear the decks' after a badminton lesson, referring to the need to clear the gymnasium of equipment, which is clearly far removed from the origin of the expression associated with clearing the deck of a ship. Metonymy is a trope in which a thing or concept is not called by its own name, but by the name of something intimately associated with that thing or concept. For instance, 'the curse' is used as a metonym for menstruation because historically it has been associated with restricting girls' and young women's human rights on the basis of biology, such as preventing young women from participating in 'unsuitable' sports. Closely associated to metonymy, synecdoche is a figure of speech which builds on a part–whole relationship where the part symbolizes the whole, for example, 'wheels' may be used to signify a car in a phrase like 'I love your wheels!' Finally, irony serves the purpose of sharpening or highlighting certain discordant features of reality by conveying a meaning which is the exact opposite of its literal meaning. For example, a pupil who loathed a PE lesson will state that 'this was the best PE lesson I've ever experienced in my life!' In so doing, the pupil aims to assert the 'truth' that all PE lessons are gruesome. I am not proposing here for a moment that we all need to become literary theorists in order to engage in narrative inquiry, yet I do believe that we need to be acutely aware of the slippery nature of language and the ways in which individuals consciously, and subconsciously, construct images of lived experience via these symbolic forms for achieving specific purposes (Ricoeur 2003). By paying attention to the multilayers of language we may be afforded multilayered insights into the experiences of equity and/or difference in PE, sport and health. As Riessman (2008) reminds us, there are many ways to narrate experience, and the ways in which individuals select the literary apparatus to construct a tale (e.g. by the use of irony or ambiguity) are not without significance; texts therefore require a 'close reading'.

Picking up on what I wrote in the introduction, every story is linked to the socio-cultural context in which it is narrated. This includes the physical and spatial environment in which the experience is lived and told, as well as the socio-political aspects of the location. A narrator situated, for example, in an area of social deprivation and a school building suffering from years of neglect is likely to tell a different tale than a storyteller in a prosperous community attending a well-maintained educational establishment. Socio-economic locations, as indeed ethnic or religious affiliation, influence the story as told in terms of the language used and the 'truths' it draws upon. As Phoenix (2008) states, individual 'small stories' or 'personal narratives' about equity and difference in PE, sport and health reflect in some way the available 'big stories' or discourses about equity and difference (Phoenix 2008). The plot structures and literary apparatus (described above) that individuals 'choose' to use in order to tell stories about their lives in PE, sport and health draw inevitably upon the plots and literary forms that their local, and national, culture provides. These storytelling resources are not equally distributed, and reflect the unequal distribution of power in society at large. We need to be conscious of the way in which some cultural stories are more privileged than others, and that some people simply do not have access to tell the story in the culturally preferred style (Gubrium and Holstein 2009; Phoenix 2008). Integral to the importance of acknowledging the context of storytelling, is the role of the listener (situated in the context) in any tale because, as stated above, particular tales are told to particular audiences for particular reasons; narratives can have very different functions and must also be understood in this light. In the words of Gubrium and Holstein (2009), 'settings are integral parts of narrativity. Whoever heard of a story being told nowhere, at no time?' (Gubrium and Holstein 2009: 22).

The functions of narratives

Indeed, let us now consider in a little more detail the notion of storytelling as social action and look at the range of functions that narratives can have in general, as well as more specifically in relation to issues relating to equity and difference in PE, health and sport. To reiterate a point from above, individuals and groups most obviously use narrative as a means of comprehending their experience and carving out their identities. By chronicling memorable events, organizations and cultural groups are able to pass on privileged values; events or stories are retold from generation to generation in order to preserve a group's shared identity. At an individual level this function of storytelling, that is to say the 'memory work' of narrative, is clearly wrought with challenges when we acknowledge that our present selves are inevitably an expression of revising and editing the memories of the past within the self of the present. In this way the story of one's self is boundless, seemingly lacking a beginning, middle or end, yet the 'narrative reality' of a particular story provides us fortunately with a temporal and contextual framework for constructing manageable units (Gubrium and Holstein 2009). Storying ourselves and being accountable to others via our sense-making is, in fact, fundamental to being human (Polkinghorne 1995; Riessman 2008). Our storytelling capability is a skill which we learn from an early age, although the skill requires practice and time (over a period of many years) to reach a level whereby we are capable of telling credible, rhetorically persuasive, socially effective narratives (Salmon and Riessman 2008). The ability to tell a good tale tends to go hand in hand with the ability to listen and to respond to prompts from a recipient, whether this listener is an actual person or an imagined audience.

The rhetorical art of persuasion brings us to another function of narrative, namely that of arguing a point of view (Riessman 2008). Competing views, or discourses, about teacher or coach professionalism can, for example, be storied with the intention of reaching particular goals (Dowling 2011). In relation to equity, a story might be used to depict instances of being treated fairly or conversely to illustrate feelings of indignation. Just recollect the number of times you have storied your frustration about incidents concerning the Hopeless Referee! In political terms, stories are narrated with the view to persuade their audiences about certain 'truths', whether this is at a national, governmental level, concerning, for example, equal rights to education, or at a micro-political level, such as arguing the case against an unjust grade in a PE exam. An associated function of storytelling is the way in which narratives can also be used to consciously *mis*lead an audience. Reflect upon the way in which war propaganda illustrates the latter: the 'story' about Iraq's atomic arsenal, with the ensuing invasion by foreign powers, is a recent case in point.

In this way, stories work to position people or institutions, and they can be told about people who are not themselves privy to the narrative; this is what power is about (Czarniawska 2004). Women's bodies, and particularly working-class women's bodies, have, for example, been, and continue to be, patholo-gized via narrativity (Skeggs 1997). As a result many women are excluded, or have been excluded, from a variety of social arenas, including different sports (Hargreaves 1994, 2001). In a similar way, tales about disabled, dysfunctional bodies can function to accomplish social exclusion (Fitzgerald 2005), whilst 'racist' narratives can be seen to serve to privilege white supremacy (Gilborn 2008). Narrative research in PE teacher education has shown how stories about initiation rituals steeped in traditional values about heterosexual mas-culinity (Sparkes *et al.* 2007) and stories about the 'non-existence' of gay PE students (Sparkes 1997) can work to position students within a traditional gender order, leaving little or no room for stories of nonconformity. Once again it is therefore important to remind ourselves that we are not necessarily in a position to tell a story as we wish, but rather we are often positioned by the available dominant storylines. Some stories dominate because they act to suppress alternative storylines (Czarniawska 2004; Goodson 1995). Narratives can function to instil conformity, and there can accordingly be a high price to pay when the storyline is altered to one of resistance (Barone 1995; Gubrium and Holstein 2009).

Narratives can thus function as powerful tools for achieving particular social goals, whether this is in a global, political capacity or in everyday encounters on the playing field or in the staffroom. As political tools, tales can operate to mobilize audiences to challenge unacceptable social practice. Feminists have, for example, long recognized this function of personal and social stories (Mirza 2009; Pheonix 2009), as indeed have other political movements fighting for social change (Connor 2008; Morris 1991). Evocative, well-crafted tales can open up unknown worlds to different audiences and persuade individuals to support a specific point of view. Of course, stories can also simply function as pure entertainment (Riessman 2008). Indeed, I think it is important to realize that many of the functions outlined here tend to overlap in practice. I am, for example, in no doubt that to mobilize PE teachers or coaches to embrace new practices requires considerable persuasive, narrative skills. In using a narrative approach to better understand our professional worlds, we will therefore need to keep these overlapping functions in mind when we analyse tales from the field.

Research methods in narrative inquiry

In turning to the question of what methods are appropriate for narrative inquiry in PE, youth sport and health, the scope of choice and the challenges of the various methods make it impossible for me to do justice to them within this chapter. Remembering, however, that interpretive and critical interpretive paradigms use research methods which are inductive, hermeneutical and dialectic, it is true to say that narrative inquiry draws upon a range of methods within 'qualitative research' (Denzin and Lincoln 2000a). Stories may be generated 'naturally' in the field in an ethnographic study (Coffey and Atkinson 1996; Denzin 1997; Delamont 2002; Patton 2001), or by engaging in autoethnography (Coffey 1999; Ellis and Bochner 2000). They can be 'activated' by the use of interviews (Gubrium and Holstein 2002, 2003; Kvale and Brinkmann 2009; Mason 1996; Riessman 2008): by online interviewing (James and Busher 2009), by life history interviews (Plummer 2001) or focus group interviews (Barbour and Kitzinger 1999). They can also be created via visual methods such as photography or film (Bach 2007), or by the use of diaries or video diaries (Banks 2007), and stories are, of course, 'naturally' occurring in social media such as blogs or Facebook (Holland 2008) or, more broadly speaking, on the internet (Hine 2000; Markham and Baym 2009). Due to the inherent need for researchers to be reflexive about their own role in the qualitative research process, as well as the recognition that they are inevitably co-producers of mediated experiences or stories, a research diary or log-book is, in addition, a very useful tool for aiding this type of reflection (Mason 1996). The type of method(s) which the researcher chooses will inevitably reflect her/his research interests and questions, as well as her/his paradigmatic beliefs (Denzin and Lincoln 2000a; Mason 1996).

With regard to the organization of narrative inquiry projects, these can be initiated by researchers but they can also be carried out collaboratively by researchers and practitioners/clients and, of course, they can be initiated and developed by practitioner-researchers, such as teachers or health personnel (Clandinin and Connelly 2000; Connelly and Clandinin 1990; Goodson 1995; McNiff and Whithead 2005; Stenhouse 1975). In relation to the latter, PE teachers, sports coaches or health officers might, for example, benefit from systematically writing self-narratives about their experiences, and the ways in which they conceptualize difference in PE lessons, sports contexts or health settings, as well as in their lives more broadly, so that they can become more aware of the 'taken-for-grantedness' of their social worlds (Butt *et al.* 1992; Cortazzi 1993; Davies and Gannon 2006). On the other hand, they may wish to systematically analyse their practice in relation to students in schools/girls and boys in sport/clients, and therefore embark upon some ethnographic fieldwork or interview research, either as a practitioner-researcher or in collaboration with researchers at a nearby university or college (Clandinin 2007). Clearly the possibilities are overwhelming, and I presume that research of this kind is often a reflection of 'personal troubles' being turned into 'public issues': the result of the practitioner's or researcher's sociological/educational imagination (Wright Mills 1959).

Despite the wide range of research methods available to the narrative inquirer, it is important to understand that their 'products' are nonetheless similar; whatever method has been employed, researchers generate texts. These texts are interpretations of individuals' social worlds and interactions, whether they are constructed from visual representations of difference in PE, sport and health (e.g. from a video diary), or whether they are transcriptions from interview talk or participant observation. Movement and embodied experiences and practices (from activities such as running, tackling an opponent and weighing oneself on scales, to taking a shower) are 'translated' into language in narrative inquiry. It is these texts that constitute data and it is these interpretations of experience that are analysed (see below for discussion of analysis). Here it is timely to remind ourselves that researchers co-produce these data: the ways in which they structure and punctuate the language of interview encounters, field notes, or texts based from film recreate imitations of these lived worlds (Riessman 2008). The texts do not, in other words, signify the 'real thing'. A reflexive stance about the ways in which researchers 'write data' is therefore essential, as discussed above, and should be incorporated into analyses of them (Denzin 1997; Denzin and Lincoln 2000b; Richardson 2000).

The moral responsibilities which accompany writing in narrative inquiry are, in fact, merely one of many ethical considerations for researchers using qualitative methods. Other ethical aspects centre on issues such as power relations between the researcher and the researched, the intricacies of 'informed consent', the inevitable co-production of multiple interpretations in the field, the researcher's power to inscribe the social realities of Others, the moral responsibility to 'give' and not to simply 'take' from research participants, to mention but a few. Once again, these crucial aspects of doing narrative research are unfortunately beyond the remit for this chapter.

Accordingly, I advise you to acquaint yourself with them in all their complexities in the research methods literature, but I will address some of them as they relate specifically to narrative inquiry in a little more detail below.

How can we analyse stories of (in)equity and difference in PE, youth sport and health?

Given the multiple definitions of narrative inquiry, and the multidisciplinary nature of the field of narrative research, it is not surprising to learn that we are faced with a number of ways with which to analyse the stories that we generate. Of course, our research interests will influence both our choice of methods and the ways we analyse the tales from the field. They will also affect whether we focus more upon the 'what' or content of the narrative data, more upon the 'how' or ways in which stories are told and to whom they are told, or whether we confine our analyses to the structural form or internal organization of the stories (Gubrium and Holstein 2009; Riessman 2008). In fact, Gubrium and Holstein (2009) distinguish between two main ways of approaching data analysis: one which focuses upon the internal organization of stories in texts (e.g. their characterization, the way they are emplotted, the themes therein) and the other which is concerned with 'narrative reality', focusing upon both the internal and the external organization of accounts, and how these two aspects of storytelling relate to each other. They position themselves as researchers interested in 'narrative reality', acknowledging that the substance and internal organization of people's stories are of interest, but emphasizing the need to analyse 'how the circumstances of story telling ... mediate what is said and how it is assembled for the telling' (Gubrium and Holstein 2009: 21). Keeping in mind the many potential functions of narratives, our analytic questions about narratives of diversity in PE, youth sport and health

> require that we step outside of narrative texts and consider questions such as who produces particular kinds of stories, where are they likely to be encountered, what are their purposes and consequences, who are the listeners, under what circumstances are particular narratives more or less accountable, how do they gain acceptance, and how are they challenged? ... We would need to listen to and take account of how stories are taken on board, consider what might be preferred tellings in particular circumstances, and explore the risks and outcomes of storying experience in conformity, or out of line, with what is expected. We would need to pay serious attention to the possibility that narrative occasions and circumstances have privileged stories.
>
> (Gubrium and Holstein 2009: 23)

Riessman (2008) argues, however, that there are three different forms of narrative analysis. First, there is 'thematic analysis' which centres upon content (e.g. what is said, what themes can be identified). Second, she refers to 'structural analysis', which is based upon social linguistics and, as its name suggests, centres upon the linguistic structures of texts and how the narrator uses form and language (e.g. how people tell stories the way they do, how they shape their accounts, how they highlight a point, or how they provide meaning within the plot they narrate). And third, she talks about 'dialogic/ performance analysis', which is akin to Gubrium and Holstein's notion of 'narrative reality' and involves examining the content of stories within the contexts in which they are produced (e.g. whom did the narrator address, when did they act as they did, and for what purposes, and how do contexts beyond the field setting impinge upon the story?).

Another useful distinction, which I think can be made with regard to analysis within the broad field of narrative inquiry, pertains to whether the researcher positions herself/himself as a 'story analyst' or a 'storyteller' (Smith and Sparkes 2008a). According to Polkinghorne (1995: 12) the story analyst uses some form of paradigmatic analysis which 'results in descriptions of themes which hold across stories or in taxonomies of types of stories, characters or settings'. Prior theory, such as theory about social class or the construction of the subject of PE, often serves as a resource with which to interpret the content of the stories in the data via a 'thematic analysis' (Riessman 2008), but researchers also work inductively to develop concepts about the phenomenon they are studying from the data themselves. Alternatively, researchers can work with 'structural' or 'dialogic/performative' analysis, as described above. Irrespective of the preferred analytic approach, the stories are then most often represented in the form of a 'realist tale' (Sparkes 2002), in which the meanings and social actions of the participants are described and then interpreted by the help of theory. On the other hand, the researcher who is a storyteller will engage in what Polkinghorne (1995) calls 'narrative analysis', whereby she produces a story, for example, from an analysis of field notes or interview transcriptions, which is not simply a representation of observations or interview dialogue, but is a tale which aims to provide a dynamic framework in which disconnected data elements can be linked together in an interesting and *explanatory* way. Smith and Sparkes (2008a: 24) write that 'storytellers show what is told and how it is performed through writing … creative analytic practices'. These explanatory stories 'do the work of analysis and theorizing … storytellers move away from abstract theorizing and explaining toward the goals of evocation, intimate involvement, engagement and embodied participation with stories' (Smith and Sparkes 2008a: 21). The researcher's project is therefore one of representation, and writing is seen as a method of analysis; the stories 'speak for themselves'. Such narratives are presented in a variety of forms, such as autoethnographies, poetic representations, ethnodramas or fictional tales (Sparkes 2002), in which theory is an implicit, rather than an explicit, feature of the story.

In Part II of the book you will find a range of narratives which reflect both the plurality of narrative analysis and the various epistemological and ontological assumptions of the researchers. You should be aware that, in the case of the realist tales, we have withheld the explicit theoretical texts from the researchers' representations, but we hope that you will be inspired to interpret them, and all the narratives, in the light of the recommended reading which you will find at the end of each tale, your personal experience, the theory presented on diversity in Chapter 1 and, of course, other theoretical lenses which you think are appropriate (Hatch and Wisniewski 1995).

Different ways of retelling stories: realist tales, confessional tales, autoethnographies, ethnodramas, poetic representations and fictional tales

Taking account of the way in which language shapes social reality and our understandings of it (often referred to as the 'crisis of representation': Denzin and Lincoln 2000a), narrative researchers strive, therefore, to recognize their constitutive role in the crafting of texts when they try to capture the complexities, tone and feeling of the lived experience of their research subjects. They reject the notion that writing is a sort of 'mopping-up' activity following data collection, and perceive writing as 'a method of inquiry, a way of finding out about yourself and your topic ... . By writing in different ways, we discover new aspects of our topic and our relationship to it. Form and content are inseparable' (Richardson 2000: 923). Indeed, researchers' texts are inescapably dependent upon the writing and reading conventions that their producers and consumers employ (Coffey and Atkinson 1996). Rejecting the notion that writing mirrors *a* social reality and that a text can have a fixed meaning, the narrative researcher is faced with the moral responsibility to write authentic, multiple, local realities which honour the subjects in their studies and provide insights into their field of research. Accepting the researcher's subjectivity in the research process must not, of course, be conflated with a ticket for being unfaithful to informants' words, a chance to lie or to deliberately omit things which run contrary to developing interpretations about diversity in PE, youth sport or health contexts (Bochner and Ellis 1996). Narratives ought to be as 'true to life' as possible to informants' talk and actions, and to their sense-making.

However, rather than taking writing for granted, researchers have to reflect upon how they write and to whom they aim to write. They need, for example, to ask: How can the nature of the data be conveyed (including both the themes and emotions from the field, as well as their own role in the generation of the data)? What theoretical points are to be made? What truths are to be told? Whose voices are to be included, prioritized or not? What is the intended purpose of the research?, and Who is the intended audience? As Sparkes (1995: 162) poignantly observes, 'how we choose to write has profound implications not just for how readable a text is, but also how the people it portrays are "read" and understood'. Researchers' choices about how they present data and analyses are not incidental, rather they are crucial and political, and moreover they have moral consequences for research informants, of which we need to be acutely aware. Following Clough (2002), narrative inquirers need to pose questions such as, 'What will this story *do*?'; 'Who is it *for*?'

Different literary styles can contribute to meeting these varied goals of the research project and broaden the scope of dissemination about issues of diversity within PE, youth sport and health. In trying to get PE teachers and educators to engage in 'emancipatory educational storysharing' about their professional worlds (Barone 1995), the researcher may, for example, use a poetic transcription (Dowling Næss 1998; Sparkes 2002; Sparkes *et al.* 2003) or a 'fictional tale' in order to persuade them to contribute to dilemmas posed by the research findings. The former has perhaps the greatest potential to remind the reader of the labour of the text: of the inevitable word reduction and the deliberate construction of the author's interpretations into a text, and of the reader's active role in establishing the meaning(s) of it. A poetic transcription may also best represent the speaker in an interview or field setting because of the way in which it honours the pauses, alliterations, narrative strategies and rhythms of such speech (Richardson 2000). In Part II of the book you will find several examples of the genre, so you can explore these claims for yourself. 'Fictional representations' are what you might expect from their name: they are 'fictional' in some sense. The 'facts' of the tale may be 'falsified' (disguised, withheld) in order to protect the identity of the informants or the social context in which research is carried out, not least in environments where realities are harsh and raw (Clough 2002). They often represent an amalgam of 'raw data' and insights from the researcher's imagination and knowledge about the social phenomenon in focus gained over a long period of time: 'they are stories which *could* be true, they derive from real events and feelings and conversations, but they *are* ultimately fictions: versions of the truth' (Clough 2002: 9). In the wake of the 'crisis of representation', authors of fictional tales use the literary style of good fiction (although clearly this is a complex field in its own right) and aim to recreate the social world through the five senses (Denison and Markula 2002; Richardson 2000; Sparkes 2002). They embrace an art form in order to engage the reader in a visceral, as well as intellectual, process of understanding the topic in hand; they show rather than tell. As Richardson (2000) candidly observes, such a form of writing is unlikely to persuade policy makers captured within 'evidence-based' rhetoric, but my own experience of using the genre in the professional development of PE teachers, such as using Sparkes's (1997) ethnographic fiction about a gay Jock in PE teacher education, has demonstrated that it can be a powerful and gripping pedagogical tool. The hallmark of a 'good' or persuasive story is that it is written in a style which prompts the reader to reflect upon the dilemmas it poses and try to contribute answers to them; it avoids providing a 'closed' reading. More importantly, persuasive storytellers can entice some readers into reconsidering comfortable attitudes and values (Barone 1995).

Ethnographic drama can similarly reconstruct the lived worlds of research projects in evocative and sensory ways. The genre offers readers the opportunity to go beyond 'simply' reading about diversity in PE, youth sport and health, and provides the means for gaining an embodied understanding via the enactment of a script. Although such an approach has a long tradition in educational and therapeutic settings, it is only recently that drama has been used to represent research (Sparkes 2002). In fact, Denzin (1997: 93) argues that, through engaging in what he terms 'performance ethnography', 'there will be a continual rediscovery of the body; that is, the performance text always works outward from the body'. He continues,

> The performance text is the single, most powerful way for ethnography to recover yet interrogate the meanings of lived experience. The performed text is a lived experience in two senses. The performance doubles back on the experiences previously represented in the ethnographer's text. It then re-presents those experiences as embodied performance to an audience. It thus privileges experience – the evocative moment when another's experiences come alive for the self ... . If performance is interpretation, then performance texts have the ability to criticize and deconstruct taken for granted understandings concerning how lived experience is to be represented.
>
> (Denzin 1997: 94–95)

There are three ethnographic dramas in the book so I advise you to enact them and see for yourself whether you agree with Denzin's claim.

Autoethnographic narratives, like fictional tales, draw upon a range of literary styles to create evocative texts and, as their name suggests, they rely heavily on the researcher-author's biographic experience. Clearly, the researcher avoids the dilemma of how best to re-present the social world of the Other because she/he relates personal experience to cultural analysis (Richardson 2000). There are two autoethnographic tales in this collection and they draw upon a combination of conventional prose and poetry to trouble your taken-for-granted worlds about diversity and inclusion. In contrast to the narrative forms in which the researcher-author's presence in, and labour behind, the text is brought to the foreground, realist tales and their complimentary genre, confessional tales (Atkinson 1991, cited in Sparkes 2002), can on the other hand be characterized by the almost complete absence of the author. Similar to traditional scientific tales, the text is crafted to give the impression that only the words of those who have been studied, their actions and their local culture, are portrayed 'as they are'. Realist tales build largely upon the informants' language and field notes, although the researcher has undoubtedly edited and structured the narrative either using time, or specific episodes, to provide the reader with a plot. The latter forms, indeed, the substance of the confessional tale in which the seemingly absent author reaffirms her presence in a complementary text to the realist tale. The confessional tale provides the reader with information about the researcher's role in the data generation and their analysis, and the choices which have been made with regard to the representation of the research on diversity. Whilst some critics argue that realist tales can be too linear, flat and fragmented, and fail therefore to reveal life's complexities in evocative and engaging ways, I would agree with Smith (2010) who purports that many realist tales can indeed achieve these ends. I think the realist tales included in Part II add weight to his observation.

Judging the quality of narrative research and ethical considerations

Following the tenets of interpretive and interpretive critical research, and in the wake of the 'crisis of representation', when it comes to the question of how we judge 'good' from 'bad' narrative research it is important to recognize the shortcomings of the simple question, 'Is it true?' Due to the dominance of positivist thinking in everyday language, such a question, if it is not deconstructed, in effect asks whether the narrative mirrors an 'objective Reality'; does it *correspond* with the real world, is it valid and reliable? Instead, it seems more appropriate to ask, 'How is it useful?' and to ask whether the researcher has made sensible theoretical and moral decisions along the research pathway (Smith and Deemer 2000; Smith 2009). Acknowledging that social reality about diversity in PE, youth sport and health can only be known through a window of theory, and that 'facts' can be constructed in multiple ways, we need to evaluate whether a narrative *coheres* (is connected and consistent) with previous knowledge about a topic, as well as contributing to 'enlivening our research and practitioner conversations' (Eisner 1997) about diversity.

In order to help us to achieve the latter, the narratives need to seem *authentic* in the sense of being 'true to life' (Bochner and Ellis 1996; Clough 2002; Eisner 1997; Marshall 1990; Smith and Deemer 2000; Smith 2009; Sparkes 2002). Do they *persuade* us to revisit our taken-for-granted values about equity and difference (Barone, 1995), and are they a spur with which to develop emphatic understandings of the Others' worlds (Eisner 1997)? Do they affect us in sensory, as well as cognitive, ways, and do they avoid closure to the tale, enabling new stories to evolve? Although the literary style of the narrative is seen as important in this context, I would nevertheless agree with Wolcott (1995 cited in Smith 2010), who observes that good writing can never compensate for poor, irrelevant research questions. Finally, we need to ask, 'Does the researcher convince us that her/his work has been carried out in an ethical and moral fashion?' In other words, evaluating the goodness and value of a narrative is a 'judgement call', and debate about its relevance and insights can only be resolved via a dialogic process (Marshall 1990; Smith 2009). I hope that the narratives in Part II will encourage you to enter just such a dialogue with your colleagues in PE, youth sport and/or health, and not least engage in 'educational storysharing' about diversity.

References

Armour, K. (2006) 'The way to a teacher's heart: Narrative research in physical education', in D. Kirk, D. Macdonald and M. O'Sullivan (eds) *The Handbook of Physical Education*, London: Sage Publications, pp. 467–85.

Armour, K. and Jones, R. (1998) *Physical Education Teachers' Lives and Careers*, London: Falmer Press.

Bach, H. (2007) 'Composing a visual narrative inquiry', in D. J. Clandinin (ed.) *Handbook of Narrative Inquiry, Mapping a Methodology*, London: Sage Publications, pp. 280–307.

Banks, M. (2007) *Using Visual Data in Qualitative Research*, London: Sage Publications.

Barbour, R. and Kitzinger, J. (eds) (1999) *Developing Focus Group Research. Politics, Theory and Practice*, London: Sage Publications.

Barone, T. (1995) 'Persuasive writings, vigilant readings, and reconstructed characters: The paradox of trust in educational storysharing', in J. Amos Hatch and R. Wisniewski (eds) *Life History and Narrative*, London: Falmer Press, pp. 63–74.

Barthes, R. (1977) 'Introduction to the structural analysis of narratives', in R. Barthes *Image-Music-Text* (translated by Stephen Heath), Glasgow: Collins.

Bochner, A. and Ellis, C. (1996) 'Talking over ethnography', in C. Ellis and A. Bochner (eds) *Composing Ethnography. Alternative Forms of Qualitative Writing*, London: AltaMira, pp. 13–45.

Brown, D. and Rich, E. (2002) 'Gender positioning as pedagogical practice in teaching physical education', in D. Penney (ed.) *Gender and Physical Education. Contemporary Issues and Future Directions*, London: Routledge, pp. 80–100.

Butt, R., Raymond, D., McCue, G. and Yamagishi, L. (1992) 'Collaborative autobiography and the teacher's voice', in I. Goodson (ed.) *Studying Teachers' Lives*, London: Routledge, pp. 51–98.

Clandinin, D. J. (ed.) (2007) *Handbook of Narrative Inquiry, Mapping a Methodology*, London: Sage Publications.

Clandinin, D. J. and Connelly, F. M. (2000) *Narrative Inquiry. Experience and Story in Qualitative Research*, San Francisco, CA: Jossey-Bass.

Clough, P. (2002) *Narratives and Fictions in Educational Research*, Buckingham: Open University Press.

Coffey, A. (1999) *The Ethnographic Self*, London: Sage Publications.

Coffey, A. and Atkinson, P. (1996) *Making Sense of Qualitative Data. Complementary Research Strategies*, London: Sage Publications.

Connelly, F. and Clandinin, D. (1990) 'Stories of experience and narrative inquiry', *Educational Researcher*, 19(5): 2–14.

Connor, D. (2008) *Urban Narrative Portraits in Progress. Life at the Intersections of Learning Disability, Race and Social Class*, Oxford: Peter Lang.

Cortazzi, M. (1993) *Narrative Analysis*, Washington, DC: Falmer Press.

Czarniawska, B. (2004) *Narratives in Social Science Research*, London: Sage Publications.

Davies, B. and Gannon, S. (eds) (2006) *Doing Collective Biography: Investigating the Production of Subjectivity*, Maidenhead, Bucks: Open University Press.

Delamont, S. (2002) *Fieldwork in Educational Settings: Methods, Pitfalls and Perspectives*, 2nd edn, London: Routledge.

Denison, J. (1996) 'Sport narratives', *Qualitative Inquiry*, 2(3): 351–62.

Denison, J. and Markula, P. (eds) (2002) *Moving Writing*, New York: Peter Lang.

Denzin, N. (1997) *Interpretive Ethnography. Ethnographic Practices for the 21st Century,* London: Sage Publications.

Denzin, N. and Lincoln, Y. (eds) (2000a) *Handbook of Qualitative Research,* 2nd edn, London: Sage Publications.

——(2000b) 'Introduction: The discipline and practice of qualitative research', in N. Denzin and Y. Lincoln (eds) *Handbook of Qualitative Research,* 2nd edn, London: Sage Publications, pp. 1–29.

Dowling, F. (2011) 'Are PE teacher identities fit for post-modern schools or are they clinging to modernist notions of professionalism?' A case study of some Norwegian PE student teachers' emerging professional identities, *Sport, Education and Society.* 16(2): 201–22.

Dowling Næss, F. (1996) 'Life events and curriculum change: The life history of a Norwegian physical educator', *European Physical Education Review,* 2(1): 41–53.

——(1998) *Tales of Norwegian Physical Education Teachers: A Life History Analysis,* PhD thesis, Oslo: Norwegian School of Sports Sciences.

——(2001a) 'Narratives about young men and masculinities in organized sport in Norway', *Sport, Education and Society,* 6(2): 125–42.

——(2001b) 'Sharing stories about the dialectics of self and structure in teacher socialization: Revisiting a Norwegian physical educator's life history', *European Physical Education Review,* 7(1): 44–60.

Eisner, E. (1997) 'The new frontier in qualitative research methodology', *Qualitative Inquiry,* 3(3): 259–73.

Ellis, C. and Bochner, A. (2000) 'Autoethnography, personal narrative, reflexivity', in N. Denzin and Y. Lincoln (eds) *Handbook of Qualitative Inquiry,* 2nd edn, London: Sage Publications, pp. 733–68.

Evans, J. and Davies, B. (1986) 'Sociology, schooling and physical education', in J. Evans (ed.) *Physical Education, Sport and Schooling. Studies in the Sociology of Physical Education,* London: Falmer Press, pp. 11–37.

——(2004) 'Pedagogy, symbolic control, identity and health', in J. Evans, B. Davies and J. Wright (eds) *Body Knowledge and Control. Studies in the Sociology of Physical Education and Health,* London: Routledge, pp. 3–18.

Fitzgerald, H. (2005) 'Still feeling like a spare piece of luggage? Embodied experiences of (dis)ability in physical education and sport', *Physical Education and Sport Pedagogy,* 10(1): 41–59.

Garrett, R. (2006) 'Critical storytelling as a teaching strategy in physical education teacher education', *European Physical Education Review,* 12(3): 339–60.

Giddens, A. (1991) *Modernity and Self-identity. Self and Society in the Late Modern Age,* Cambridge: Polity Press.

Gilborn, D. (2008) *Racism and Education: Coincidence or Conspiracy?,* London: Routledge.

Goodson, I. (1995) 'The story so far: Personal knowledge and the political', in J. Amos and R. Wisniewski (eds) *Life History and Narrative,* London: Falmer Press, pp. 89–98.

Groves, S. and Laws, C. (2003) 'The use of narrative in accessing children's experiences of physical education', *European Journal of Physical Education,* 8(2): 160–74.

Gubrium, J. F. and Holstein, J. A. (2002) *Handbook of Interview Research,* London: Sage Publications.

——(eds) (2003) *Postmodern Interviewing,* London: Sage Publications.

——(2009) *Analyzing Narrative Reality,* London: Sage Publications.

Hargreaves, J. (1994) *Sport Females: Critical Issues in the History and Sociology of Women's Sports*, London: Routledge.

——(2001) *Heroines of Sport: The Politics of Difference and Identity*, London: Routledge.

Hatch, A. and Wisniewski, R. (1995) 'Life history and narrative: questions, issues and exemplary works', in J. Amos and R. Wisniewski (eds) *Life History and Narrative*, London: Falmer Press, pp. 113–36.

Hine, C. (2000) *Virtual Ethnography*, London: Sage Publications.

Holland, S. (ed.) (2008) *Remote Relationships in a Small World*, New York: Peter Lang.

James, N. and Busher, H. (2009) *Online Interviewing*, London: Sage Publications.

Krogh Christensen, M. (2007) 'Biographical learning as health promotion in physical education. A Danish case study', *European Physical Education Review*, 13(1): 5–24.

Kvale, S. and Brinkmann, S. (2009) Interviews: *Learning the Craft of Qualitative Research Interviewing*, 2nd edn, London: Sage Publications.

Markham, A. and Baym, N. (eds) (2009) *Internet Inquiry. Conversations about Method*, London: Sage Publications.

Marshall, C. (1990) 'Goodness criteria. Are they objective or judgement calls?', in E. Guba (ed.) *The Pardigm Dialog*, London: Sage Publications, pp. 188–97.

Mason, J. (1996) *Qualitative Researching*, London: Sage Publications.

McNiff, J. and Whitehead, J. (2005) *Action Research for Teachers*, London: David Fulton.

Mirza, H. (2009) *Race, Gender and Educational Desire: Why Black Women Succeed and Fail*, London: Routledge.

Morris, J. (1991) *Pride Against Prejudice. Transforming Attitudes of Disability*, London: The Women's Press.

Oliver, K. (1998) 'A journey into narrative analysis: A methodology for discovering meanings', *Journal of Teaching in Physical Education*, 17: 244–59.

Patton, M. (2001) *Qualitative Evaluation and Research Methods*, 3rd edn, London: Sage Publications.

Phoenix, A. (2008) 'Analysing narrative contexts', in M. Andrews, C. Squire and M. Tamboukou (eds) *Doing Narrative Research*, London: Sage Publications, pp. 64–77.

——(2009) 'De-colonising practices: Negotiating narratives from racialized and gendered experiences of education', *Race, Ethnicity and Education*, 12(1): 101–14.

Plummer, K. (2001) *Documents of Life 2. An Invitation to a Critical Humanism*, London: Sage Publications.

Polkinghorne, D. (1995) 'Narrative configuration in qualitative analysis', in J. Amos Hatch and R. Wisniewski (eds) *Life History and Narrative*, London: Falmer Press, pp. 5–23.

Richardson, L. (2000) 'Writing: A method of inquiry', in N. Denzin and Y. Lincoln (eds) *Handbook of Qualitative Research*, 2nd edn, London: Sage Publications, pp. 923–48.

Ricoeur, P. (2003) *The Rule of Metaphor*, trans. R. Czerny London: Taylor and Francis.

Riessman, C. Kohler (1993) *Narrative Analysis. Qualitative Research Methods, Series 30*, London: Sage Publications.

——(2008) *Narrative Methods for the Human Sciences*, London: Sage Publications.

Salmon, P. and Riessman, C. Kohler (2008) 'Looking back on narrative research: An exchange', in M. Andrews, C. Squire and M. Tamboukou (eds) *Doing Narrative Research*, London: Sage Publications, pp. 78–85.

Skeggs, B. (1997) *Formations of Class and Gender*, London: Sage Publications.

Smith, B. (2010) 'Narrative inquiry: Ongoing conversations and questions for sport and exercise psychology research', *International Review of Sport and Exercise Psychology*, 3(1): 87–107.

Smith, B. and Sparkes, A. (2005) 'Men, sport, spinal cord injury, and narratives of hope', *Social Science and Medicine*, 61: 1095–1105.

——(2008a) 'Narrative and its potential contribution to disability studies', *Disability and Society*, 23(1): 17–28.

——(2008b) 'Changing bodies, changing narratives and the consequences of tellability: A case study of becoming disabled through sport', *Sociology of Health and Illness*, 30(2): 217–36.

Smith, J. K. (2009) 'Judging research quality. From certainty to contingency', *Qualitative Research in Sport and Exercise*, 1(1): 91–100.

Smith, J. K. and Deemer, D. (2000) 'The problem of criteria in the age of relativism', in N. Denzin and Y. Lincoln (eds) *Handbook of Qualitative Research*, 2nd edn, London: Sage Publications, pp. 877–96.

Sparkes, A. (1992) 'The paradigms debate. An extended review and a celebration of difference', in A. Sparkes (ed.) *Research in Physical Education and Sport: Exploring Alternative Visions*, London: Falmer Press, pp. 9–60.

——(1994) 'Self, silence and invisibility as a beginning PE teacher: A life history of lesbian experience', *British Journal of Sociology of Education*, 15(2): 93–118.

——(1995) 'The textual construction of goodness in interpretative inquiry: Research writing as persuasive fiction', in T. Tiller, A. Sparkes, S. Kårhus and F. Dowling Næss (eds) *The Qualitative Challenge. Reflections on Educational Research*, Landås: Caspar forlag, pp. 155–91.

——(1996) 'Interrupted body projects and the self in teaching: Exploring an absent presence', *International Studies in Sociology of Education*, 6(2): 167–89.

——(1997) 'Ethnographic fiction and representing the absent other', *Sport, Education and Society*, 2(1): 25–40.

——(2002) *Telling Tales in Sport and Physical Activity. A Qualitative Journey*, Champaign, IL: Human Kinetics.

Sparkes, A. and Silvennoinen, M. (eds) (1999) *Talking Bodies*, Jyvaskyla, Finland: SoPhi.

Sparkes, A., Partington, E. and Brown, D. (2007) 'Bodies as bearers of value: The transmission of jock culture via the "twelve commandments"', *Sport, Education and Society*, 12(3): 295–316.

Sparkes, A., Nigles, L., Swan, P. and Dowling, F. (2003) 'Poetic representations in sport and physical education: Insider perspectives', *Sport, Education and Society*, 8(2): 153–77.

Squire, C. (2008) 'Experience-centred and culturally-oriented approaches to narrative', in M. Andrews, C. Squire and M. Tamboukou (eds) *Doing Narrative Research*, London: Sage Publications, pp. 41–63.

Squire, C., Andrews, M. and Tamboukou, M. (2008) 'Introduction: What is narrative research?', in M. Andrews, C. Squire and M. Tamboukou (eds) *Doing Narrative Research*, London: Sage Publications, pp. 1–21.

Stenhouse, L. (1975) *An Introduction to Curriculum Research and Development*, Oxford: Heinemann Educational Books.

Templin, T., Schempp, P. and Sparkes, A. (1991) 'The professional life cycle of a retired physical education teacher: A tale of bitter disengagement', *Physical Education Review*, 14(2): 143–55.

Tinning, R. (1997) *Pedagogies for Physical Education: Pauline's Story*, Geelong: Deakin University Press.

——(2004) 'Conclusion: Ruminations on body knowledge and control and the spaces for hope and happening', in J. Evans, B. Davies and J. Wright (eds) *Body Knowledge and Control. Studies in the Sociology of Physical Education and Health*, London: Routledge, pp. 218–38.

Wright Mills, C. (1959) *The Sociological Imagination*, London: Oxford University Press.

Part II

Stories of difference and (in)equality

Run rabbit, run

Lisette Burrows

Tom and Casey leave school at 3.05pm. Home to Tom's by 3.10pm, dump their bags and head for the fridge. The milk is cold. It tastes good – straight from the cow. Casey doesn't have a cow. He's got Tom, though – best mate in the world. He's been waiting all day for this, waiting for that giraffe[1] to shut up. Waiting for spelling to end. Waiting for the bell to ring. Waiting to go hunt rabbits.

'What was it that giraffe said?' Casey asks Tom.

'You are a customs officer and your body is a country,' Tom imitates. 'What stuff would you stop at the border and what would you let into your country?' He moves himself like a puppet and Casey laughs. 'Yep, that was it,' he says, gulping down the rest of his milk. 'Do you reckon milk's allowed in?' Tom shrugs. 'Yeah, dunno … who cares? That giraffe was gay … let's go. I've got the catapults.'

Casey takes his catapult. It's nothing like he thought. Tom had been talking about it all week. He had imagined a Buzz Lightyear kind of contraption – something shiny and fierce. This was just a two-pronged stick with a piece of rubber stretched across it. He runs his hands over it – it's a bit rough and twisted. How's this gonna get a rabbit?, he wonders.

They crouch low to squeeze through the hole in the Macrocarpa hedge. Sheep shit everywhere on a burnt brown paddock with holes, holes all over the place. 'Over here,' Tom hisses. 'If we hide behind this trough they won't know we're here.' Casey follows, and they stay low. 'There's heaps of stones here,' Tom says, clutching his catapult. 'Lemme show you how it works.' Carefully he places a stone in the centre of the rubber, holding it firm with his thumb and forefinger … pulling it back, controlling the tension, then 'ping' the stone flies straight into the hedge. 'Hey. It works!', Casey cries.

It's harder than it looks. Get the tension wrong and the stone plops to the ground like a failed rocket launch. Too much, and the stone is out of control. 'See that hole we just crawled through?' says Tom. 'Line up with that, focus, pull it back … just to here … then fire in the hole!! …. ' Five failed missions later, Casey gets it. 'Hey you're good,' says Tom. 'It took me hours to get the hang of it.'

They stuff stones in their pockets, load their weapons, and peer out over the trough. To their left a lone rabbit bounces over the hard ground. 'Go!' yells Tom. Casey springs up over the trough, heart racing, bunny in sight, catapult front and centre, lines his eye up with the rabbit – peow! He misses. Dust flies. The rabbit runs.

Regrouping behind the trough, Tom's got his eyes fixed on the centre paddock – 'sssshhh – see them there?' he whispers. Heart thumping, Casey follows Tom's line of sight – there's *heaps* of them. He didn't know he could feel like this. It's not like he's got anything against rabbits, but ... 'Go!' yells Tom, and just like before, on starter's orders, he's over the trough ... aim – fire – aim – fire. Casey skirts to the left – they're everywhere ... bobbing white tails. Tom's to the east, crouched low, eyes on the prey. Casey fumbles for stones in his pocket, wipes the dust from his eyes, slings his catapult like a pro. No sign of dead rabbits yet. Who cares. It doesn't matter. They're warriors him and Tom. Fighting the war of the rabbits.

The paddock is turning a dark shade of rust. The sun is going down. Heading home, their legs are heavy, eyes gritty with dust. The smell of sausages wafts toward them. They squeeze back through the hole in the Macrocarpa hedge – a barbecue!

The strum of a guitar beckons. It's Tom's dad, Mr M. 'Hey boys – was just about to send out a search party for you. I saw your mum down the street, Casey – she says it's fine if you want to stay the night with us.'

'Sure, that'd be great Mr M.' Casey hopes he keeps playing the guitar.

Tom's mum comes out of the house juggling bread, plates and drinks. She smiles wide. 'Come eat boys, but wash your hands first, eh?'

Awesome, Casey thinks. Nothing like a sausage wrapped in white bread. Tomato sauce dripping down his chin. Casey watches Tom's sister Sarah munching through her third sausage sandwich. Mrs M. is dishing the pudding – big slabs of ice-cream and chocolate sauce.

'Hey, come see my pet rabbit, Casey,' Sarah calls. 'I'm gonna give him his dinner.' He's huge, white and furry. Rustling around in a hutch. Casey reaches for his catapult. 'Hey. What are you doing?!' screeches Sarah. 'He's a sitting duck,' says Casey. 'He's a rabbit, and he's mine!' Sarah declares. 'You can't hurt him.'

'OK you lot, I'm cleaning up now,' Mrs M. interrupts, 'and best leave that one alone, Casey. He's a pet. Right, hot chocolates then bed for you boys, and Sarah ... you're on dishes.'

The next day Tom and Casey are full of it. 'We'll get one next time ... Mum will make us rabbit stew,' says Tom. 'Dunno if rabbit stew's allowed into your country, Tom,' laughs Casey. 'Best we check with Harold the Giraffe ... .' 'Nah – that giraffe is *from* another country I reckon!' Tom declares. On they go, beating up their rabbit-hunting stories ready for the telling ... but they won't tell – it's private – some good shots, some stink ones ... nothing nobody else needs to know about. They're the rabbit raiders now. Casey can't wait for the weekend – another sleepover at Tom's ... rabbits, barbies ... waiting ... .

First up, it's health. Casey's somewhere else. Back at Tom's. Cargo pant pockets loaded with stones. Rabbits bouncing all over the paddock ... . 'Casey – I am asking you a question. What did Harold tell us yesterday? Are you listening?' Arrrgh – that damned giraffe again, he thinks, as his white-tailed rabbits dive into their burrows ... . 'Um ... "Only let good things into your body",' he choruses. 'Yes, that's right,' says Mrs Tam – 'so what are the "good" things we should put in our bodies, kids?'

'Milk', Casey sings out. He's not usually one to talk in class, ' ... and sausages.'

'Well now ... thanks for your answer, Casey, but I think what Harold would ask us next is what KIND of milk? Blue top, green top, calcium rich? And HOW were those sausages cooked?'

'All I know is they tasted good, miss, can't be that bad if they taste that good?' he fires back.

'Yes, well, um ... that's something Harold might not agree with. Lots of things we *think* taste good aren't always good for our bodies are they? Let's just open up our own lunch-boxes shall we? – cross-country run this afternoon – Harold will be hoping you have some healthy things in there to give you energy for the race,' declares Mrs Tam.

'Oh no ... ,' gulps Casey. He hasn't even checked what's in his. He wonders if Mrs M. has read the nutritional guidelines for healthy kids, like his Mum has. *His* Mum knows about this stuff. She gets those 'Healthy Food' maga-zines, has a healthy food magnet on the fridge, portion plates in the cup-board, and the food pyramid poster on the pantry door. She goes to the gym, gets the weight-watchers meals at the supermarket. She *knows* what he should have in his box. She reads the messages that school sends home. She always puts the right stuff in his box. 'Does Mrs M. know about this?'

Gingerly he peels back the plastic lid on his lunch-box – a single shrivelled sausage lies limp on a paper towel, two bits of buttered bread, fruit, chippies, a big soft scone and milk – a whole bottle full of cow's milk. What? he gasps, heart racing. Mrs Tam edges closer, scanning the boxes ... . 'Ah, a sausage for you, Casey ... oh, chippies too, and a scone ... what would Harold say about this, do you think?' The muffled laughter of his classmates drowns out the thumping in his chest. Head down, offending sau-sage grinning up at him. 'What would a stupid giraffe (or Mum) know anyway?' he mutters.

Lined up by the blue gates at school – Mr Potter raises his starter pistol – ready, steady, 'crack' and they're off – 100 students round the corner heading for McGregor's Ridge – Tom, aka Peter Rabbit, at the front, Casey chasing his tail, gasping for breath ... already ... five bunches behind ... feeling sick. It's a war of the rabbits. He's the rabbit now. A slow rabbit. Dodging catapult shots. Giraffes gallop by while he gasps for air. Cows watch on. A lone sau-sage struggles past border control. He's tired, oh so tired ... left his asthma inhaler at home – hasn't taken his doses ... the end in sight ... lost all air, throat dry, sweating like a pig, stumbles over the finishing line – second to last … rabbits flash before him as he dives into his burrow. Tom's voice reaching through the dust – 'Casey, Casey – you OK? Casey!'

Run rabbit, run – yeah right, thinks Casey before he blacks out.

Research context

The research that informed the composition of this narrative was an ethnographic study working with nine- and ten-year-old students from a rural area in New Zealand. The study focused on exploring what young people know, do and feel about health and physical activity both within and outside school contexts. We were interested in understanding how children thought about health, what kinds of physical activities they participated in and what influenced their experiences of physicality in rural settings. Children were interviewed in pairs and took photos of things and people that were important to them. Their testimonies and pictures yielded rich and evocative stories about the role of physical activity in their lives and the ways school, culture, family and socio-economic factors contour the nature of their engagement in health and physical activity practices.

Note

1   The giraffe referred to here is called 'Harold'. It is a puppet used by the LIFE education agency, a contracted health provider that regularly delivers health education programmes in New Zealand primary schools. Harold communicates messages about healthy living, including what comprises a healthy diet, avoiding drugs, good hygiene, and so on.

Recommended reading

Burrows, L. (2010) 'Kiwi kids are Weet-Bix kids: Body matters in childhood', *Sport, Education and Society*, 15(2): 235–51.

Burrows, L. and Wright, J. (2007) 'Prescribing practices: Shaping healthy children in schools', *International Journal of Children's Rights*, 15(6): 83–98.

Leahy, D. (2009) 'Disgusting pedagogies', in J. Wright and V. Harwood (eds) *Biopolitics and the Obesity Epidemic: Governing Bodies*, London: Routledge, pp. 172–82.

Wyn, J. and White, R. (1997) *Rethinking Youth*, St Leonards: Allen and Unwin.

Young men, sport and sexuality: A poetic exploration

David Carless

What do we know – at this point in time – about the experience of same-sex attraction and desire for young males in sport and physical education settings? What does the existing literature tell us about the characteristics of this particular avenue of human experience? *Invisibility* is one possible characteristic: 10,708 competitors from 204 countries took part in the 2008 Beijing Olympics. Among all these competitors there was only one openly gay male (Buzinski 2008). *Concealment* might be another: according to Anderson (2005: 43), sport can be 'a safe space for those desiring to deeply conceal their same-sex desires. Athletes (particularly in team sports) are shrouded in a cloud of heterosexual assumption, while simultaneously engaging in a highly charged, homoerotic environment.' *Isolation* as a result of perpetuated myths could be a third characteristic: 'It was all such a cruel joke. I recognized guys from the wrestling team, from track, from all over school,' write Amaechi and Bull (2007: 113), 'to acknowledge one another and our minority status threatened doom – unless there was some way we could coordinate our message. And that's exactly what discrimination prevented.' Within a culture characterized by (near) invisibility, concealment and isolation, what *can* we hope to know? And, perhaps more to the point, *how* can we know? Who will do the telling, the showing, the sharing?

Men – Sport – Sexuality

I live and breathe within all three (problematic) descriptors
And you want me to try to make sense of it?
Right here on this page?
But how can I make sense of something if it doesn't make sense?
How can I word what can only be felt?
How can I explain – to you – what is rarely even spoken?
And how can I be sure that *you* are ready to hear?

Is it about desire?
Is it about touch?
Is it about becoming whole?

Is it about (sexual) orientation?
        (sexual) behaviour?
        (sexual) identity?

It is *in* my body ... realized and expressed through my body (sometimes)
It has coloured my soul and spirit over the years ... more than I ever knew before
It separates and isolates ... in the coldest of ways
Yet it connects and fulfils ... in the most important of ways

***

In poetry I am not trying to close anything down; I am not trying to understand everything; I am not seeking control. Instead, I am open to the world, open to process and mystery, open to fragmentariness, open to understanding as an archipelago of fragments. This does not mean I am not trying to make connections in understanding, but I am no longer pretending that I understand what I do not know. I am fundamentally *agnostic*, knowing above all that there is much I do not know and will never likely know (Leggo 2008: 168).

Orientation/Body Desires

Matt lives among the silvered machines
The plates, the bars, the dumb-bells, the steel
The crunch and the clang – *Gasp! Muted scream!*
It's a procession of bodies, it's a daily routine

Matt's pleased with his reflection, he likes what he sees:
Pectorals that curve beneath the close cloth of his vest
Deltoids rounded yet cut, shimmer with sweat
Matt grabs a hold of his biceps, he gives them a squeeze

Pumped for an hour, almost ready to leave
Matt walks around the lat pull-down machine
Then: *BANG!*   ... it happens ...
Everybody freeze

The music goes silent, bodies vanish from sight
Matt's focus is narrowed, the thought he had disappeared
Stood three feet away from this shaved-headed guy
Who is looking at Matt ... right in the eye

Fight? ... or ... Flight?
Or is there another option the physiologists have missed?
The guy searches Matt's eyes for a clue, a reveal
Together for a moment they're too scared to steal

Matt looks away at the wall, the guy looks down at his watch
Shoulders twist sideways, dance round the machine

But in one of many mirrors Matt watches him still
Desire and attraction ... the fear, the thrill

Behaviour/Solitary Bodies

Laughter, joking, shouts and slammings – the male changing room is crowded with 20 or more bodies in various stages of undress. Matt unlocks his locker, takes out his bag and searches for a spare hook to hang his clothes. He peels off his vest, kicks his trainers under the bench, pulls out his towel and turns round to sit. As he turns, Matt sees the shaved-head guy standing there across the changing room, eyes fixed on him again, perfectly clear and in-focus among the blurred crowd of changing bodies ... .

His face: chiselled, smooth, unreadable
        but looking at Matt
His body: lean, muscled, wrapped in a blue towel
        walking now into the showers

Matt pulls off his shorts and wraps the towel round his waist
Ba-boom, Ba-boom, Ba-boom
He walks the few steps, through the bodies, to the showers
Ba-boom, Ba-boom, Ba-boom
Hangs his towel next to the blue one which is already there
Ba-boom, Ba-boom, Ba-boom
Shower and shampoo, under warm running water, stood side by side
 ... but Matt, unable to look, fixes his eyes on the tiles
He wants to turn to this stranger, he's desperate to speak

But something much bigger – unspoken, unknown
Seems to have frozen them both – their bodies, their tongues
No words, no action, no connection at all
Just a resistance to risk, the fear of a fall

By the time they're both dressed all that remains
is a dull sense of frustration, another chance gone astray
Why ...
        ... is it always like this?

The guy walks from the room, with a brief parting glance
No smile, no phone number, no coffee, no chance
Not even the barest flicker

        of hope
                    for
                            love?

Identity/Connecting Bodies

It's the story, you see, that maketh the man

Without a plot line, a template, a very rough plan
How can Matt ever build a self that feels like it fits?
It's by connecting to others that identity exists

Not the roles of Kenneth Williams or John Inman
You know: the joke, the alone, the effeminate ham
Growing up in the 80s were these the roles
for gays, for bisexuals, for every queer man?

Well, they didn't fit Matt …
and they didn't fit me

Now there are new identities outside sport and within
Try, if you're looking for a place to begin:
Mark Tewkesbury
John Amaechi
Gareth Thomas
Steven Davies
Anton Hysen
Matthew Mitcham … who I think (*if I may utter a subjectivity here?*) is gorgeous!

All of these sportsmen have taken the brave step
That in 1990 football showed it couldn't accept
Justin Fashanu died and we all shoulder the blame
I want to do what I can to contribute to change

Of course, you don't have to pay attention to any of these stories … . But help yourself to one if you like … . It's yours. Do with it what you will. Cry over it. Get angry. Forget it. But don't say in years to come that you would have lived your life differently if only you had heard this story. You've heard it now (King 2008: 25).

References

Amaechi, J. and Bull, C. (2007) *Man in the Middle: My Life in and Out of Bounds*, New York, NY: ESPN Books.

Anderson, E. (2005) *In the Game*, Albany, NY: SUNY Press.

Buzinski, J. (2008) *In Beijing Olympics, Only 10 Openly Gay Athletes*. (Online.) Available from: <www.outsports.com/os/index2.php?option=com_content&task=view&id=111&pop=1&page> (accessed 4 June 2010).

Frank, A. (2000) 'The standpoint of storyteller', *Qualitative Health Research*, 10(3): 354–65.

King, T. (2008) 'The art of indigenous knowledge: A million porcupines crying in the dark', in J. Knowles and A. Cole (eds) *Handbook of the Arts in Qualitative Research*, Thousand Oaks, CA: Sage, pp 13–25.

Leggo, C. (2008) 'Astonishing silence: Knowing in poetry', in J. Knowles and A. Cole (eds) *Handbook of the Arts in Qualitative Research*, Thousand Oaks, CA: Sage, pp 165–74.

Research context

This piece utilizes an autoethnographic methodology through which I aim to connect my own experiences to more general cultural and social issues by privileging action, emotion and embodiment. Through this approach, I turn the focus of my narrative enquiry away from others towards myself and my own experiences as 'a political and ethical act of self-reflection' (Frank 2000: 356). By writing autoethnography, I follow an emerging tradition in sports studies and physical education through which researchers share moments of their own personal experience, often by using storytelling elements. On this occasion, I have chosen to utilize a poetic form of representation as a way to explore and distil selected moments which – together – speak to the complexities of same-sex attraction among young males in sport. At certain points, I have included quotations from relevant literature as a strategy to link this particular, situated piece with other cultural perspectives.

Recommended reading

Anderson, E. (2011) 'Masculinities and sexualities in sport and physical cultures: Three decades of evolving research', *Journal of Homosexuality*, 58(5): 565–78.

Carless, D. (2011) 'Negotiating sexuality and masculinity in school sport: An autoethnography', *Sport, Education and Society*, DOI: 10.1080/13573322.2011.554536.

Connell, R. (2008) 'Masculinity construction and sports in boys' education: A framework for thinking about the issue', *Sport, Education and Society*, 13(2): 131–45.

Sparkes, A. C. (1997) 'Ethnographic fiction and representing the absent Other', *Sport, Education and Society*, 2(1): 25–40.

Inclusion in National Curriculum policy and physical education

Dawn Penney

This narrative takes inspiration from and adopts the genre of a legendary BBC[1] comedy series, *Yes Minister*. The series was produced between 1980 and 1984 and managed to convey, in and through comedy, the somewhat 'crazy reality' of policy issues and policy processes in government.[2] It vividly 'rang true' with, for example, Ball's (1998) contention that:

> National policy making is inevitably a process of bricolage: a matter of borrowing and copying bits and pieces of ideas from elsewhere, drawing upon and amending locally tried and tested approaches, cannibalizing theories, research, trends and fashions and not infrequently flailing around for anything at all that looks as though it might work.
>
> (Ball 1998: 126)

The series centred on three characters, Jim Hacker, Minister for Administrative Affairs; Sir Humphrey Appleby, Permanent Secretary (senior civil servant); and Bernard, Private Secretary to the Minister. Particularly pertinent to this narrative is the observation that Sir Humphrey's stance and political skills epitomized government as 'a machine that has no gears, only brakes' (BBC n.d).

Here, a cabinet reshuffle sees Jim Hacker taking on a new portfolio, Education, within a Labour government widely regarded as reaffirming rather than challenging policy agendas that had their origins in the preceding Conservative government. The cabinet reshuffle comes at a time when a revision of the National Curriculum is once again pending, five years after its introduction in 1988. Taking up his new post (having previously held junior positions within both the Department for Culture, Media and Sport, and the Department of Health), the Minister has declared a particular interest in physical education.

BERNARD (enters the Minister's office): Yes Minister? (he says quizzically).

MINISTER: I've been thinking about my new role. I've decided it's a tremendous opportunity to make a real difference Bernard, not just in government, but to young people's lives! And I've decided I want to do that, Bernard. I want people to look back in time and recognize this as a turning point in education in Britain, when finally education policy caught up with the twenty-first century.

(Bernard has been looking increasingly worried. He interjects nervously.)

BERNARD: Err, what do you have in mind, Minster?

MINISTER: Well, I'm concerned that the sort of education we're providing is really only serving the needs of a very few young people, Bernard, and that it hasn't really moved with the times has it? I mean, you have to agree that education critics have a point when they say that the 1988 National Curriculum looked remarkably similar to the 1904 curriculum and that, since then, so called revisions haven't really changed things much have they either?[3]

BERNARD: Yes Minister, you're quite right, that's always been government policy.

MINISTER: Err, sorry, can you explain that Bernard?

BERNARD: Well, as you know Minister, we don't want to upset the status quo do we?

MINISTER (somewhat frustrated and becoming animated): Well actually Bernard, yes, I've decided that that is precisely what I want to do! We're due for a revision of the National Curriculum soon and I think it is an ideal opportunity for us to take a fresh look at what sort of a curriculum young people in Britain need for the twenty-first century. I think we need to recognize that the social make up of Britain is very different from a century ago and that perhaps we shouldn't be surprised that many young people are 'disaffected' or struggle to see how the curriculum relates to their lives, values or their interests. We may talk of a multicultural society, and one in which technological changes are happening at a tremendous speed, and where young people need skills, knowledge and understanding that neither you or I can probably relate to, but what are we *doing* about it all when it comes to education? Can you organize a meeting with Sir Humphrey – I'll need him to coordinate things with other departments.

BERNARD (who is now seriously worried about the Minister's intentions): Other departments, Minster?

MINISTER: Yes, I'll explain when we meet with Sir Humphrey. (He ushers Bernard out of his office with a sense of urgency … .)

(Bernard exits to hurriedly locate Sir Humphrey and explain the emerging crisis. He soon locates him in the corridors of Whitehall.)

BERNARD: Sir Humphrey, the Minister wants to see you urgently to discuss his plans for revising the National Curriculum.

SIR HUMPHREY: Revising the National Curriculum? Plans? What plans, Bernard?

BERNARD: I don't know, he just said that he saw this as a chance to make a difference, for young people in Britain in the twenty-first century, and he wants you to coordinate things with other departments.

SIR HUMPHREY: Make a difference? Young people in the twenty-first century? Other departments? What is he thinking?

(They both walk briskly back to the Minister's office, knock and enter.)

SIR HUMPHREY: Minster, you wanted to see me?

MINISTER (enthusiastically responding and beckoning Sir Humphrey to take a seat): Yes, Sir Humphrey, sit down, I want to run through my plans for education with you.

SIR HUMPHREY: Plans, Minister?

MINISTER: Yes, Sir Humphrey, as you know we're approaching a revision of the National Curriculum and I want to make sure that this time we take a serious look at things that I think haven't really been addressed before. Now I know that you'll be a bit nervous and not want me to change too much too soon ... .

SIR HUMPHREY (interjects with a nervous laugh, speaking with both a hint of enthusiasm and sowing a seed of caution): Not at all Minister, we just need to make sure that whatever you are proposing aligns with the government's election commitments and also that it will connect with the *tone* of the nation currently.

MINISTER (in a puzzled tone): The *tone* of the nation currently?

SIR HUMPHREY (reaffirming the emphasis of caution and hinting at potential risks that may be involved in whatever the Minister is thinking): Well, yes Minister, it's something that we always have to keep an eye on, but don't let me interrupt you ... .

MINISTER: No, you're right Sir Humphrey, it is vital that we do take account of what people across the country are thinking, and as Minister for Education I'm particularly concerned with Britain's young people – our so-called 'disaffected youth', young men and women from various ethnic groups ... . I'm not convinced that the National Curriculum really reflects their needs, either now or for the future. I think that it's probably meeting the needs of a relatively few young people, but is failing *many*. So I've decided it is time to do something about that and I am going to start with something that most Education Ministers seem to have avoided engaging with ... .

(At this point Sir Humphrey and Bernard glance sideways at one another, waiting to hear just where the Minister has decided to direct his misconceived attention.)

MINISTER: ... *Physical education*!

SIR HUMPHREY AND BERNARD (in unison): Physical education, Minister?

MINISTER: Yes, physical education. It's a subject that is part of the core of our curriculum and yet all the attention recently seems to have been on other areas – particularly numeracy and literacy. Physical education is crying out for change! I mean, from what I have been reading, it hasn't really changed significantly for decades, and many schools still focus on a small range of traditional team games. Now these may align with hopes and ambitions for national success on the world stage in soccer or in the Rugby World Cup, or to ensure that we retain the Ashes, but they probably aren't going to connect with the youth of today, or certainly not many of them. I mean, we've known for decades that the so-called 'traditional' PE curriculum succeeds in putting so many people off physical activity for the rest of their lives. Just how many people reflect back on their physical education and see it as having provided them with the skills, the confidence and the inspiration to participate in various activities at different stages of their lives? No, it's time for change! And we need to look at this from an integrated policy perspective.

SIR HUMPHREY (who has been trying to interject to point out some political truths to the Minister, and finally manages to do so): Integrated policy perspective Minister? And why are you so concerned with young people's views? Or change for that matter? And physical education?

MINISTER (with a hint of frustration): Sir Humphrey, in case you have forgotten I am now Minister for Education! My job is *fundamentally* concerned with young people's education and, therefore, also their lifelong health and well-being!

SIR HUMPHREY (rapidly interjecting): Yes Minister, but you seem to be forgetting that they can't vote. Ultimately, as Minister for Education, young people below voting age are *not* your prime concern. Parents and teachers – now they might justifiably be your concern, and of course we need to recognize that their views may be very different to those of their children, but ... .

MINISTER: Yes but young people are our future voters and they are the future of Britain.

SIR HUMPHREY: Precisely, which is exactly why we need to make sure that we do everything we can to make sure that they appreciate our history, our cultural heritage, our core values as a society. You wouldn't want to do anything to jeopardize that would you Minister?

MINISTER: Who suggested that I was?

SIR HUMPHREY: Well, at this stage nobody did Minister, but you hinted at changing the curriculum didn't you?

MINISTER: Yes, but ... .

SIR HUMPHREY (interjects again): Precisely Minister! I'm really just pointing to the questions that are likely to be raised in the corridors if your ideas get out ... .

MINISTER (now recognizing Sir Humphrey's resistance and wanting to challenge it): Hear me out, Sir Humphrey! I see real potential here, not just for this office, but for the government as a whole. You see I want to bring others into this, to help us try to really do something that will mean that *all*, rather than just a few young people, have positive, meaningful experiences in physical education. I mean, think of the impact – it'll be good for education but also for sport and health. This thing is much bigger than Education, Sir Humphrey, and we should be responding to that. We need to be looking at the *whole picture*, not just part of it. We need to look at *what's* being taught, and also *how* – Do PE lessons *meaningfully engage* all students – or are some left pretty much 'on the sidelines'? How do children who come to school with limited physical skills, having had few opportunities to develop those in family or community settings, then feel in physical education? We need to look at what it will take to have a curriculum that genuinely extends *beyond* the school gates and has relevance well beyond school years – and not only for the able few young people who're selected for representative sports.

(As the Minister draws breath, Bernard sees a chance to assist Sir Humphrey in 'applying some brakes' to the Minister's enthusiasm.)

BERNARD: Yes Minister, but you do realize that if you raise issues such as those, you are in danger of getting into debates about pedagogy, don't you?

MINISTER: And your point is, Bernard?

SIR HUMPHREY (seeing an opportunity): Err, Yes Minister, Bernard raises a very good point. It really comes down to respecting policy boundaries, which clearly, you, as all Ministers, will be concerned about. I'm not sure it is advisable to tread on the toes of your colleagues in Sport and Health, is it Minister? And while we might be able to begin to take a look at some of 'what' is included in the curriculum, we really can't be seen to extend to matters of 'how', which are *clearly* the domain of teachers. Indeed, many of your predecessors have made a point of emphasizing the flexibility of policy in that regard, to ensure that whatever changes we make to the official curriculum, teachers will be able to make their own interpretation of things and adapt things to suit their particular school contexts.

MINISTER: Yes, but doesn't that mean that in reality nothing might change?

SIR HUMPHREY: Well, perhaps Minister, but it does also reflect your concern that we need teachers to respond to the needs and interests of all students. I mean no Minister can really do that, can they? But teachers can.

MINISTER (now somewhat puzzled by the policy direction that the discussion is leading towards): So, you don't think I should be looking at major changes in this revision and that I'm better off maintaining the current structures?

SIR HUMPHREY AND BERNARD (in unison): Yes Minister.

Notes

1   British Broadcasting Corporation.
2   If you are not familiar with *Yes Minister*, extracts can be viewed on YouTube: www.youtube.com/watch?v=jNKjShmHw7s (accessed 30 September 2011).
3   See, for example, Lawton (1993).

References

Ball, S. J. (1998) 'Big policies/small world: An introduction to international perspectives in education policy,' *Comparative Education*, 34(2): 119–30.

BBC. (n.d.) *Yes Minister*. Online. Available from: <www.bbc.co.uk/comedy/yesminister/index.shtml> (accessed 6 September 2010).

Lawton, D. (1993) 'Is there coherence and purpose in the national curriculum?', in C. Chitty and B. Simon (eds) *Education Answers Back. Critical Responses to Government Policy*, London: Lawrence and Wishart, pp. 61–69.

Research context

This narrative is informed by policy research undertaken by Dawn Penney and John Evans that explored the initial development and implementation of the National Curriculum for Physical Education in England and subsequent research exploring revisions in both England and Wales. The research sought to extend understandings of the processes of policy and curriculum development, and to investigate factors shaping the content of official policy texts and their interpretation and expression as physical education curricula and pedagogy. The research involved data collection at various sites of policy and curriculum development, including central government departments and agencies, local education authorities, schools and physical education departments. Documentary data, interviews, questionnaires and participant observation were utilized across the research sites. Theoretically the research was informed by work in the fields of education policy sociology and the sociology of education.

Recommended reading

Curtner-Smith, M. D. (1999) 'The more things change the more they stay the same: Factors influencing teachers' interpretations and delivery of national curriculum physical education', *Sport, Education and Society*, 4(1): 75–97.

Kirk, D. (2010) *Physical Education Futures*, London: Routledge.

Penney, D. (2002) 'Equality, equity and inclusion in PE and sport', in A. Laker (ed.) *The Sociology of Sport and PE: An Introductory Reader*, London, Routledge, pp. 110–28.

Penney, D. and Evans, J. (1999) *Politics, Policy and Practice in Physical Education*, London: FN Spon, an Imprint of Routledge.

'Miss Whitney' and 'Miss, are you a terrorist?': Negotiating a place within physical education

Anne Flintoff

Miss Whitney

The bell for next lesson rings loudly, followed by hundreds of pairs of feet hurtling down the corridor. The noise is deafening. 'Walk slowly! Don't push, you'll not get there any quicker!,' I shout, but there's no order; I've lost the battle. 'All right, Whitney?' shouts Tim, the head of department, rudely pushing two boys out of his way to reach my side. 'Can you manage this lot do you think, being such a youngster? Dance? Well, you've got the advantage anyway, natural rhythm, and all that, eh, and especially with *your* body!' His eyes sweep slowly down the top of my shirt, then he glances quickly up at me and grins. 'You'll love it, won't you Darren?', elbowing one of the bigger, stockier boys nearby. I recognize him as the captain from last night's winning cricket team. His shirt tail hangs out over one side of his trousers, mud colouring both knees, testimony to the morning break kick-about. A large, loose knot on his tie, offering up a defiant challenge to the school's dress regulations. The team's win had been announced in assembly. Darren had collected the cup from the Head to loud cheering and clapping. Cricket's *the* game here, apparently, and it was the first time we'd won the league. A proud moment for the whole school … . 'Do we have to, Sir?' Darren complains loudly. 'Dance is for puffs! Why can't I do athletics with you, Sir?' Tim smacks him playfully on the head, laughing as he responds. 'You'll be OK. Miss Whitney knows how to dance, don't you Miss Whitney? She'll give you boys a good time I'm sure!'

A hot flush sweeps slowly up my face and I turn away struggling to hide my embarrassment, anger, try to regain composure, as Tim – all six foot of him – strides purposefully towards the equipment cupboard, swinging his whistle, clipboard under one arm, oblivious to my discomfort. What's worse, the nickname, the throw-away line undermining me in front of the kids in one quick move, or that it's always dance he seems to have a problem with? I'm not sure. Well all of them, actually! I feel a hard knot of frustration gathering in my chest, like a bad bout of indigestion, only worse. I know I won't do anything, say anything, to challenge him. I can't. First teaching practice and challenging the head of department – get real! But all this stuff from uni about 'learning from experienced teachers' – bloody hell! I'm really learning *such* a lot from him! Jonathan seems to be getting on OK with him, though. Seems like they're best mates, especially since Friday night's drinking session celebrating the cricket. I thought it would be good, having two of us going to the same school – we could support each other – but I never see him. He's always off to football practice or rugby practice or something, with Tim, all matey matey.

Coaxing the stragglers into the gym, I tell myself, again, just a few more weeks and then you'll be back in university, stick it out, laugh it off – just *survive*. Helen had to explain the Whitney stuff to me. I didn't get it at first. '*You* know,' she said, laughing. 'Whitney Houston, the black singer? Her song, I Wanna Dance with Someone?' Right. OK, great. So what if I *am* a bit different from the average PE teacher, being mixed 'race' – I'm certainly the only one on my course anyway! And in this school, well, I do stand out. But get over it, I want to tell him, there's a multicultural world out there, you know. You ought to open your eyes a bit more! But of course I don't. I daren't. *He's* writing my report. *He's* the expert! Joanne's good, she tried to intervene once, but he laughed it off, saying she needed to chill out, that she was being an 'old woman' and couldn't she see it was only a joke. There's obviously no love lost between those two. I'm so glad Joanne's my mentor and not Tim! She's really helpful, doesn't have a problem. Treats me the same. And the kids are OK. They were always asking at first, 'Oh Miss, you've got a good suntan, where's that from? How do you do your hair like that?' But that's different. Kids are just like that, it's the way they are. That one kid saying, yesterday, that it was great to have a PE teacher like her was fantastic. That's what really counts!

Just keep my head down and try and fit in. That's what Mum says I should do. Of course it's different for me, I *can* fit in more that she can. She doesn't say much but you can tell it was bad for her when she was training – there weren't many black people around there then at all. And especially when she met Dad and moved to Barnstock, which is totally white. In a way, college has been no different for me – my school was all white, my friends were all white, so university wasn't anything new really. I didn't expect there to be hundreds of us, so it was OK. But then sometimes it all comes back, hits you slap bang in the face. When we talk about 'race' at uni, it's like they totally forget I'm black or that I'm even in the room! They say oh people aren't racists nowadays, and then the stuff they come out with, I can't believe it! Asians don't want to do this because of their religion or culture or stuff. And when James said that his PE teacher had told him he wouldn't get a place at this uni because they would pick people from different 'races' over him because of filling their quotas – that hurt. Hurt a lot. I just sat there, sat on my hands, waiting for the lecture to end; I couldn't say anything. Why should I say anything, anyway? Tony did try to challenge him, but I didn't hear his comments – there was too much blood pounding in my ears. I was just thinking, let me get out of here! It wouldn't have made a difference whatever Tony had said – James had said it, hadn't he?

'Miss, do we have to go in bare feet or can we wear trainers?' My attention snaps back to the lesson, and I move into the studio, encouraging them to choose bare feet, better for dance. Two girls sit huddled against the wall at the far end, near the CD player. As I turn on the music, I hear, 'I'm so fat I have been to the gym three times this week!' 'Well, look at this, ugg!' – Lucy, I think she is called – responds, pinching her midriff between thumb and forefinger. Worrying about body fat at twelve! But I can't deal with this right now … . Turning back to the group I start the lesson. 'OK, remember the warm up we did last week. Let's try it again … OK, find a space and follow me!' Peter gets to his feet. He'd been sitting patiently – he always does – waiting quietly for the lesson to begin, with his hands wrapped around his bony knees, his long legs folded into his body. No one is sitting with him, he seems a bit of a loner, but sometimes, I see him really come out of himself, like he connects with the music and really begins to move well. I think he's beginning to enjoy dance. Too late, I see the elbow dig hard into his ribs followed by Peter's 'ouch', and see him turn to identify the culprit. Stuart, Darren's mate, is smirking 'Hey spasso, watch it, that was my space! Go find your own!' I pretend not to see, turning to adjust the music instead. I cop out, all the while, thinking I shouldn't have ignored that. But I can't do everything. I remember my mentor's feedback from last week. 'Concentrate on getting a good start – get them active quickly, with a brisk opener that will set the scene.' Easy for him to say … . Anyway, what *I'm* learning is that becoming a teacher means a hell of a lot more than just teaching kids how to dance.

Miss, are you a terrorist?

I've reached the door, but stand outside, uncertain whether to go in. I shiver, suddenly cold, clammy skin, though the evening's warm. Minutes pass. Pull yourself together, come on now, breathe, it's fine, I tell myself. It's not that bad. My hand shakes as I reach up to explore my swollen cheek. The now-useless, sodden tissue leaks blood which runs slowly down my arm onto my coat sleeve. A dull, throbbing headache begins behind my temples. Why? Why me? I begin to cry again, I can't stop myself. I know I have to go and face them, but I know what they will say, well what Mum will say. But I'm already late and they'll be expecting me. I need to go in.

I struggle with the key in the lock, push open the door and move into the warmth of the kitchen. Cooking smells linger. I had hoped they'll be out for the evening. But they're sitting at the table finishing their meal, talking over their day. Their quiet conversation halts abruptly as they turn to greet me and see that something's wrong. Dad rushes over, and his arm around my back feels comforting; I collapse heavily onto the nearest chair, my college bag dropping to the floor. I can't look at Mum's face, but know she is beginning to cry. She asks me over and over again, 'What's happened love, oh Nadia, what's happened?' Dad rushes to get the first aid box, and wets cotton wool at the sink. 'Here use this, gently now,' he says, handing it to me to replace the tissue.

I try to explain, but it's hard, I don't really know. One minute, I'm walking home from uni saying goodbye to Lucy, next I'm sprawled on the floor, dizzy and disorientated, a half-brick lying next to me on the ground. The weapon, I guess. 'I didn't see what they looked like. They were on the other side of the road, we're talking, we didn't take much notice.' 'Let's take a look at that, now,' Dad interjects as he slowly peels away the cotton wool and inspects the wound. 'I don't think it'll need a stitch, but keep pressing to stop the blood for now. You were obviously just in the wrong place at the wrong time,' he adds reassuringly, but I notice the concern showing in his eyes nevertheless. 'I'll be OK, I think they must've been drunk or something,' I respond weakly, lying. I know full well it was my headscarf that had marked me out for their target practice. I'd heard their taunts. But whatever I say, it's still not what Mum wants to hear, and we slip into the conversation we've had so many times before.

'I just don't understand why you want to put yourself in that situation. How can you be a good Muslim and be a PE teacher? Your sister is fine, medicine's different, different people down there, nice people. Why choose to mix with non-Muslims all the time? Look what happens when you do.' I try and suggest that what's happened this evening has nothing to do with my choice of career. That it could happen anywhere. She's not convinced. 'Why don't you stop?' she pleads quietly. 'Won't you stop now?'

Sighing, I glance at Dad for support. He was the same initially, didn't want me to teach, but after he saw I was getting good at sport, that I was serious about it, he's been really good. I've wanted to be a PE teacher since I was 14! I know he's had to put up with a lot of grief, particularly from his mum and dad and the cousins. Teaching was OK as a career, but teaching PE? Spending three or four years learning how to throw a ball? For what? No way could they get their heads around that! All they see is footballers on the tele, getting into fights, singing and drinking after the game. I'd not dared tell them that there's some of that at uni, too. It's the most difficult thing for me, not the lectures, not the learning, that's great! I've enjoyed every minute of that. It's just, it's difficult, the social side, if everything is about alcohol – I'm not seen as a team player because I can't join in. Even at school, teachers want to talk to you about your lesson down the pub. I haven't told Mum and Dad that, of course.

I respond firmly, 'But Mum, it's important I'm there, I can educate kids, so things like this don't happen in the future to other people. Remember when I told you about my first few minutes at Brackenridge school, the all-white school in Easingby where I did my first practice, when that kid called me a terrorist and asked whether I believed in killing people because I was Muslim? I made a difference there, just by being there, I know I did. Being a Muslim and a woman and teaching PE! But also, you know, I told you about those sessions I taught with Mr Brown's PSHE[1] group on stereotyping and Islam, remember that? Using us as the example?'

'I wasn't too pleased you'd used that photo of me, though!' Dad joked, trying his best to lighten the atmosphere. 'It was hardly me at my best.' 'Yeah Dad, but it got the message across!' I responded. 'When I put it up next to the picture of Bin Laden, they could see that you both looked the same, but that's all. I could show them that that was how stereotyping worked, through ignorance, and fear. It is important, Mum, it really is. I can educate them, and give them a different story to their Daily Mail front pages – "Muslims and The War on Terror!". They need people like me in teaching. I'm actually a real resource for schools if they choose to look at me that way. Mr Brown certainly saw me that way.'

Note

1   Personal, social and health education.

Reference

Turner, D. (2007) 'Ethnic diversity in physical education teaching', *Physical Education Matters*, 2(2): 14–16.

Research context

These ethnographic fictions draw on research exploring black and minority ethnic (BME) physical education students' experiences of teacher education in England. Funded by the Training and Development Agency (TDA), the government agency responsible for teacher education, the study was set within a wider, government policy agenda concerned with increasing the diversity of teacher education cohorts. Physical education teacher education (PETE), as a specific teacher education context in England, is overwhelmingly white, a situation that has shifted little over the last decade or so. Eleven per cent of students opting into teaching across all subject areas are from BME backgrounds, compared to PETE at 2.94 per cent (Turner 2007). The research involved in-depth interviews and questionnaires with 25 BME students from across four teacher education institutions and sought to explore how their ethnic, religious and gendered identities impacted upon their experiences of PETE.

Recommended reading

Benn, T., Dagkas, S. and Jawad, H. (2011) 'Embodied faith: Islam, religious freedom and educational practices in education', *Sport, Education and Society*, 16(1): 17–34.
Flintoff, A., with Chappell, A., Gower, C., Keyworth, S., Lawrence, J., Money, J., Squires, S. L. and Webb, L. (2008) *Black and Minority Ethnic Trainees' Experiences of Physical Education Initial Teacher Training*. Unpublished report for the Training and Development Agency, Carnegie Research Institute: Leeds Metropolitan University. Available from: <www.leedsmet.ac.uk/carnegie/F7DDB88DA13F477E9E5 78A028E96FDB4.htm> (accessed 3 October 2011).

Gilborn, D. (2008) *Racism and Education: Coincidence or Conspiracy?* London: Routledge.

Harrison, L., Jr. and Belcher, D. (2006) 'Race and ethnicity in physical education', in D. Kirk, D. Macdonald and M. O'Sullivan (eds) *The Handbook of Research in Physical Education*, London: Sage, pp. 740–51.

Kay, T. (2006) 'Daughters of Islam: Family influences on Muslim young women's participation in sport', *International Review for the Sociology of Sport*, 41(3): 357–73.

The spark and discouragement of an innovative male physical educator

Nate McCaughtry and Kimberly Oliver

The scene for this fictional tale is an advising appointment/tutorial meeting between a university physical education teacher education (PETE) advisor/ mentor (Dr S.) and an increasingly disillusioned undergraduate pre-service teacher called Pete. It blends together some of the most important and current themes in physical education, including: the limits of sports-based PE, the interplay of masculinities, the reproductive role of PE teacher education, and the fragility of different visions in our field.

Prologue: Pete has cautiously scheduled a meeting with the PETE programme co-ordinator Dr S. He thinks that, if anyone can understand where he's coming from, it would be him. However, he's somewhat intimidated by Dr S. and worried he will feel offended when he explains that he thinks the PETE programme is too traditional and team sports-focused, and that it is not preparing him to teach different groups of students, especially boys that are like he was when he was young.

DR S.: Hi Pete, why don't you take a seat? Now, how can I help you?

PETE: Hey, Dr S. Thanks for seeing me today. I'm sorry I haven't come to see you in a while. I've had a lot on my mind. I've been trying to think things through, but it's like I'm stuck in a maze, you know, like I've tried every route and still can't find my way out. I feel so lost. I don't know if you've noticed, but I've been pretty down lately and my work is suffering.

DR S.: Yes, I have to say I've noticed a pretty big change since you joined the programme. You used to be so energetic and passionate. I remember you used to sit in the front row and eagerly contribute to every class discussion, and now you sit near the back of class and rarely contribute. What's going on?

PETE: I'm starting to think this programme isn't for me.

DR S.: Really? But you have so much potential! Why are you thinking it's not for you now?

PETE: I'm not really sure, maybe it's this programme, maybe it's being a PE teacher at all. I started here wanting to be a different kind of teacher. But, I'm starting to fear that this programme won't prepare me to do what I believe in. Who knows, maybe no programme would?

DR S.: Whoa, you've got to help me understand a bit more. I'm not sure that's a fair statement. You gotta give me more to go on.

PETE: It's like, well, when I started, I hoped that it would be different from the PE I'd had when I was a kid. PE in grade school and middle school was really difficult for me. I wasn't very sporty. Don't get me wrong. I loved to play with my friends. We lived on the outskirts of town, so we'd hike the fields and forest for hours. We rode our bikes and played everywhere, just being active with my friends without a care in the world. The trouble was I didn't like structured sports and my parents never got me into any. Both of my parents worked and I had a sister and two brothers, so I don't know if it was a time thing or a money thing, or what. And the only real organized physical activities I did was dance because they had dance classes at our church. Those classes were so fun because I could just be with my friends and really let my body go, you know, I felt free to express myself.

DR S.: OK, but what was it about PE that made it difficult?

PETE: For one, I never knew what I was doing and I wasn't very good at the things they played. It seemed like all the other kids, especially the boys, knew how to play basketball, soccer, softball, volleyball. I didn't play these at home and I wasn't part of a team, so I always just sat there wondering what I should be doing. The other thing was I really didn't like playing against my friends. Like, at home my friends and I played all sorts of games – it was never me against you, but us doing something, discovering something, accomplishing something together. Like we used to play this game together called Sharks and Minnows. It sounds kind of dumb, but some of us would be sharks and we'd pretend to swim around the fish tank after the minnows. But, in PE all we ever did was play sports against each other and I didn't really like that. We weren't playing with each other, but against each other. There was just a different feel about playing.

DR S.: Help me understand, it sounds like the PE you're describing was pretty normal. They covered a range of sports. Maybe the problem was your teachers?

PETE: I guess it was partly all the sports, and partly that everything was so competitive. No matter how hard I tried, I just couldn't get skilled in sports. I mean we practiced skills a little but, when games started, they were way too fast and all the other boys seemed to know what they were doing. I just wanted to ride my bike, or run through the woods, or play tag. It made no sense to me how into the competition they got, and how the teacher got so excited when they did! Sports just weren't my favourite things to do, so I tried to hide as much as possible. Oh soccer, I remember soccer. When it was soccer I used to position myself wide on the wing and that way the ball never got passed to me. It was like an invisible sideline had been created exactly where I was standing and that meant I wasn't really on the pitch. I wasn't the only one, there were lots of us boys who felt that, because we couldn't do the sports in PE. We all thought something was wrong with us.

DR S.: Well some kids don't really like sports at first, that's why your teacher should have taught the skills more and de-emphasized competition. Now tell me, do you think your feelings have to do with how the sports were taught or was it the sports themselves you didn't like?

PETE: It's more than that. Like, in high school, we had to take two semesters of PE. There was this new teacher, Mr Davis, who taught the PE classes. He changed my life.

DR S.: How so?

PETE: You know, I've thought a lot about this and I think the biggest thing was the activities we did. We did these individual fitness things like yoga, Pilates, Tae Bo and Tai Chi. We also did stuff outdoors. I remember orienteering at the park and going on an inline-skating adventure. Oh, and the best was the dance, not the old-fashioned square dancing crap, but hip hop and stepping. This one time we even got to make our own dance to *Jump Around* and perform it at the football pregame celebration to help the whole school get in the mood for the big game. But it wasn't just the activities, it was the atmosphere they created. We were all there doing these things together and having fun together while we exercised. For me, it was awesome because these were the kinds of activities that fitted the kind of boy I was, and I didn't get made fun of or feel inferior. It wasn't about skill or status, just learning to be physically active together.

DR S.: I'm still trying to understand what made this experience so life changing for you. Was it the different kinds of activities, or was it the teacher, or was it something else?

PETE: I think it was the whole package. Like I said, I was a pretty active kid. I was good at these new things because I liked to move around. Before it was that I didn't know how to play the sports and I didn't have any of the skills that most of the other boys had. These new activities were more social and fun, we weren't trying to outdo each other with some kids dominating others or getting mad at each other when they lost. Sure, Mr Davis was a big reason, too. He actually talked with me, he didn't ignore me because I wasn't the 'right kind' of boy. I didn't get the sense that he was disgusted with how unskilled I was. Frankly, I think the biggest thing was how different PE *felt*. I just felt like I belonged. No one knew most of the new activities and, with my dance background, I learned things like yoga quickly. I guess if I had to sum it all up, there was just a completely different feel to PE. It was more about having fun doing physical activities so you could get more healthy, than beating each other up on the sports field.

DR S.: So, was it these classes that made you want to be a PE teacher?

PETE: Absolutely! I took Mr Davis's second class at the end of my junior year. It was this adventure PE class where he taught us about different types of biking, you know, mountain biking, road biking, cross-tour biking. It wasn't just about doing the biking, though, we learned how to buy a bike, how to fix it, maintain it, how to find trails and safe roads, and the etiquette. It was the whole package of what you needed to learn to make biking part of your life. We also learned how to hike, orienteer, canoe and camp outside. You know what, we even did some skateboarding and inline skating. This class opened the world to me. It made me see that PE could be more than competitive sports, it could be something that I loved, that was part of me.

DR S.: Did Mr Davis encourage you to become a PE teacher?

PETE: Oh yeah! I talked with him all the time about it. I was scared because I knew I wouldn't make a good PE teacher if it was like the PE I had in grade school and middle school. I just wasn't a sporty person, and that's all I knew about PE until high school. But Mr Davis convinced me that PE could be what I wanted it to be. About getting kids to love physical activity and you could create all kinds of different classes to accomplish that goal. I came to university wanting to learn how to become Mr Davis, and be the kind of life-changing PE teacher he had been for me.

DR S.: So why quit now?

PETE: To put it bluntly, it's because I'm not being taught how to be like Mr Davis. I just feel the programme here is far more like the PE I endured during grade school and middle school.

DR S.: What do you mean? Give me some specific examples, because I'm not sure you are being completely fair.

PETE: Well, look at the classes we take. I took team sports one and two, dual sports one and two, individual sports one and two. The only thing other than sports that I took was a one-credit dance class where I learned the hokey-pokey, chicken-dance and square dancing. Those are hardly what I'd call contemporary, cool dances! I mean there's no outdoor stuff, like hiking, biking, camping, anything in the outdoors. There's no individual fitness activities like running, stepping, elliptical, Zumba, yoga, Pilates, BOSU. You know, things you'd do at a fitness club. It also has to do with my classmates and the instructors. Don't get me wrong, they're nice people for the most part. But, they're different than me. When we learn activities in our classes, my classmates are really competitive and they get mad at me when I cause their team to lose. They don't want me with them for group assignments like basketball units because they don't think I know what I'm doing. Most of them openly say they're only getting their PE certificates so they can coach. It's really clear when we peer teach or go out to the schools that most of them have no idea what it's like to be a non-athletic kid, or a kid who isn't sporty. Every time the instructors in our courses explain things or use examples, they talk about sports, how to teach sports, why sports are good, how to make sports palatable for kids. We haven't even taken a class about teaching the things like I loved in high school PE or understanding the different kinds of students we'll be teaching. It's like we played a bunch of really competitive sports last year, and now this year we're learning how to teach them to kids. All I hear is drill, drill, drill, game! No one even questions whether PE has to be like this.

DR S.: I can see your point. And yet, in our defence, you should understand that, around here, in our communities there are lots of youth sports, and the kids around here love it, so that's why it's a big part of our programme. We have particular facilities, resources and faculty, and changing that would be really hard. The local schools where you're going to get a job, and cooperative teachers where you go to practice, expect that our pre-service teachers can teach sports well. The high school programme you described sounds great and we might work toward that, but there's a lot of liability issues to consider, as well as things like staffing, expertise and accreditation. I'm not sure you understand how much of a complete shift it would be to do what you're talking about. Not to mention, I'm just not sure there's enough kids in the schools who would want that kind of programme. In the end, PE teachers teach what they know, and most of our students know sports, they played them as kids and want to teach them to their future students. It's our job to make sure they do it well.

PETE: I hear what you're saying and I didn't mean to offend you. I know you're just looking out for the best interest of the programme. I guess I'm just very disillusioned with what I thought the programme would do for me. I thought it would be more, sort of, intellectual, you know, ask really important questions about different kinds of PE, what's best for kids, how to teach different kinds of activities, and most of all how to teach different kinds of kids. I know this might sound bad, but sometimes this programme seems like it's more about athlete production.

DR S.: Pete, I think you're missing the bigger picture here. Most kids like competitive sports and there are many good things they can learn from them. Instead of focusing on what's bad about them, you might consider embracing the positive things. You can be the teacher who makes sports great for a lot of kids, the same way Mr Davis did for you.

PETE: Well, I guess that's one way to look at it. OK, maybe I'll try to start looking at it more like that. I have to run, secondary methods is about to start. Thanks, I really appreciate you taking the time to help me out.

DR S.: Glad I could help.

PROLOGUE: Pete left the meeting very discouraged. To him, Dr S. hadn't really heard or understood him, nor was he willing to question the mission and practices in the PETE programme. The programme was too deeply engrained in a sports-based PE philosophy, without really questioning the kinds of students that those programmes often underserve, namely many boys and girls who aren't competitive by nature or simply aren't as skilled or experienced as others in highly organized team sports. Pete grew increasingly disillusioned and completed the semester in a very withdrawn fashion. He didn't return.

Research context

Our narrative is a fictional tale that is based in part on discussions we have had with physical education teacher education candidates and in-service teachers reflecting on their teacher training in American universities. To build the narrative we reconstructed past conversations and identified common themes to reflect the kinds of experiences that progressive-minded would-be physical educators face as they navigate traditional physical education teacher preparation programmes. The narrative highlights the tensions between competitive, sports-based teacher preparation and non-traditional students whose views of physical activity and educating the young in the context of school physical education differ both in content and process.

Recommended reading

Aldous, D. and Brown, D. (2010) 'Framing bodies of knowledge within the "acoustics" of the school: Exploring pedagogical transition through newly qualified physical education teacher experiences', *Sport Education and Society*, 15(4): 411–29.

Brown, D. and Rich, E. (2002) 'Gender positioning as pedagogical practice in physical education', in D. Penney (ed.) *Gender and Physical Education: Contemporary Issues and Future Directions*, London: The Falmer Press, pp. 80–100.

Dowling, F. (2008) 'Getting in touch with our feelings: The emotional geographies of gender relations in PETE', *Sport, Education and Society*, 13(3): 247–66.

Gorely, T., Holroyd, R. and Kirk, D. (2003) 'Muscularity, the habitus and the social construction of gender: Towards a gender relevant physical education', *British Journal of Sociology of Education*, 24(4): 429–48.

Tischler, A. and McCaughtry, N. (2011) 'PE is not for me: When boys' masculinities are threatened', *Research Quarterly for Exercise and Sport*, 82(1): 37–48.

Second toe syndrome

Catherine Morrison

Leo's story (now 16 years old)

At first, they made me play Saturday soccer. Before every game, Mum would tell me, when the ball came towards me, not to run away. 'Run *to* the ball, Leo, not *away* from it,' she'd say. I'd go out on the field and be OK at the start of the game, but then the ball would come straight at me: 'What do I do again?'

I'd get distracted easily. I'd forget about the game. The field was so green and muddy. I used to wish I had my digger there. I would build a huge trench around the outside of the field to drain the water. I'd roll the field flat. The landfill would be used to build a viewing platform for the spectators. I'd need scaffolding for that. And ... then Mum's voice would interrupt. '*Leo*!! The ball!!! Run *TO* the ball!!' My plans would be blasted to smithereens. The ball would go belting past me. Everyone would groan.

Halfway through that season, Dad said to Mum that I should have played rugby right from the start. 'Soccer's a waste of time – it's a girls' game anyway,' I heard him say.

The next year, Dad signed me up for rugby. Dad said I'd like it. I wasn't so sure. I've never been good at that catching and throwing stuff. Mum said I'm like that because of something that sounds like a *really* flash vegetable. It's called 'Dyspraxia'. My brothers don't have it. Mum said you can call people lots of names. She said I also have the name 'Expert Scaffolder and Digger'. My brothers haven't got that either. I am not sure which one I caught first.

I hated rugby after a while, but I couldn't tell Dad that. Everyone yelled heaps more at rugby. 'Tackle, tackle!' 'You're playing like a pack of pansies.' 'Ruck the ball.' 'Rip the ball.' 'Stop playing like a girl's blouse.' 'Get *in* there.' 'You're like flies 'round dog shit.'

After a few games, no one yelled to pass the ball to me. That was good. I always hated it when the ball came my way, anyway. *Pass the ball? Set it up? Run with it? Lay it out?* Far too confusing. I liked talking to the players from the other team though – Dad said, don't do that. My rugby socks never stayed up and I had to keep pulling them up over and over – Mum said don't do that, either.

I got a cake when I scored my first try. I actually just happened to be there and I fell on the ball. Everyone was really pleased. Dad looked chuffed. I only ever got one cake, though. My youngest brother, Fergus, he got lots of cakes.

Mum didn't think rugby was working for me – I heard her say it to Dad. Dad didn't want to talk about me and rugby any more. Sometimes I'd look at my short second toe and wish it would grow longer like Mum's and Dad's and my stupid brothers'. Maybe that would've helped.

One day, Mum and Dad said maybe we would try something different. Something less confusing, they said. But I had to play some kind of team sport on a Saturday. Everyone in our family did. Diggers didn't count.

I joined Cadets. It was my idea. Mum and Dad didn't know anything about Cadets. Mum said I could give it a go. Dad said it wasn't really a sport. I guess war isn't really. It's about parades, marching and uniforms immaculately pressed with no 'train lines' visible. We travel in Unimogs, do rifle shooting and stuff like that. John, my younger brother, his long second toe stuffed into his flash new rugby boots, clattering down the driveway, would give me a flick as he ran past on his way to the car. 'Retard,' he'd hiss. He said I looked like one in the uniform. I didn't say anything back.

There's no parents' shouting on the sidelines at Cadets. The Sergeant Major is who I listen to, and she tells us exactly what to do. I like that. I like her.

When we collected for ANZAC day – that's the Australian and New Zealand Army Corps – bigger boys pushed and shoved me on the street. Someone even fired BB bullets at us when we were standing on the corner. I didn't care.

An old man bought a poppy and told me how he lost his best mate in the trenches at Gallipoli. He bought two for $10. He was taking a poppy to put on his friend's headstone at the cemetery. I heard a lot of stories that day. I'm proud to be in the Cadets. Short second toe 'n' all.

Leo's Mum's story

We were a sporty family. Dad, a former provincial rep, was proud of us.

'It's all about the second toe,' Dad said. He knew exactly how to tell who would be a fast runner, who would succeed, and who wouldn't. 'Your second toe has to be longer than your big toe,' he said, showing us his to prove his point. After every bath time, we'd check. Thankfully, just like Dad, we all had a second toe longer than the rest. We were sure then, we were destined to be fast, to be first, to be the best.

Practice was in the front paddock every night. The lawn-mower was heaved over the barbed wire fence. The sheep scattered with the inevitable roar, and the running lanes magically appeared.

Dad coached us to be great starters. He had his very own set of starter clappers, fashioned from two bits of four-by-two.

'I'm going to change the pace of the "ready, set and go" each time. Those buggers in town never start a race properly,' he muttered. 'So, be on your toes.'

I was, in fact, a fabulous starter, but then would have to zigzag my way to avoid the sheep droppings. Meanwhile, my brother, Joseph, a slower starter, never minded the green squish and splurge between his toes. He would run the straight line to win. Dad said the scotch thistles peppering the paddock were the best thing out for us. They spurred us over the finish line. 'Makes you tough,' he reminded us as the thistles needled our bare feet.

At the town champs, I knew I could win. I always did. At the finish line, proud as punch, I'd pull off my socks and shoes. My second toe winked at me. Dad was always right: my second toe was my secret weapon.

Leo's Dad's story

Winter rugby practice was in the back paddock. I'd get Dad's rugby boots out of the storeroom. They had leather studs, were a million years old and way too big. Even with my elongated toes, the bootlaces had to be pulled so tight to stop them falling off my feet. I played a special game of rugby. I called it One Man Rugby. I'd pretend to be Barry John, the famous Welsh fly-half. I'd sometimes pretend to be Bryan Williams, the All Blacks winger. I'd spend hours scoring tries all over the field. I was always on the winning side, no matter what.

Mum and Dad would take me into town for the games. That's what you did on a Saturday. We played all over the province. We were a *real* team. Tough. Confident. Tactical. We'd thrash the townies, easily beat the boarders and, when we took on the Dooleys, we had them quaking in their boots before the whistle even blew. After the game, we'd show each other our battle wounds. The more ruck marks you had, the tougher you were. In those days, only sooks wore helmets. Only sissies wore singlets under their rugby jerseys.

When I got picked for a rep team, it was another step closer to wearing the famous All Blacks jersey; in front of the screaming crowds; inside the stadium at Twickenham; my hand on my heart; Dame Kiri Te Kanawa singing the New Zealand national anthem; the team performing the haka ... ; I imagined being the great All Blacks lock, Colin Meads. I always wondered if Colin's second toe was longer than his big toe, just like mine. Dad said it would be.

But ... enough of that stuff.

It's not just about getting out there on the field. It is about *how* you play the game when you get there that is important. Ready for action. Skilled. Strong. Focused. Aggressive. Man to man. You look them in the eye at the start of the game. You stare them out. Only then is the game *really* on. 'Read my lips,' you say slowly as you bring out ... the deadly double-barrel-shooter sign! 'Bite the dust. 'cause you guys are going down ... down ... down!'

You know what? I think I'm going to keep my boots for a million years too.

Leo again

Mmm … don't think I'll keep my rugby boots. When I'm a Dad though, I'll probably still inspect my children's feet. You never know what you're going to get, I guess. But I'll probably be pleased if their second toe is longer than the first.

It's a family tradition.

Research context

Poststructural theoretical resources inform this narrative. How does one experience physicality when one is 'less able' to engage in traditional sporting activities valued within the family? It would seem imperative to understand the experiences of those whose habits, dispositions and physicalities differ from the 'norm'. By interviewing Dad, Leo and then the writer (Mum), reflecting through writing this narrative, we question how one young man with a dyspraxia label negotiates and understands his physicality and sense of 'self' in a family where physical competence and masculinity are inevitably linked. The narrative enables us to interrogate the discourses around physical culture: whose interests are privileged (or not) in what sports, and which physical activities count?

Recommended reading

Connors, C. and Stalker, K. (2007) 'Children's experiences of disability: Pointers to a social model of childhood disability', *Disability and Society*, 22(1): 19–33.

Fitzgerald, H. and Kirk, D. (2009) 'Identity work: Young disabled people, family and sport', *Leisure Studies*, 28(4): 469–88.

Martino, W. and Pallotta-Chiarolli, M. (2003) *So What's a Boy? Addressing Issues of Masculinity and Schooling*, Maidenhead: Open University Press.

Morrison, C. (2009) 'Deconstructing a narrative of physical culture', in H. Fitzgerald (ed.) *Disability and Youth Sport*, London: Routledge, pp. 132–44.

Pringle, R. and Markula, P. (2005) 'No pain is sane after all: A Foucauldian analysis of masculinities and men's experiences in Rugby', *Sociology of Sport Journal*, 22(4): 472–97.

Gendering running, gendering research: a collaborative trans narrative

Heather Sykes and Satoko Itani

Heather

In the fall of 2009 Itani came to the University of Toronto to do doctoral research into trans issues in sport, and I am serving as Itani's doctoral supervisor. Soon after Itani arrived, I received the invitation to contribute some of my earlier research in a narrative form to this book. I have been increasingly drawn toward the potential of collaborative writing based on some inspiring co-authored autobiographies that students had written for my curriculum theory courses. So, quite rapidly, Itani and I decided to collaborate in writing, sharing and discussing our own narratives about gender and transgender in relation to sport and physical education. We began by talking to one another about what gender and trans-ness meant to each of us. This was a valuable, intense and intimate conversation early on in our relationship. Over several months Itani then wrote several versions of [their/his] narrative. It took a while for me to write my narrative, but when I did it came tumbling out of a place in between my memories and fantasies, my body and my language, the lived and imagined stories I tell myself about my gender and sexual identities. This was a process of talking about ourselves, writing our individual narratives separately and then discussing how to bring them together within this text.

Methodologically, my approach was informed by the poetry of trans activist Eli Clare (2007), a respectful engagement with the anti-colonial poetic research of indigenous scholar Peter Cole (2006). I have also been encouraged by feminist scholars such as Patti Lather (2007) to be open to that which is yet to come, to collaborate and share, and to search for trust and queerness within research relationships.

This was also a collaborative process of writing about and across our multiple differences, our relations of power and relations of trust. We wrote between the institutional power relations of 'supervisor' and 'student'. Heather wrote in her only language, English, with all the colonizing legacy and white privileges this enabled. Itani talked and wrote in between the translation of Japanese to English, with all the losses and emotions that requires.

These narratives lie somewhere in between truth and fiction, between research and remembering, between Toronto, Kobe and Yorkshire, between male and female, between Itani and myself. We seem to have an initial, yet deep respect for the other person's trans/gender identity, although there is much that Itani and I do not know or discuss with each other about our own gender identities and gendered bodies. The two poetic narratives that follow portray how each of us has lived our genders as boku, boi, transgendered or transsexual with (almost) as much clarity, trust and emotion as we have developed between us.

Heather: articulate boi syndrome

For my eighth birthday, Auntie Frances gave me a cowboy outfit.
Fake Stetson hat, tasseled waistcoat, gun holster without the gun.
'Yeeeeeehaaaaaaaaaaaaaaw,' rang across our green, middle-class, Yorkshire lawn
Followed by a river of angered tears rolling down my cheeks.

A cowgirl skirt?

Where were the tasseled chaps?

What sort of cowboy wears a skirt?

My manners fell away under my gender devastation.
It took me 35 years to eventually buy my butch, boi leather chaps in Toronto's Kensington Market.

***

Throughout my 20s I made surreptitious trips to the Green Mushroom,
Nottingham's radical bookstore.
Scouring the shelves for diagonal black and white stripes on the spines of Women's Press books.
Reading my gayness into existence through
  Radclyffe Hall, Jeanette Winterson, Minnie Bruce Pratt, Audre Lorde.
Reading over the transgender existence of Stephen in Radclyffe Hall, Bobby in Enid Blyton.
  Recognizing lesbians
  Misrecognizing transmen
Furtively, I read my gayness into existence through Jeanette Winterson
  Oranges were no longer my only fruit
Ferron sang my-lesbian into existence through shady gate
Furious, I rode my butch dyke into existence through Patrick Califia's s/m biker dyke
I now get paid to read my white boi into existence, thru Toronto's queer pretensions.
Reading in deference to whiteness
  Getting three degrees without getting into debt
    Getting hired without living in war

***

Moments of gender devastation
A far cry from a lifetime of gender dysphoria

My cry detoured through pain
Monthly screamingPain, erupting from my belly
Finding, while not seeking, a syndrome

Irritable bowel syndrome
Irritable boi syndrome
Endometriosis

It'll be the end of me
Endo me
Endo me being together
Pain disrupted my classes, my sleeping, my driving, my orgasms
Pain illuminated another self inside me
Pain illustrated the arrogance of complete explanation
My pain refuted psychology
and exercise physiology
My pain ruptured rationality
of sports science
of Western enlightenment
How could I play rugby for England
How could I be a 1980s white granola lesbian
How could I be a Loughborough trained PE teacher
And yet fall apart?
And be filled with pain for 25 years.
I still have no clear link between being queer and being in pain
Am I intersex? I still don't know but I'd like to get tested.
What if there is a link between so much pain
What if progesteron levels in childbirth, during menstruation, during orgasm,
during anger
ARE Linked to my body's gender devastation?
What if progesteron levels in the closet, during rugby, as a stressed teacher
ARE linked to being a tomboy, becoming lesbianBoi?
I ran away from the genderizing, pathologizing physiologists and endocrino-
logists who
Roar, in positivist certitudes, their patriarchal cigendered explanations and
prognoses.
What if I had been a good enough athlete to have been sex tested?
What of my dreams of finding testes inside my labia?
They told me endometrial tissue might have fused my bowel to my
abdomen
If they had looked, would they have found spermatozoa confusing my endo-
metrium?
Was this confusion screaming through my pain?

athlete
PE teacher
professor

Screaming for years from inside just pain don't explain
What if diverting my career away from exercise physiology and VO2max
toward critical poststructural postcolonial studies of everything
is my body talking through my head?

***

I settled Canada.
Not single-handedly
Christian missionaries, British merchants, English elitism paved my way
AngloGenocides of language
>   From lost language of the cranes
>   To lost language of Tagish
>   Paving the way for my Anglo accent
>   My easy domain name.edu
I settled into Canada
Becoming a white lesbian amidst Yukon's First Nations
Running rivers, no running from gunfire, Indian Agents, Christian Brothers
Female masculinity in the Yukon, under the aurora borealis
Taking too long to make the connections between aurora borealis, Turtle Island and
Aotearoa
Slowly, almost geologically, learning the difference of my whiteness

***

My pain settled down in Canada
Alleviated by laminated layers of Anglo settlement
By moving to a new latitude
By my latitude to move
To leave the british dying empire's collective depression
>   With its brutish psychoses infecting the british isles.
Diagnose the sickness of empire
Not the irritability of my gender.
Now in my manly menopausal years, my pain has gone
Medicated by doses of whitened liberalism
>   and my choice migrate, to move

***

Was that gender pain?
Irritable bowel syndrome became articulate boi syndrome
It matters who we read.
It matters how we move.
It matters who we read as we learn to move.

***

You write, Itani, that when you arrive in Toronto you feel some freedom

You look around, you go running.
You also write to remember, your rainy season.
We are just beginning to talk with each other, write with each other.
You just wrote a brilliant paper about the sociology of diagnosis,
Diagnosing how Gender Identity Disorder travelled and settled to Japan.
Will our writing, this writing, this trans narrative
Diagnose the sickness of gender science, of DSM syndromes, of APA style.

Itani: 僕 私は **running chameleon**

背景に合わせて僕.　私の体は読み替えられる、*as they please*
競技に青春を捧げる陸上選手
Boyish Japanese tiny girl
運動神経のいい女子
おてんばな少女
性同一性障害者
Gender queer
Transgender
Asian man
Gay man
Queer
娘

People read my body and my life
「男の子二人でいいですね」（見知らぬ女性1）
「ここは女子トイレよ」（見知らぬ女性2）
「ボーイッシュでかっこいいね」（同級生）
「大変だったんだね」（友人）
"Jap" (stranger 1)
"Hello Sir" (stranger 2)
"Hi ladies" (stranger 3)
"You are our secret weapon" (a classmate in a University PE class)
"I hate Chinese men!" (A woman screaming at my face on the street in
Toronto)

In their eyes, 僕.　私は
I'm gay.
I'm trans.
I'm tomboy.
I'm a daughter.
I'm a track athlete.
I'm a small Asian girl.
I'm a poor person with GID.
I'm a colonizer and a colonized.
I'm a man who invades women's washroom.
I'm a confused Asian guy who shops for sports bra.

I'm a tiny Asian girl who could not possibly play volleyball better than
white classmates.
I'm a Chinese man who had done something wrong to a white woman who
I've never met before.

***

27回目の夏を久々に日本で過ごしている。近所の山に走りにでかけ、ふ
と途中の坂で立ち止まり、はるかに連なる六甲山を眺める。梅雨の雨は
止んだばかりで、まだ山の上はうす雲に覆われている。が、東の方から
空が明るみ始め、生ぬるい空気が初夏の訪れを告げていた。べそ顔を拭
い切れぬ梅雨の空が、まだ痛みを知らない幼き頃の記憶を思い出させ
る。初夏の太陽と林を掻き分け走り、蒸すような新緑の香りを胸いっぱ
いに感じていた幼少時代。六甲山は美しく輝いていた、自分がカメレオ
ンであると知るまでは。

***

Every time I cross a border, from Japan to the USA, to Canada, to South
Korea, I open a map, take a deep breath, and go for a run. Firmly grasping
the ground with my feet, I feel a sense of freedom. I feel I am alive and exist
there. The stranger the place, the better it feels. In a new city, there is no one
who knows my past or the trace of my old image that I want to break free
from. Here I construct my identity from scratch. I change my colours and
keep running. The only identity I take across borders and that people never
fail to see – I'm a runner.

***

故郷の山に背を向けて、地球の裏まで走って10年。
故郷の山々が輝いて見えたのはいつぶりか。

僕．私は変幻自在なカメレオン。
And I'm running.

Itani

Words always fail to fully capture the bodily experience, especially when it is
translated from one language to another. Personal history and the very culturally nuanced meanings of the words are lost in the process. The easiness of
speaking the English 'I' erases my complicated relationship with *boku*, the
masculine first person in Japanese, and the unspeakable emotional pain it
requires for me to even say 'I' in my language.

Conventional academic writing, scientific writing, rational writing, etc. are
meant to communicate a particular dimension of things to a particular group
of people. My in-betweenness – my gender, physique, languages, and my
relationship to the colonial history of North America and of Asia – and the
emotional toll it requires cannot be written in a neatly organized scientific

writing. Let's leave it to the doctors who want to diagnose my in-betweenness as a disorder. And I have no interest in talking to them about my 'symptoms' in their language.

Heather wrote his physical and emotional pain, but does the simple word 'pain' fully tell us what it means to him? I highly doubt that I can even understand 1 per cent of what he had gone through. Yet, one thing is certain – his pain, tears, anger, and his eventual border crossing paved a way for me to come to Toronto to be his student and to co-write this narrative, which has been a blessing experience. Heather taught me to write back against ever-colonizing English language and diagnosing science through his relationship with aboriginal people in Canada and through his pain. Our bilingual narrative with an unsettling format is a small resistance to the colonization and the diagnosis of our language, our body, and our pain.

What I hope is that someone somewhere in this world will find a connection to our fragmented words, to our pains, to our languages, and to our experiences. もしあなたが日本語を読めるなら、僕 私のナラティブの一語一語にまた英語とは違った繋がりを見出してもらえるかもしれない。そしてその繋がりが小さなレジスタンスの輪となって広がることを期待してやまない。

References

Clare, E. (2007) *The Marrow's Telling: Words in Motion*, Ypsilanti, MI: Homofactus Press.

Cole, P. (2006) *Raven and Cayote Go Canoeing: Coming Home to the Village*, Montreal, QU: McGill University Press.

Lather, P. (2007) *Getting Lost: Feminist Efforts Toward a Double(d) Science*, Albany, NY: SUNY.

Recommended reading

Caudwell, J. (ed.) (2006) *Sport, Sexualities and Queer/Theory*, Abingdon: Routledge.

Lather, P. (2007) *Getting Lost: Feminist Efforts Toward a Double(d) Science*, Albany, NY: SUNY.

Sykes, H. (2006) 'Transsexual and transgender policies in sport', *Women in Sport and Physical Activity Journal*, 15(1): 3–13.

——(2011) *Queer Bodies: Sexualities, Genders and Fatness in Physical Education*, New York: Peter Lang.

Looking and 'feeling' the part

Anne Flintoff and Sheila Scraton

'But Mum, please! It's really awful this term – we're doing gymnastics and I've got my period. I really, really hate athletics! It's stupid. We have to wear shorts! And it's with the boys! I can't do it! Pleasssssse – you've just got to say I'm not feeling well. It doesn't have to be long, but she'll make me do it if I don't have a note!'

Sonia covered her lower belly with both hands, pressing gently on the dull ache that had appeared overnight and was sure to worsen over the course of the day. Of all the days to 'come on'. Athletics – that was bad enough, without this as well! Minutes later, she was gratefully stuffing the note into her school bag and calling a hurried 'goodbye', as she ran to catch the bus. Her Mum hadn't liked PE, either. Well, what was the point? Who's going to do athletics or hockey when they leave school?, thought Sonia. Once she'd gone to aerobics down at the local leisure centre with her Mum. Now that'd been a right laugh. You could wear what you wanted, and it was 'all female'. You could make a fool of yourself and no one really minded, people were really nice. There were a lot of mirrors, though. Her Mum had started going with the hope of losing weight, but she hadn't been for weeks. She claimed she'd too much to do, what with her ironing and stuff, so Sonia hadn't gone since, either. The bus jerked to a halt and her thoughts were interrupted by Maria pushing up the gangway and plonking herself down on the neighbouring seat.

'Hiya, alright?' she asked Sonia.

'Yeah, suppose so. Feeling like shit, actually, 'cause I've just "come on", but at least I've got a note for PE.'

'Lucky you, I'll have to do it this week. I skived last week, so she's on my case. A nightmare!'

'And it's athletics 'n shorts as well!'

'Well, you're on the Council, aren't you? Aren't you doing stuff to change it?' responded Maria, glancing up from her iphone.

'Well, we are talking about the kit, yes. But you know Mrs Robinson, she says we have to listen to everyone, and not just suggest things that we want ourselves,' explained Sonia.

'And I bet Beccy and her lot think it's OK as it is? Miss bloody Fitness Freak! She loves it, prancing about in her skirt or her little tight shorts! Have you noticed?'

'Yeah,' Sonia sighed, 'I know. And Tina's OK with it, too, *obviously.*'

'Butch lessie! She's always going to like it, isn't she, what with her playing rugby an' all! Anyway, I can't see why we can't just have a choice. My cousin at Brownlea's can wear leggings or trackies, or whatever they want. Not hoodies, mind. Apart from that though, as long as it's black, no big logos, you know, they can wear what they like. I mean, does the uniform have *any* affect on my performance in PE? No! I don't see the point of it! It's so childish!'

Sonia shuddered, remembering last week's lesson. She did actually like some bits of PE. The swimming was good last term, for example. She was good at swimming. She'd gone to the local baths every Saturday with her brother when she'd been at primary school. As soon as she was in the water, she felt OK. She could swim quite well. But athletics! In front of the whole school. The windows all looked out onto the field, so it was like being in a goldfish bowl! You could just feel the boys staring at you, and imagine their comments. It just made her feel small somehow, not herself, and it was even worse when they did PE with the boys. That'd been one of the reasons she'd agreed to join the School Council – to try and change things. She'd been amazed how many people wanted to have their say on the kit for PE. It wasn't just her. Loads of girls had come up to her, sent her texts; particularly the year 10s. All wanting different things, all wanting their views heard! Year 7s and 8s didn't seem quite so bothered, though.

Following Maria off the bus, she felt a pull on her sweater from behind, followed by the sharp twang of her bra strap. She turned around and looked at the boy grinning in her face, his hands held up in front of her. 'What? What's the problem, Sonia? Don't like a bit of attention?' Before she could respond, Maria pulled her away.

'Just ignore him, Sonia, it's not worth it.'

Once off the bus and out of earshot, Sonia responded, 'But that's a good example. That's exactly what we have to put up with from the boys here. I'm sick of it, and that's what I want to change at this school! I just want us to be able to be ourselves, without the hassle all of the time.'

***

Jenny let her gaze come to rest on the untidy notice-board on the end wall of the cramped, over-hot, PE office and stopped herself from sighing out aloud. Out-of-date notices, the latest Head of Year missive, telephone numbers scribbled on bits of torn paper, and a lone black plastic whistle, hung by a frayed cord, jostled for position on its now faded, felt surface. A fly buzzed irritatingly around the room. Her colleagues looked at her and waited, silent. She noticed their folded arms across their chests and their posture, sitting back on their chairs, looking defensive. Danny tapped one foot, impatiently, grains of sand dropping from his shoe and collecting in a small pile on the floor. This wasn't going to be as easy as she'd thought and, for a moment, she hesitated. Did she have the energy, the determination? Getting everyone on board would take time, and a quick glance at the clock told her that, if she didn't hurry up, her time would be up, and her chance gone.

Taking a deep breath, she reiterated her point: 'so to summarize, this is not about change for change's sake – it's important for girls' participation in PE as a whole, for who takes part, for how they feel, whether they view PE as something they feel comfortable doing – want to do. Surely we all want every pupil to feel like that, don't we? We all know we struggle with some of the girls, and I just think we ought to consider the whole package – not just what we offer – we've made some good changes to the kinds of activities we're doing ... but now I am proposing we go one step further. Research in the UK shows that one of the key things that puts girls off PE is the kit they're asked to wear, and the whole changing room/showering thing.'

'Research!' Danny snorted, 'great – so now we're going to change everything because you're doing your masters and have read some article! Our kids all go out for PE looking the part, looking smart, all the same. We've worked hard over the years for that. But now we're gonna relax our standards and let kids do what they like? Just because a few girls don't like it, and some academic or other – who I bet's never been anywhere near a school in the last 20 years – says so! Bloody marvellous!' Danny tightened his arms still further, frustrated at the way in which Jenny was pushing them to agree the change, and her power to impose it, regardless of their views. Although he'd not admit it, he was still smarting over the fact that she'd been appointed to the head of department's post two years ago. At the time he couldn't be bothered to apply. He thought he didn't need the hassle, what with his coaching and everything. Now it seemed his decision had come back to haunt him.

Peter, in his second year of teaching and still finding his feet in the politics of the department, did as he often did, and aligned himself with his senior male colleague's position. He chipped in, 'Danny's right, we shouldn't be changing the whole kit policy just because of one or two kids. The boys don't complain. In fact, in my experience, most of the girls don't, either. We already allow the Muslim girls to wear leggings, if they want to. So they're sorted. And if we do make a change, it's no guarantee that the others are going to get into PE anyway, so why bother upsetting things when most kids are OK? We know the kids who don't want to do PE and, whatever we do, they're always going to be like that!'

Danny, who wasn't going to give way easily, added, 'And anyway, OFSTED[1] didn't say anything about it! They clearly don't think we're doing anything wrong by having a kit for PE. And the head's always saying that part of the reason we've moved up the league tables is because of our uniform policy and the way we enforce it. Our kids look smart, and parents like that!'

Jenny tried a different angle. 'It's not a question of us doing anything wrong as such. And I'm not suggesting that we shouldn't get kids to change for PE. But I do want us to consider how we can improve our practices, and that we avoid getting stuck in a rut. And our kit policy is one of those things I'd like us to consider. It's not just research that suggests kit is an issue, government policy guidelines do, too. Look at the handout. I think this statement here is really helpful. OK, it was written some time ago, but it's still useful.' Jenny pointed to a line on a page of the National Curriculum guidelines that she had printed off for everyone that morning. 'It says "considerations of safety, comfort and freedom of movement should override conventions associated with being female or male" and that's just it, I don't think our current kit does. We've all seen the way in which the girls don't like even walking down the corridor in their skirts or shorts if the boys are there, let alone when it's athletics or something on the field. And I think it's much more than making an exception for Muslim girls. *All* girls' bodies are maturing and changing, more so perhaps than the boys really. Regardless of their religion or culture – I think that's a red herring anyway – you can tell that a lot of girls are really embarrassed in front of the boys. You know as well as I do the kind of comments that are thrown about, particularly from some groups. It's a constant battle. We need to respect that all kids are different. Some are happy with their bodies, but others aren't, and that goes for some of the boys too, you know.'

Sarah interrupted, 'I can see what you're saying in some ways, Jenny, but I don't see how we can change the kit from skirts for games, even if we wanted to. If they want to play for a netball club outside school, or for the County, they'll have to wear them anyway. It's not just netball. I know they're allowed to wear shorts underneath for hockey but they still have to wear a skirt or they can't play. It's the Governing Bodies. You know as well as I do, Jenny – so we're going to disadvantage those girls playing County if we do this. And anyway, look at the women in high-level sport these days – they show off their bodies, and they're the role models for our kids! Look at the volleyballers, or the golfers! Even they're wearing really short shorts, and there are no complaints there, are there?'

Although she'd anticipated some resistance to her suggestions, nevertheless Jenny's heart sank at her colleague's lack of support. If she couldn't convince Sarah, she knew she'd struggle to convince the rest. It *was* difficult with the Governing Bodies, and Sarah did have a point there. But, on the other hand, this was PE, not sport, and the reading she'd done for her masters had really got her thinking. It helped her make sense of some of the things she'd been struggling with, and given her a different perspective. A gendered perspective. She could see how some of the things they did could be partly why some of the girls were switching off PE. Of course, she could hardly talk about a gendered perspective and 'discourses of heterosexual femininity' here, could she? Jenny acknowledged to herself. Pity they weren't all reading the same stuff as her! Even so, she was determined to get them to reflect a bit more. We're professionals after all and it mattered for the girls' sake – but also for the boys', she thought. It wasn't as if there wasn't an issue with the boys too, at least for some of them anyway. It's easy for us to sit here thinking everything is OK. We're sporty, we enjoy physical activity. We're OK about our body image. But that's the point, we're not like most of the kids we teach!, Jenny reflected, before continuing.

'I am not saying that we should just be changing the girls' kit either. I think we need to review the choices we offer to everyone. Not all of the boys are happy with wearing shorts and a T-shirt on a freezing cold day either. We could simply have a list of different clothing in school colours and give kids the choice about what they wear. That way, we acknowledge everyone's different. And everyone's comfortable because they get to choose what to wear. Surely that's worth thinking about?'

At that moment, the bell for the next lesson drowned out her voice, and before she could bring the meeting to any kind of conclusion, Peter stood up, pushing his chair backwards, legs screeching on the floor, and strode to the door. 'Sorry, we gotta go!'

***

Turned inwards towards the bench, Louise hunched her shoulders forwards, trying to cover her way-too-small breasts as she swopped her white school blouse for her PE shirt. An Asda supermarket special, which her Mum had got her at the weekend! Two for one. A good deal, she'd claimed; although Louisa couldn't help thinking she'd never use either of them if she could have her way! She hated PE. Pulling on her school sweatshirt quickly, she shivered as a stream of cold air filled the changing rooms from an open window. To get rid of the smell, Miss Cooper said. True, it did smell, but it would take more than fresh air to make this place bearable, she thought. Cold, dirty, crowded. Who in their right minds would choose to change in here, let alone have a shower afterwards? At least showers were optional now they were in Year 10! Glancing up, she saw Sonia, and remembered the School Council meeting later that day. She must talk to her about it at break.

'Right girls, are we all ready? Let's have some hush for the register, please.' Miss Cooper interrupted the noise and, once she'd gained order, quickly read through the names. 'OK, it's lovely and warm today, so there's no need for sweatshirts, girls. Out to the field please, quick as you can!' Thinking that here was a real live situation where she could practise her arguments for the Council meeting later in the day, Sonia responded politely, but firmly, 'But Miss, why can't we just choose whether we want sweatshirts or not? I think one or two of us are actually quite cold and would prefer to keep them on today.'

Research context

This ethnographic fiction draws on data collected as part of a qualitative study exploring young people's active lifestyles, and specifically the relationship between their out-of-school physical activity involvement and school PE. We were interested in how young people's experiences of school PE related to, if at all, their out-of-school physical activity engagement. The research took place in four case-study schools, all co-educational, comprehensive schools with multi-ethnic intakes, located in the inner city area of a large north-eastern city, and consisted of group and individual interviews with 60 young people in total. The young women's stories revealed rich insights into their active negotiations of gender and class relations in their quest to be physically active, in and out of school. Discomfort around their PE clothing and their experiences in mixed-sex lessons were significant parts of many of the young women's interviews.

Note

1   The Office for Standards in Education, Children's Services and Skills (OFSTED) is the government body in England responsible for standards in services that care for children and young people, including schools.

Recommended reading

Flintoff, A. and Scraton, S. (2001) 'Stepping into active leisure? Young women's perceptions of active lifestyles and their experiences of school physical education', *Sport Education and Society*, 6(1): 5–22.

——(2006) 'Girls and PE', in D. Kirk, D. Macdonald and M. O'Sullivan (eds) *The Handbook of Physical Education*, London: Sage, pp. 767–83.

Garrett, R. (2004) 'Negotiating a physical identity: Girls, bodies and physical education', *Sport, Education and Society*, 9(2): 223–37.

Hills, L. (2007) 'Friendship, physicality and physical education: An exploration of the social and embodied dynamics of girls' physical education experiences', *Sport Education and Society*, 12(3): 317–36.

Scraton, S. (1992) *Shaping up to Womanhood: Gender and Girls' Physical Education*, Buckingham: Open University Press.

Holly goes to school to become a PE teacher … and doesn't!

A three-act play

Antony Rossi

The characters

HOLLY: an elite kayaker, children's coach and student teacher at a university in Queensland, Australia. Holly is about to undertake her final professional placement (teaching practice or practicum).

TED: an ageing health and physical education (HPE)[1] teacher, senior soccer coach, coordinator of the senior programme (years 11 and 12).

SANDRA: a teacher of 12 years' experience, senior netball coach and regional district coach, Holly's supervising teacher.

JENNIFER: head of health and physical education, senior examinations officer, head of the district review panel.[2]

KIRSTY: a health and physical education teacher with two years' experience.

Act 1: The material space: crushing reality

SCENE 1: The action takes place in the staffroom allocated to the HPE Department of an all girls' riverside school in a town somewhere in Australia. The staffroom is in the part of the school known as the 'sports block'. There is a territorial demarcation of space that is very apparent, and clearly everyone has *their* place. It is Holly's first day in the school and it is the morning break. Some departmental members are sitting around in chairs drinking tea or coffee. Others are standing and attending to administrative tasks. Holly walks in; she doesn't really know anybody other than Jennifer with whom she met a few weeks ago. Jennifer is in the staffroom but is more often found in her office above the staffroom.

(*Ted leans over to Sandra in order to speak quietly.*) TED: Who's the blonde Sheila?

SANDRA: It's the new student, she's a rower or … um … no … what's it called … kayaker, that's it.

TED: Again? We had a student last term! How come we've got another one? How about those lazy bastards across the courtyard taking one? (*He gestures with his head, over to the Art Department, which can be seen through the window across a small courtyard.*)

SANDRA: Well Ted, I know it's a drag, but someone's got to take them. The Art Department actually took three last term and Science took five.

TED: Yeah, yeah, I know, but they just take up so much of your time. It's more of a nuisance really – you know, telling them where this is and where to find that. Can't they think for themselves? And what do we get out of it? Hardly a king's ransom and, by the time you've paid the tax, it's not worth the while.

SANDRA: Yeah, but you know Ted, that's not quite the point. I take your meaning though; they are soooo labour intensive. I'm not sure I have the time this term with all the sport we have on. By the way, don't use that term 'Sheila'! (*Ted groans and heads over to make another cup of instant coffee.*)

HOLLY: Hi everyone! (*There is muted response and Holly feels like the guest who stayed too long at a party.*)

KIRSTY: Hi, you must be Holly.

HOLLY: Yep, that's me.

KIRSTY: Awesome! You're taking some of the classes I took last year! They're pretty crappy, actually, but Jennifer said they had to be given to you. You know, earn your spurs as it were. They're year 9 this year, mostly recreation classes.

HOLLY: Yeah, I have it on my timetable. What's a recreation class, anyway? I didn't really 'get' that on my visit. Sandra didn't really say much about them, either. What are they like?

KIRSTY: No, I don't suppose she did. How can I put this? Well, you know, they're mostly kids who're not interested, or are no good at sport. The fat kids or the unco[3] kids (*a longish pause ensues as Kirsty realizes what she has just said*) ... but they're OK girls, you just won't really teach them much, that's all. Loads of them bring notes, so just let them play something easy and then they tend to be reasonably cooperative.

HOLLY: So what shall I plan for them, then? I left it 'til now so that ... (*Kirsty hastily interrupts.*)

KIRSTY: Oh, I shouldn't worry about that too much. I think Sandra just does whatever she's in the mood for. We stream the girls here so, for this lot ... umm ... well, mostly, try to get them to do some simple games. Something where there's not too much running about or some simple relays that require little in the way of thinking. Anyway, that'll give you more time to focus on your better classes where you can really get some good stuff done AND on your science classes where there's probably a bit more scope to be adventurous in your teaching.

HOLLY: But Kirsty, don't all the girls follow the State syllabus? I mean it ought not to be a matter of whether they're good or bad at sport! The syllabus is structured in a way that aims to make young people physically educated citizens, who're able to make good health choices. At least that's what we've learned at Uni and ... (*Kirsty hastily interrupts again but keeps her voice low.*)

KIRSTY: Yeah, look, don't worry too much about the syllabus thing here, it's not a big issue. If I were you, I'd keep your teaching pretty much along the old 'command style'. They 're not too big on inquiry-based learning type stuff here, either.

HOLLY: But …

KIRSTY: OK gotta go! Oh here comes Jennifer, anyway. Haven't you got a meeting with her next period? Let's catch up later. Good Luck!

HOLLY: OK, thanks.

JENNIFER: Hello, Holly! Great to have you with us! Let's go to my office upstairs, and we'll talk though the classes and duties we've assigned to you.

HOLLY: OK great.

SCENE 2: Jennifer's office; a conversation is taking place between Jennifer and Holly.

HOLLY: Kirsty was just telling me a little bit about the recreation classes. I was wondering if I could try some different stuff that might get them interested?

JENNIFER: Like what?

HOLLY: Well, I'm not sure. Off the top of my head maybe some dance or even some kayaking. I remember you showed me the kayaks when I came on my visit. I just thought doing something different might help the girls connect a bit to physical activity.

JENNIFER: Out of the question! We can't have these girls in the river; that would be insane! Anyway, only qualified personnel can use the boatshed. And as for dance, we don't do dance here because it's not part of the inter-collegiate sports competition.

HOLLY: Yeah I know, I went to one of the schools in the Association, but I thought it might be a way to get them active. As for the boatshed, I'm a level two coach with full certification in rescue and assistance, first aid and resuscitation. I did them when I was part of the elite programme. (*Holly is cut off before she can develop her case.*)

JENNIFER: Look Holly, I know you want to try new things and so on. But you need to understand, our programme has a particular focus. We ensure the better girls are competition ready. As for the rest, well we just try to ensure they get a bit of physical activity, are reasonably happy and are well behaved.

(*Holly thinks to herself, clearly 'busy, happy and good', it seems, is still alive and kicking.*)[4] HOLLY: OK, will do.

JENNIFER: Excellent.

Act 2: The imagined space: what it could be like

SCENE 1: It's four weeks later. At the morning break the usual people are gathered in the departmental staffroom plus a few teachers from other departments, mostly to talk about sports teams they coach. Over in the corner, Holly is excitedly talking to Kirsty about something she has been trying in the last two weeks with the recreation classes.

HOLLY: So, in the first session they have they do a sort of 'Sport Education' model. However, I got them to decide on the activity and asked how they might adjust it to suit everyone. I know we didn't get much physical activity done in the session but they came up with some great ideas and so this week we got started and it went pretty well.

KIRSTY: That's awesome, what did Sandra say about it?

HOLLY: Well, not too much actually. I think she was surprised that I had them sit there planning the programme instead of playing tunnel ball! In fact, on the way out of the gym she said something that I thought was really sarcastic.

KIRSTY: What do you mean?

HOLLY: She said something like 'Ooo that was physically active, I must say … not.' I mean she was smiling when she said it, as if to suggest she was just kidding, but I thought she came across as a real bitch.

KIRSTY: Yeah, Sandra's a bit 'old school'. She probably hangs around with Ted too much, but this school is a lot like that anyway. So what do you do in the second session?

HOLLY: OK, well I decided we should do some fitness activities.

KIRSTY: Whoa! How did that go down?

HOLLY: Well yeah, I was a bit anxious, but I tried a combination of circuit training to music and sort of aerobics, I guess you'd call it. So first, I had them try to figure out what the large muscle groups are. We then considered the ways we could exercise them, and then organized these activities into stations. So the girls had options at each station, both in terms of activity and level of intensity. We do that for about 20 minutes and then we do a 15-minute warm-down using some calisthenics, some walking and some modest stretching. I call this aerobics because it's a term they're familiar with. It's cool because either they bring in the music to play, or tell me what they want. I then download it and play it on my iPod through the system in the gym.

KIRSTY: And?

HOLLY: Well, we've only had one session after the initial planning process, but they seemed to think it was OK.

KIRSTY: I bet it was fantastic! (*They are interrupted, as Sandra calls across the room to summon Holly.*)

SANDRA: Holly, we need to have a chat about these recreation classes.

HOLLY: Yeah, I'm really pleased with how they're going and … (*Holly is quickly interrupted.*)

SANDRA: Well I've been talking to Ted here, and we're not sure you're on the right track with 'those' girls.

HOLLY: What girls?

TED: The recreation classes missy, you know what we're talking about. They are all over the place, either sitting down or some even lying down writing, then prancing about, refereeing their own games. You even have a score-keeper for goodness sake! What on earth ... ? (*Holly quickly interrupts, knowing she is sure to be chastised for it.*)

HOLLY: Well, that's the whole point, Ted! The idea is to get them involved at all levels, with different responsibilities, to develop an understanding of what they're doing, and why they are doing it. In the process they might get a bit sports literate and develop some useful health literacy skills along the way. I would have thought ...

TED: Sports what? What does all that ... ? (*Sandra hastily interrupts Ted.*)

SANDRA: Ted, it just means that they can understand various sporting move-ments – it doesn't mean they can do them, of course. Anyway, let me handle this.

HOLLY: Well that's not exactly it (*she pauses*), it's more about ... (*Holly is cut off again.*)

SANDRA: Look Holly, I see where you are going on this. But we are worried about their discipline, your class organization, and you hardly ever use a whistle.

HOLLY: That's because I don't have to ... (*Holly is lost for words.*)

TED: What Sandra is saying lass, is try and do as you were asked and it will all be fine.

SANDRA: We just think that it would be best if you stuck to what we sug-gested. In fact, Holly, I have to warn you that if you don't follow our advice, we may not have any option but to put you 'at risk'.

(*The school bell sounds to signal the end of the break, Holly gathers up her stuff quickly to walk through the door with Kirsty.*)

KIRSTY: You OK, Hol?

HOLLY: I hate this fucking place.

Act 3: The space of resistance: coaching beginners' kayaking and teaching science

SCENE 1: It is two weeks before the end of the professional placement (practi-cum). Holly is in the boatshed putting the lifejackets away, having run the lunchtime kayak club for the year 10 girls. Some of the girls are expertly putting the kayaks up on the racks; others are putting the paddles away. Kirsty suddenly enters the shed looking for Holly.

KIRSTY: Hiya Hol, we don't see too much of you these days. Nearly done, eh?

HOLLY: Yep, can't come too soon. I'll miss these girls, though. You know, since I started this kayak club, the girls have shown up religiously. I run a club now on every day except Monday and that's because we have our 'oh-so-wonderful staff briefing'. An excuse, if ever there was one, for Ted and Sandra to bitch and moan. If I didn't have to be at that, I wouldn't step foot in that crappy staffroom.

KIRSTY: Oh come on Hol, it's not that bad, is it?

HOLLY: Yeah Kirst, it is. Did you know they put me 'at risk'?

KIRSTY: Oh shit! Are you going to fail?

HOLLY: No, Jennifer told me yesterday that I was going to pass. She said, 'Sandra can see the potential in you, but you need lots of practice.' Like she's doing me some big favour.

KIRSTY: Well, at least you won't fail.

HOLLY: I know, but what's my rating going to be like? You know, as well as I do, that this will affect my employability and, do you know what, Kirst, I don't give a shit! I got more out of the so-called 'less able' girls down here in the boatshed than I ever could in that pathetic programme they wanted me to teach. Here, they wanted to listen, learn about safety. They asked me a million questions: 'Miss, how do I get stronger for this?', 'Miss, should I lose weight?', 'Miss, who will teach canoeing when you leave?', and so on. And you know, Kirst, they were the same kids from the recreation classes. They weren't the 'able' netball and hockey girls. Gee, those kids weren't even allowed to come down here in case they got hurt! Got hurt for goodness sake – what do they think I'm doing down here?

KIRSTY: Yeah, but Hol, we didn't even see you during the morning breaks.

HOLLY: Nah, luckily I drew a playground duty one day and then, the way the timetable worked out, I was either free before morning tea-time, or I was over in Science. So I hung out in the Science Department. Do you know the Head of Department over there, Doug? What a great bloke.

KIRSTY: Yeah, I know him. He's a really nice guy.

HOLLY: He was brilliant, Kirst. I asked if I could experiment with teaching methods. He said, 'My dear, you can do what you like providing it's safe and you don't lose control of the kids. You're here to learn not only about teaching but also about yourself. So see what works for you, and for the kids'!! I couldn't believe it! Like, I mean, what a difference!

KIRSTY: What will you do now?

HOLLY: No idea! I might look for science teaching jobs, or maybe I'll do a Master's degree in sports science and coaching. But I sure as hell know what I'm not going to do, and that's teach PE!

KIRSTY: That really sucks, Hol. Come on, lock up, we've got just enough time for a cuppa before afternoon school starts, and don't worry (*Kirsty's face creases into a wry smile*) we don't have to go to the staffroom. I've brought a thermos!

HOLLY: Awesome!

End.

Acknowledgement

The project on which the narrative is based was funded by the Australian Research Council (Discovery Project 2008–10).

Research context

The narrative draws upon data generated in a project which focused upon the PE departmental office as a site of learning. Motivated by stories from the practicum of deep-seated sexism and motor elitism, and what we perceived as other socially unjust practices, we were keen to ask, 'What is learned, by whom, and where?' in the context of a PE major practicum. Adopting a case-study approach, 18 student teachers participated during their 10-week practicum, and 8 of them were later followed up during their induction year in the profession. We drew upon the following concepts and ideas in the project: communities of practice, workplace learning and social theories of learning; identity formation and becoming a teacher; performing the role of student teacher; and spaces for professional learning. Holly is a composite character based upon four student teachers, who had shared similar experiences. Whilst the teaching staff portrayed in the play are also based upon fieldwork observations during the students' practicum, they are in addition based upon insights gleaned during the researcher's lifelong career in PE teaching and teacher education. Some of the events depicted here are, in part, fictional, but they are 'true to life' and fully informed by the data. The actual setting is 'real'.

Notes

1   Health is an equal component of both the curriculum and the job descriptions of teachers of this subject in Australia.
2   In Queensland, all senior work is assessed internally and then samples of senior work are submitted to a review panel (one for each senior school subject eligible) for external moderation.
3   'Unco' is an Australian slang term and is a shortened version of the word uncoordinated.
4   This is a reference to Judy Placek's well-known, and now oft-cited paper: Placek, J. H. (1983) 'Conceptions of success in teaching: Busy, happy and good', in T. Templin and J. K. Olson (eds) *Teaching in Physical Education*, Champaign, IL: Human Kinetics, pp. 46–56.

Recommended reading

Dowling, F. (2011) '"Are PE teacher identities fit for postmodern schools or are they clinging to modernist notions of professionalism?" A case study of Norwegian PE teacher students' emerging professional identities', *Sport, Education and Society*, 16(2): 201–22.

Rossi, T., Sirna, K. and Tinning, R. (2008) 'Becoming a health and physical education teacher: Student teacher "performances" in the HPE subject department office', *Teaching and Teacher Education*, 24(4): 1029–40.

Sirna, K., Tinning, R. and Rossi, T. (2010) 'Social processes of Health & Physical Education teachers' identity formation: Reproducing and changing culture', *British Journal of Sociology of Education*, 31(1): 71–84.

Tinning, R. (2006) 'Theoretical orientations in physical education teacher education', in D. Kirk, D. Macdonald and M. O'Sullivan (eds) *The Handbook of Physical Education*, London: Sage.

Wrench, A. and Garrett, R. (2011) 'Identity work: Stories told in learning to teach physical education', *Sport, Education and Society*, DOI: 10.1080/13573322.2011.607909.

Them, us, we, me

Negotiating being a Muslim girl in Australia

Kelly Knez and Doune Macdonald

Zeena

I barge through the PE locker-room door; the pile of Cosmo magazines I've been carting around all day slip out from under my arms, sending a startling echo through the empty space. I ignore the magazines, now at my feet, looking around the cold, deathly quiet, locker room. The locker room itself hasn't changed since I was here last; it's the fact that I'm the first one here that is different. I'm always late for lunchtime netball training, but our class finished early today. I collect up the magazines – my favourite glossies – before walking over to the bench to put my things down. The emptiness is short lived and in no time the room has transformed with the scent of hair spray and Impulse deodorant – lots of it.

I open my bag to take out my clothes for training. Oh, shit! Where have I put my singlet? I'm sure I put it in my bag after Mum searched it before school this morning. She has this stupid thing about monitoring what I wear for school sport. Well, really it is my step-dad and she is just doing what he says. I don't know why he's worried; it's not like there are hundreds of boys watching us at lunchtime netball training. I play for the interschool netball team. I just love netball. I love the way it makes me feel, you know, alive, I guess. Mum and Dad don't really know about me playing interschool sport; I faked my Mum's signature on the permission slip.

Tasneem

Ah, saved by the bell! The ringing sound echoing across the school signals the end of my Australian Politics class and the beginning of lunch. I sweep my books from the desk and pick up my bag in one rushed movement. I have interschool netball training during lunch and Miss Briggs gets really pissed if we're late. I head towards the school gym. My mind is moving as fast as my legs are – 'Math assignment due Wednesday, science test Friday, German presentation next week, touch football training Wednesday, game on Monday night, tennis on Wednesday after touch, pennants on Saturday'. I'm just too busy! I've been hoping that things sort themselves out, but I know I have to drop something, and deep down I know that sport has to go; it's taking up too much time, and I have to do well in my exams this year to prepare for my senior studies. My dream is to become a doctor, and maybe work for an aid agency in Pakistan or Africa. I'll still have school netball, I remind myself, as I catch up to some of my other teammates. I follow them into the locker room and feel the cool, damp air move over me; the familiar smells of musty air, shoes and girly deodorant are strangely comforting. I walk past the sinks and put my bag on the wooden bench next to Zeena's. I pause to admire Zeena's hands, which are covered in a beautifully complex pattern of henna. Zeena mentioned she had a wedding on the weekend. She's Indian and she lives and breathes everything Indian. Her bedroom walls are covered in Bollywood posters. I contrast the image

They're so worried about what the Indian community will think about them if I'm running around outside with a short netball skirt on. Like who cares anyway! They're fine with me doing PE and school sport, though. We have lots of Muslims at our school and the PE department designed another uniform for us to wear, which really sucks because it looks soooo gay. I just want to look like everyone else, nothing special.

'Oh my god, what am I going to wear for training – it's not here,' I mumble loudly enough for Tasneem to hear me. Tasneem is a Muslim too, she's really good at sport, and has parents who are way better than mine. Her parents don't care what she wears.

'Mum must have busted me again and taken my singlet out,' I reply, feeling rather defeated.

'Here, take this T-shirt, I was going to wear it to the mall after school, but I can just wear my uniform.'

'You're so lucky, my parents never let me do anything,' I reply as I take her T-shirt.

'Yeah, but that doesn't stop you – can you imagine what they would do to the school if they knew you were playing netball?'

'Who cares about the school! They would probably make me go to St Mary's Ladies College or something. Arrgh, school without boys – how boring!' I scream, covering my mouth at the horror of such a thought.

I quickly put the T-shirt on and am about to ask Tasneem about Saif, a guy at school who has the hots for her, when I'm interrupted by Miss Briggs, our netball coach.

of her room to mine, which is pretty plain in comparison, except for the giant Edward Cullen poster above my bed. Before Edward it was Harry Potter, hmm, I wonder if anyone will replace Edward? My dreaming of Edward is short lived.

'Oh my god, what I am I going to wear for training – it's not here,' Zeena mumbles, loud enough for me to hear.

'YOU don't have your clothes?' I ask. I'm surprised, well, shocked actually. Zeena's school bag is like a rotating wardrobe. She is always wearing something new. It's pretty handy because it means that I don't need to ask Mum and Dad for new clothes all the time as I just borrow hers. I look through my bag to see if I have anything I can lend her – ha, this is a first!

'Mum must have busted me again and taken my singlet out,' Zeena replies.

'Here, take this T-shirt, I was going to wear it to the mall after school, but I can just wear my uniform,' I offer. I can't believe how much Zeena gets away with. She worries that they'll send her to an all girls' if her parents found out about interschool sport. If her parents did ever find out though, I'm pretty sure she'd be lucky if they did only change her school. Her aunty and uncle sent her cousin to live with their grandmother in India … Zeena might find herself closer to India than she wishes if she keeps this up.

Miss 'Barbie Doll' Briggs shouts at us to get on to the court and I wander out, continuing my thinking … I don't know what my parents would do. Our family came from Turkey a long time ago. Mum and Dad still talk about their distant cousins who live there, but I've never met them. Maybe they'd just ground me? I catch the netball Miss Briggs throws to me as I pass through the gym doors and head towards the goal ring, bouncing the ball every three or four steps.

'Come on ladies, let's get going. We need to make the most of every training opportunity if we want to give Blackstone High a thrashing next week.' Miss Briggs is such a typical Aussie – so competitive when it comes to sport and she's so into showing her long legs – we call her 'Barbie Doll Briggs'. I wonder if she uses fake tan? I quickly zip up my bag and head across the breezeway to the gym. The squeaking sound of sport shoes rubbing against the polished floorboards echoes throughout the gym, interrupted by the thumping of the netballs on the floor and the occasional whistle. Everyone is moving, like a well-oiled machine, I jog over and take my place.

When I'm playing netball, my body feels as though it knows what to do, when to move, without even thinking about it. It feels so automatic, even when I'm breathing so hard my lungs feel like they're going to explode. I hope my body also knows how to burn off the calories from the sausage roll I ate for morning tea! Mum commented last night that my Indian clothes are getting tight. She told me to just diet if I want to lose weight, but I'm always dieting! I know she worries about finding me a good husband, always wanting to make sure I look pretty, if I'm not pretty-y-y-y, no one will want me-e-e-e. But I've had seven marriage proposals already; I don't know why she worries. Oh, there's Saif looking! I might just try a shot at goal.

I notice Saif, a guy from my class out the corner of my eye, trying to watch us through the glass window of the gym doors. Oh crap! He is with his friends. I told him not to watch. Sport is something I do for me, my health, my body, not for him and his mates to get their thrills. I don't like being watched, certainly not by them. Arrgh! Maybe it should be me that gets moved to the all girls' school. It would make things so much easier sometimes.

Research context

This narrative is based upon data collected from the *Life Activity Project*, which sought to explore the place and meaning of physical activity in the lives of young Australians. The project worked with cohorts of young men and women from a variety of geographical, socio-economic, cultural and ethnic backgrounds. In this arm of the project, 11 young Muslim women, who attended two different state high schools in an Australian capital city, were each interviewed seven times over a two-year period. Interviews were based upon different themes, for example, physical activity, health and fitness, mapping and the use of neighbourhood space, magazines and popular culture. This research was conducted at the University of Queensland, Australia.

Recommended reading

Benn, T., Pfister, G. and Jawad, H. (2011) *Muslim Women in Sport*, London: Routledge.

Dagkas, S., Benn, T. and Jawad, H. (2011) 'Multiple voices: Improving participation of Muslim girls in physical education and school sport', *Sport, Education and Society,* 16(2): 223–40.

Hargreaves, J. (2007) 'Sport, exercise and the female Muslim body: Negotiating Islam, politics and male power', in J. Hargreaves and P. Vertinsky (eds) *Physical Culture, Power and the Body*, London: Routledge, pp. 74–100.

Knez, K. (2010) 'Being Muslim and being female: Negotiating physical activity and a gendered body', in J. Wright and D. Macdonald (eds) *Young People, Physical Activity and the Everyday*, Oxon: Routledge, pp. 104–18.

Macdonald, D., Abbott, R, Knez, K. and Nelson, A. (2009) 'Taking exercise: Cultural diversity and physically active lifestyles', *Sport, Education and Society*, 14(1): 1–19.

It's not for the school to tell us, Charlie … after all, to us you are healthy big

Emma Rich

The gymnasium at Harkfield comprehensive middle school was sorely in need of a touch of paint, as was the remainder of the school. Nestled between the green fields and the back-to-back terraced housing so typical of this part of England, the drab school buildings, housing the village's 10–14-year-olds, were a constant reminder to the local inhabitants of Huddleton about the dismal state of public funding for education. Despite her physical work environment, Mrs Oliver, the PE teacher, is nevertheless feeling pleased with herself as she walks around the Year 7 class today, helping students to record fitness results, to weigh themselves and to measure 'fatness'. For years, she'd faced jibes in the staffroom from her colleagues who questioned the status of her subject. 'What is it you actually *do* in those lessons, Jackie, just kick a ball about?' Well, not any more, she thought to herself. PE's status in the school has risen in recent years, as Harkfield has marketed itself as a 'healthy school', in line with the National Healthy Schools Programme.[1] A smile transformed her face as she reflected upon the way in which she now gained kudos from her subject. How PE is enjoying the limelight! PE's the subject which really contributes to the 'Healthy Schools' agenda, complementing the initiative of the monitoring system in the canteen and the extra-curricular physical activity programmes.

A clique of loud, boisterous boys, racing each other out to the changing rooms, jolts Mrs Oliver back to the present. 'OK, OK, boys! I can see the time's getting on and we'll have to bring the lesson to a close. Get changed and then come back here to take a few notes,' she commands. Craig and Ben eagerly pull off their sweat-soaked T-shirts, making a show of tensing their abs as they pass Elise and Chloe. The girls are too busy to notice, staring intently at their fitness results, recorded on the now greasy and slightly crumpled lesson handout.

At the other end of the gym, Charlie and Mark amble towards the exit, oversized T-shirts covering their measured, poked at and exposed bodies. They stare enviously at Craig and Ben, 'the peacocks'. 'Oh god, my belly is spilling over. Just cover it up and get out. Just get out, Charlie! Just pass the girls and get into the changing rooms!' Mark tells himself, fixing his eyes firmly on the ground as he moves gingerly to the door. Next to him, Charlie feels the peering eyes of all the others around him, closing in and staring at his body. He tries to move quickly, wants to move quickly. Get to the safety of the changing rooms! But it's like someone's hit the slow-motion button. His feet produce slow, echoing ripples of sound, vibrating off the old wooden gym floor. Or so he believes. Lydia sniggers to her friend, 'Look at them, no wonder they get pushed around and no one wants to be friends with them!' Catching the sniggers, Mark hugs his body, trying to cover it, but surreptitiously grabbing the rolls of fat around his belly, thinking to himself, 'Feels like blubber. It's too soft. It's moving around again. Got a mind of it's own, my belly! Wish I could just push it back in!' Yet, the tighter he hugs, the more the soft, fleshy surplus seeps through his fingers.

A mix of pungent sweat and deodorant begins to heavy the air as the class return to the gym and get seated for the lesson round-up. After a few minutes of summarizing, Jackie tries to stress the importance of today's lesson in a couple of sentences:

> Well done today, class. Now, I need to remind you that if you want to maximize your lifespan – barring accidents or illnesses, of course, over which you have no control – then you need to eat healthily. The repercussions – if you don't – are cancer of the colon, to diverticulitis, and heart attacks. This is for a lifetime – and if you get it wrong for the rest of your life, then you've got nobody to blame but yourself! You need to have plenty of fitness, you need lots of exercise, lots of energy and a good basic diet. If you eat too much and you don't exercise, you'll get fat. If you eat a sensible diet and you exercise enough, that's good for you. That's the end of the message for today!

'End of the message!' Mark sniggers. 'It's all she bloody goes on about. Wait 'till next week – what will she say then?' glancing across at Charlie. 'Shut up Mark, I'm trying to listen,' says Marie, who is studiously taking notes on what to eat. She's surprised at how much she's actually listened and taken notes. She stares intently at her notes, etching, 'Will I die because I'm overweight?' in capital letters, and frantically scribbles patterns around the edges of the words. 'Don't worry Marie, just skip breakfast or have a banana for lunch like you normally do, hahahaha!' Mark responds.

'Boys! Quiet!' Mrs Oliver reprimands Mark and Charlie.

It's been a long day. Charlie strides past rows of once red-brick terrace houses, now darkened through years of grime and traffic fumes. He studies his body's reflection in the windows. He reaches further past the cracks in the pavement with each stride. Puffs out his chest, then his stomach. By the time he's powered his way to number 137, he loses it, can't sustain it any longer. His expanded stomach deflates, like a balloon losing air, his body shrinking back to its normal size. Frustrated, Charlie catches a glimpse of his thick mass of black hair in a window. 'Well, I'd rather be bald than thin! When people say bald, you've got no hair, but bold is when you're strong. I want to be bold!' With his ego deflating with each step, Charlie grabs his earphones, shutting out the world with his favourite radio show.

'Charlie! Charlie!' shouts a boy across the road, arms flailing. He runs over to Charlie and punches him on the arm. Charlie's zoned out.

'Shit, Tom. Sorry mate, I was listening to Moyles, didn't hear you,' pointing at his ear. Tom pats his stomach with both hands, 'That fat lard?!' They carry on down the street, laughing together.

'Actually I wanna be like Chris Moyles,' Charlie announces. 'Yeah, you know, grow up like that.'

Confused, Tom asks, 'Why? He's a fat lard.'

Charlie scoffs, 'Not too fat to climb Kilimanjaro! It's just the thought of being big. Big and powerful and all of that. I'm gonna be a lawyer, I'm gonna be a solicitor in criminal law, hopefully. That's why I wanna be big as well. I see people coming out of court in ... big, big people in suits ... and I think I wanna be like them. Because they stand out and they're powerful.'

Curious, Tom looks intently at Charlie's body and replies, 'How can you get like that, though?'

'Guess I'll have to eat stuff. You know, eat more than what I normally eat which is more than an adult's meal – so an adult's meal with seconds!' Charlie laughs. 'I might have to eat some more burgers and Big Macs to look like that.'

Tom laughs, 'Man you'll never get to be that size – nor as funny as him!'

'Well, I will some day. I mean, I've been around big people all my life. My Dad's big, my step-dad's bigger and my Aunty Caroline's big. No, my Aunty Caroline's *really* big because she's had three babies and not lost any weight. It's important I'm big too. Mate, I went kick-boxing Saturday. I weigh 6.1 now – I'm getting bigger.' Charlie pauses. 'I don't know if that's stones or kilograms!' They both laugh. 'But, you know – I don't feel I'm big enough yet. Thing is, I weighed more than most of them skinny kids in PE today.'

'Yeah ... skeletal Simon! Haha.'

'I'm not surprised there are so many skeletals. Everything the school is doing. Look at skinny Marie and her bananas!'

Tom quickly loses interest in talk of school and runs to the adjacent fields. 'Charlie, come on.' Charlie and Tom begin climbing trees, daring each other to climb higher and swing across bigger and bigger gaps between the branches.

'Charlie, look at this one!' Tom points towards the gap between two strong branches. Tom clambers up the tree, grabs a branch and kicks his legs out, but he can't get enough momentum to even get close to the other branch. His fingers slip and he falls into a pile of leaves. Both boys laugh.

'This is how it's done! You're too small Tom, you're not strong enough. Watch me!' Charlie grabs the branch, throwing his body into the swing, feeling his body glide through the air. Stretching out an arm, he reaches the target with an ecstatic 'yessss!' Swinging through the air laughing, he forgets the stares, the comments, his overflowing body of earlier in the day. He's strong. He's Charlie. He's successful!

The feeling doesn't last long.

'Charlie, is that you?' Charlie's Mum's sat on the sofa, still dressed in her work uniform. 'Where've you been?' Charlie slumps his rucksack in the corner of the living room.

'What's up, you look like right mardy?' she enquires.

'Nothing. They just went on a bit at school.' Charlie's Mum sits bolt upright, recognizing the familiar tale that's beginning to feel uncomfortable.

'About your weight again, was it? Look, it's none of their business. I keep telling you, your Dad's big, I'm big, your Auntie, your Gran … ' Charlie's Mum becomes more animated, pointing an accusatory finger at the 1980s wallpaper, then the television, then the cat. Charlie begins looking around the room for the missing culprit. 'I mean your Gran's, she's 86 Charlie, 86! It's not for the school to tell us what to feed you!'

'It's stupid Mum, the school. We can't even have pizza and chips occasionally. I like pizza. Most people like pizza and burgers. And chips. Everyone wants burgers, chips and pizza. You should have a right to choose what you like, not be told!' Charlie sits down in the armchair and undoes his school tie, throwing it on the floor.

'What did you have today, then?'

'The usual. You'll see it on my printout, you can't escape it!' Charlie tries to explain the monitoring system in operation at the canteen.

'It's like a bit of this and that, making sure you have your carbs and protein and all that other stuff, but we can't eat too much. Too many red foods and you're done for! It's like they're trying to build us, like lego bricks!'

Charlie's Mum replies, 'Did you have them tests today, then?'

'Yeah, they were like pinchers, those things. Grab your skin. Did fitness tests too. Boring. What's the point? Running up and down?! We got weighed as well. They don't get that I wanna be an ultimate fighting champion. If we did kick-boxing, they would see how good I am. I can do some serious moves. I'm not like that hospital man we saw on the telly the other day, you know, the really obese man who had to have the op to make his stomach shrink? I still keep my healthiness.'

'Well there you go then, Charlie. You're healthy big, aren't you?'

Research context

This ethnographic fiction draws on research exploring how 'new health imperatives' and their associated strategies are being adopted, adapted and recontextualized in schools, and their impact on young people's identities, health, well-being and rights. These include government-funded health policies and school-based initiatives designed to prescribe the 'lifestyle' choices young people should make, particularly in relation to physical activity and diet (for example, annual weight checks and fingerprint screening in school canteens). The study formed part of a wider, international collaborative research project with partner institutions in New Zealand and Australia and was grounded in case-study methodology. In the UK study, this involved in-depth interviews and questionnaire responses from 1,176 9–16-year-old young people across a diverse range of backgrounds; teacher interviews across eight 'Healthy Schools' (see note 1); and analysis of health and PE programmes, school policies, textbooks and websites.

Note

1   The National Healthy Schools Programme is a UK school-based scheme focused on awareness of health-related policies and practices. The programme seeks to increase the knowledge, skills and behaviour of pupils. For schools to achieve Healthy School status they must meet criteria in four themes (personal, social and health education; healthy eating; physical activity; and emotional health and well-being).

Recommended reading

Evans, J., Davies, B. and Wright, J. (eds) (2004) *Body Knowledge and Control: Studies in the Sociology of Physical Education and Health*, London: Routledge.

Evans, J., Rich, E., Allwood, R. and Davies, B. (2008) 'Body pedagogies, P/policy, health and gender', *British Educational Research Journal*, 34(3): 387–402.

International Journal of Qualitative Studies in Education (2010) Special Issue: Health Surveillance, The Body and Schooling, 23(7).

Pringle, R. and Pringle, D. (2011) 'Competing obesity discourses and critical challenges for health and physical educators', *Sport, Education and Society*, DOI: 10.1080/13573322.2011.607947.

Wright, J. (2008) 'Biopower, biopedagogies and the obesity epidemic', in J. Wright and V. Harwood (eds) *Biopolitics and the 'Obesity Epidemic': Governing Bodies*. London: Routledge, pp. 1–14.

Them special needs kids and their waiters

Hayley Fitzgerald

Josh Munroe's race to lunch and the special needs table

The bell goes and a sea of pupils surge towards the school canteen, a disorderly sight of impatience as they bustle and barge to secure a prime spot, the queue already snaking halfway down the hall. Michael slyly pulls on Josh's backpack, quickly bypassing him to join the back of the queue. As Josh stumbles, his bag and contents spill over the red tiles. On his knees he frantically grabs at football cards as they get kicked out of his grasp, a mix of scuffed shoes and dirty trainers unaware of the damage they cause to his collection. Annoyed, he yells, 'Hey, watch it, look where you're stepping, hey look out!' His voice dies in his throat as he watches a departing boot leave a clear and distinguishable mark on one of his prized possessions, 'Ryan Giggs'. Panic begins to bubble on top of the layers of frustration and irritation as he notices his dinner money has escaped, tantalizingly out of reach on the other side of the corridor. Desperately he tries to beat the next braying surge, but the stray coins roll and swirl on their edges, before finally disappearing. Frantically he scans their faces to see which one wears the smug smile, but the thief hides their actions well. 'Come on lads, own up, whose taken it, it's me lunch money.' Some giggle and some laugh out loud as the waves of bottle green blazers engulf him and soldier on. Still on all fours, Josh gathers the last of his belongings, stray footy sock, planner, house keys and, as he stands, he sees a group of sixth-formers laughing in the corner. Has to be one of them, he thinks, they've had words before. Boldly he begins to make his way towards them, shoulders back, chest out, ready for confrontation, but Mr Taylor promptly materializes as if from the cracks in the walls. They all scurry off, their mutterings travelling down the corridor, 'Bloody idiot, who does he think he is?' 'Rocky, Rocky, Rocky,' they chant, nearly falling over themselves with laughter, punching the air as they make their way to the playground. 'Move on quickly, Munroe,' Taylor's voice booms at him and eagle eyes send out their warning message. 'There will be no trouble on my watch.'

Resignedly Josh swiftly turns round and barges his way through the canteen doors, all of his senses suddenly assaulted. The smell of greasy burgers and salty chips, the cacophony of shouts, laughter, knives and forks clattering, the pushing and shoving, bumping and tripping, and the sight of constantly moving bodies rushing between tables, counters, cash registers and back out to the playground. The queue steadily grows behind him, beginning to ease some of the frustration he feels at being so far at the back. Being in the front half of the queue is paramount to achieving the food of your choice. Those at the back end up with the things no one really wants to eat, like an overflowing bowl of thick stew packed with carrots or, worse still, curry, all spicy and sloppy. The thought makes Josh crane his neck to see what's still left. Matthew Smith bags the last burger, grinning as he walks away with his prize. Still half a tray of lasagna, mounds of pies and a steaming pile of freshly cooked chips to be snapped up by the 20 or so people in front of him. Big, fat Billy Reynolds, sweat dripping off his face, red and flustered, seems to be getting agitated at the painfully slow progress of the queue. Theatrically he wafts his arm and gestures to those in front, 'Can we get a shifty on here? I'm starving. Don't anyone have the last chicken and mushroom or they'll be answering to me.' Further back in the queue a group of Year 7s snigger behind their hands at his outburst.

Josh's frustration levels begin to rise again, quickly, like a thermometer in the midday sun. If only he hadn't dropped his bag, he thinks. Huh, better idea, don't let the retards in before everyone else. Make them come in when the rest of us have eaten. The thought of them beating the queue irritates Josh further. 'Fuckin' retards. Really bugs me how they fuckin' queue hop. Can't even eat properly, dribbling and slobbering. Seriously, who wants to have to look at that when you're having your lunch?' he mutters to himself. Reaching boiling point, Josh has to vent, and tries to engage Andy Smart behind. 'You know, they don't have to fuckin' queue. It's just not fair. Who wants to watch that eat?' he whines, as the queue shuffles forward, inch by painful inch, getting closer to the table reserved for the special needs kids. As Josh's vent gathers momentum, his grumblings get louder; not seeming to care who hears, he unleashes another rant: 'Look at them, jammy bastards. No pushing and shoving for them to get their food and table. First choice of food every day, probably don't even have to pay. And there's more bloody staff than students. Have you seen the support workers, it's like they've got their own waiters at lunchtime and footy coach in PE! Huh, not like that helps, can't kick a fuckin' ball if it's lined up for them. Seriously, I don't know why they bother.'

Andy nods, tries to say something, but only gets as far as opening his mouth. There's no stopping Josh when he's on one of his rolls. 'I mean, if they need so much help they shouldn't be at our school, 'cause like this is a normal school, not one of them special schools.' He gestures with his index fingers when he says 'special school', which only serves to emphasize his contempt at the concept. 'They go round in their groups and just get in the bloody way. I swear, last week one of them rammed me on purpose. Wouldn't bloody move his wheelchair to the side, expected me to walk round him. He could've got out of my way. And like yesterday they were all stood waiting inside the main entrance, by the teachers' photographs, ready to go on one of their special trips, and no one could get in or out. Like, helloooo. Fuckin' move! None of their waiters to be seen then, was there? I think the waiters are as thick as the retards, probably do their homework and that's why they don't get good marks!'

As he nears the serving area Josh grabs a tray and scans the scarce remains. Spotting the head teacher talking to one of the dinner ladies, the mean one who gives you small portions of chips and big portions of peas, even when you haven't asked for them. He lowers his voice. 'If you think about it, they can't do lessons like us. They just can't. So, why make them try? It's a waste of our time and it's holding us back. Look at PE. All we seem to do is practise passing and shooting and everyone has to pretend the retards have scored by letting their goals in. It makes me sick! I'm gonna refuse to do it; I don't care if I get a bollocking from their bloody support workers. They aren't my teacher. And then you have to "include" them in the game.' His knife and fork stab the air as he tries to gesticulate his contempt again. 'Inclusion? That's a fuckin' joke! It's us that end up being excluded!'

The special needs kids talk about their waiters

They look up from their empty pudding bowls, chocolate sponge nearly a distant memory, as Josh's words intrude on their own conversations. Nathan, and the others on the special needs table, have heard most of Josh's vitriolic diatribe. Not wanting to cause a scene, Anthony whispers under his breath, 'Seriously, what is he on? He's got no idea, no idea at all.' Nathan's heart rate spikes with anger, intent on pulling Josh up on his remarks. Craftily, he bides his time, and just as Josh begins to head their way, tray loaded with chips that'll add more pimples to his spotty face, Nathan takes a fork full of leftovers from his plate, holding it up as if making a toast, 'Yum, yum, lovely lunch today, burger and chips, my favourite! Did everyone else get what they wanted? Hey Joshie, what about you?' Not waiting for an answer, he continues, 'Ah, sorry mate, looks like you got the scabby ends, again! Can't you get to the front of the queue? Too slow are you?' Unable to resist, Jonny joins in, his eating actions purposefully exaggerated as he gulps the last of his trifle, mouth slowly stretching and squeezing as it motions up and down, 'Mmm, mmm, mmmm. Delicious, just delicious! Hey guys, any leftovers let's donate to Josh. Just scrape them on this plate here.' 'He can fuck right off! He makes me sick. Ignorant shit!,' Nathan turns his back on Josh, dismissive, point made, conversation over, battle won. The brief encounter lasting just a few seconds … until the next time.

The scraping of cutlery against empty bowls is the only sound left at the table as Josh moves silently on, his face bright red. Time seems to stand still as everyone around the table looks miserably at the congealed remains on their plates, reflecting on what has just occurred, again. Helen plays with her mobile, wondering why such comments still upset her despite them being a daily occurrence. Her thoughts are broken as Jane stops chugging back Coke. 'I know Josh's a bit of a dick but, well, what do you think? Don't you think our support workers are a bit like waiters?' Anthony, ever the mediator, quickly scans the canteen and spots the three support workers chatting at the teachers' table across the hall. The coast is clear, let the gossiping begin. Somewhat defensively, Anthony replies, 'Well it ain't exactly easy with my crutches. I can't hold a lot of stuff. I'm OK with one bag, but the trays, forget it. I'd struggle without a waiter, ha, ha.' Jonny joins in. 'Well, if Clare's your personal waiter, what does that make Stuart? Your personal trainer?' 'Huh, well he ain't a very good one is he? I mean, the guy looks like he's about to have a heart attack,' says Nathan. They all stifle their laughter as Stuart walks past, tray crammed with pizza, chips and apple pie and custard. Tension eased, they all look up and smile politely as he gives them a wink and a beaming smile, bustling along in his shiny tracksuit that won't zip up, too small for his frame. Anthony offers a silent prayer, 'Please don't come and sit with us.' Stuart has a bit of a reputation for being a Clive Cling On, trying to be cool and hanging out with the students at break and lunchtimes, but Anthony's prayers get answered as Stuart plonks himself down heavily next to Miss Christopher. Feeling slightly guilty for his thoughts, Anthony continues, 'Yeah, but at least he tries, you know, at least he wants to be with me. Not like that one I had last year.' Jonny groans, 'Oh man, you mean that beast, Barry Morgan. He was one mean dude. I hated having him in PE. He was like, so bossy and horrible. Had no idea of what I was capable of and never bothered to ask, either. Just thought I was useless most of the time. He was like the complete opposite of Martin who I've got now. He knows when and how to help me, knows what I'm good at and what I'm rubbish at. He's like a mate really, looks out for you. You can chill and hang with him a bit in PE if you don't want to do it.' 'Yeah,' Anthony adds, 'Martin's great for that. Let's me go and play pool in the sixth-form common room during PE, if it's too cold outside. Stuart's OK, but he's a bit boring, and he is a bit of a laughing stock in footy, takes the focus off me though, I 'spose. I swear he can't hit a barn door five metres away with the ball. It's me who supports him half the time. Like when we're in the gym, it's me who has to show him how to pro-gramme the machines and how to work them. He gets in the way a bit, to be honest.'

The girls turn away, bored and disinterested, as the conversation turns to football and tonight's Champion's League clash between Man U and Barcelona. 'What's Clare like in PE?' Jane asks Helen, as she spins the empty Coke can on the table, watching as drops of the brown liquid spill onto the cream, scratched surface. 'Urm, well I don't know,' says Helen as she checks her mobile phone again, before dropping it back into her bag, 'it's not like she's helping me. She's just like watching out for me really. I don't need help.' 'Well, you must need it more than me,' Jane chips in, 'she never watches out for me in PE.' Helen bites her lip as she feels her anger start to build. She knows what Jane's game is. She's been down this rocky road before and she promised herself last time she wouldn't have her feelings trodden on again by Jane. 'Yeah, well, what it is like, the teachers don't think of you, erm, don't think you've got talents and think there's no need to help you. You know, you can't be helped, like there's no point. But like, for me and Sophie, the teachers see we'll get better and need their help, so that's why Clare works with us,' garbles Helen, trying to sound casual, trying to keep the anger out of her voice. 'Huh, well I wouldn't want her help anyhow,' Jane replies sulkily. 'I mean I wouldn't be able to hang out with me mates if she was on me back all the time.' Jane conveniently forgets that she never really gets to hang out with her mates in PE. More often than not, they're split up and put on different teams. And that means not being part of the game, not being passed to, 'cause all the really sporty girls just pass to each other. Not wanting to get into an argument, Helen looks away to see if Sophie's around, desperate to get some back-up support from her 'gifted and talented' friend. But Sophie's nowhere to be seen, probably at some lunchtime club somewhere. Huh, it's bad enough getting the snide glances and sarcastic comments from the rest of them, but Jane should know better, Helen thinks to herself, but opts to let it lie. She's said her piece, made her thoughts known. That should keep Jane quiet for a while. Before the awkward silence can stretch out any longer the bell shrills, signalling lunchtime is over. Grabbing her bag Helen stands quickly, before turning back to the group. She shouts to be heard over the scraping of chairs and the excited chatter of the exiting masses, 'See you later guys. Jonny, I'll see you at the normal spot, Jeff's our driver tonight.' Without waiting for a reply she turns sharply and joins the surge of green channelling itself through the glass doors. As she disappears into the crowd the 'waiters' reluctantly rise, trays in hand, ready to escort their pupils to the next lesson.

Research context

This narrative was developed with data generated from one mainstream secondary school located on the outskirts of a city in England. The school has special designation for special educational needs (SEN) and received a number of awards for 'good practice' in relation to inclusion. The study primarily sought to explore the nature of young disabled pupils' experiences of physical education and school sport. Data were generated through a series of focus-group discussions and interviews with disabled and non-disabled pupils, teachers and support staff. Whilst physical education was the focus of the study, wider school experiences were also observed in order to capture institutional embodied disciplines and discursive practices contributing to disabled pupils' identities. I deployed Pierre Bourdieu's thinking tools, including practice, field, habitus and capital, to help make sense of the social experiences of the disabled pupils in this study.

Recommended reading

Fitzgerald, H. (2006) 'Disability and physical education', in D. Kirk, D. Macdonald and M. O'Sullivan (eds) *The Handbook of Physical Education*, London: Sage Publications, pp. 752–66.

——(2011) '"Drawing" on disabled students' experiences of physical education and stakeholder responses', *Sport, Education and Society*, DOI: 10.1080/13573322.2011.609290.

Fitzgerald, H. and Kirk, D. (2009) 'Physical education as a normalising practice: Is there a space for disability sport?', in H. Fitzgerald (ed.) *Disability and Youth Sport*, London: Routledge, pp. 91–105.

Haycock, D. and Smith, A. (2011) 'To assist or not to assist? A study of teachers' views of the roles of learning support assistants in the provision of inclusive physical education in England', *International Journal of Inclusive Education*, 15(8): 835–49.

Slee, R. (2011) *The Irregular School. Exclusion, Schooling and Inclusive Education*, London: Routledge.

Making the grade

Fiona Dowling

Fatima's tale

Fatima's hand reached up under her armpit and then slowly traced down her taut, hour-glass body as far down as her hips. Had her younger brother been watching her closely, his intimate and affectionate knowledge of his sister would have enabled him to detect a hint of a smile light up what, to him, was her beautiful face. At this rushed breakfast time, his head was as usual practically in the cereal bowl and he remained therefore oblivious to the fact that she was sizing up her current body shape. Like most 11-year-old boys, Rashid paid little attention to the morning newspaper and preferred instead to muse over the cartoon or latest offer on the back of the Kellogg's packet. He remained thus in ignorant bliss about the latest findings of yet another national survey concerning the Norwegian population's body mass index. On reading the headline, Fatima's thoughts had immediately returned to last night's Facebook exchange, and she'd began to wonder how she'd look in Pia's new designer dress. She rather fancied herself in the sixties, Jackie Onassis-style shift dress and she concluded that the ivory linen with its graphite top stitching on her mocha-coloured skin would, quite simply, be stunning. Theodor couldn't fail to notice her in that outfit!

A swift glance at the wall clock jolted her back to reality, 'Rashid, we're going to be late again! Grab your rucksack, we have to leave for school immediately. No time for teeth this morning! And don't forget your packed lunch!' Fatima pointed impatiently at the small, greaseproof paper package with an apple on top of it, lying on the Formica kitchen counter beside the rice cooker. How she longed for the day when she could reasonably expect her youngest brother to assume responsibility for this daily chore.

Having deposited Rashid at the primary school gate, Fatima hurried on her way to the senior college. She'd have to take the short cut through the woods again. Why had someone decided to steal her old, battered bike? Couldn't they have taken someone else's? She made a mental note to readjust the alarm clock for the remainder of the semester because there'd be no chance of bumping into Theodor this morning, either. He certainly didn't walk through the woods at this hour of the day. The challenge of finding something appropriate to wear simultaneously paled into insignificance, as the sickening thought of failing to find a partner for the school dance once more reared its ugly head. And even were she to pluck up enough courage and invite Theodor, he might reject the offer. If he said 'yes', she'd nevertheless still have her Mother to contend with. A 'no-win situ', she thought. She hoped that she and Rashid hadn't awoken their Mother this morning. She needed to rest after being on the late shift at the supermarket. Why people needed to shop as late as midnight was beyond Fatima's comprehension but, as her Mother reminded her often enough, late-night opening hours put bread on her table. Alas, they don't put Jacki-O dresses on the table, she thought.

A rustling noise startled her, but her momentary increased alertness receded at the sight of a black Labrador retriever, stick in mouth and wagging tail. 'Morning!' boomed the owner, who was a 40-something businessman, as he ran past her so fast that he couldn't possibly have heard her soft greeting in reply. Pia's family have a dog and Fatima began to imagine what it must be like to have to take it out for daily walks. Perhaps it's almost as much as a tie as it is to have to help Rashid with his homework? Mind you, Pia's Mother was so keen on running that she more often than not seemed to exercise the dog, so Fatima couldn't muster much sympathy for her friend. She felt a bit guilty for having these thoughts, but somehow she couldn't seem to dam them up. She tried to rationalize Pia's position. After all, it's not as if it's Pia's fault that she has a Mother who runs a lot and exercises the dog. Nor is it her fault that her Dad earns so much money that a designer dress for the end-of-school dance is seen as normal. And Pia's extremely kind and fun. Why else would I spend so much time with her?, Fatima reflected.

But take today, she thought, today she'll have an inbuilt advantage compared to me in this silly PE test. She's bound to get 6 out of 6 for doing a handstand and executing a perfect cartwheel, but little old me, if I'm lucky, I'll get a 3. Fatima feared with good reason that Nasir's crash course at the weekend wasn't going to help her much in her PE lesson. She could feel adrenalin begin to rush around her blood vessels. The indignity of it all, and the sense of helplessness she felt at being forced into a no-win situation! It's not as if a person needs those kinds of skills! And we've barely spent a single lesson on gymnastics over the past two years! I suppose I could have practised a little more, but I'd be a laughing-stock had I done that in our public yard behind the flats. It's so unfair to think that she'll get a 6, when the most I can hope for is a 3. How can I compete with the likes of Pia when they've spent half their childhood being driven to Rhythmic Gymnastics competitions? A 3 today can drag my average mark down to 4, and that means my overall grade average will suffer. And who gets into medicine these days with less than a 5.2 average?

Fatima felt her breathing restricted as this realization swept through her body. All her hours of studying thrown away because she couldn't bear to have her head lower than her feet? Perhaps she should have let Nasir help her earlier? Panic was gaining the upper hand. She couldn't fail her Mother's dreams. Not after all the sacrifices she's made. She couldn't possibly let her Mother down. She's managed to keep us on an even keel after Father deserted us. Fatima so admired her Mother's dignity and strength. No one could deny that it's taken courage and determination to be a Pakistani divorcee. Rejected from the Pakistani community and still standing on the threshold of the Norwegian society. She would be eternally grateful that her Mother had chosen to leave the Pakistani community in Eastern Oslo. Sure they didn't own their flat, and many neighbours still stared at them in their western borough, but thank goodness she's not ended up like her cousin. Not allowed to go out, not allowed to play football, not allowed to play with Norwegian friends. What a wretched life her poor cousin must lead. And what's more, she's putting on weight.

Another pang of guilt engulfed Fatima. How could she have such damning thoughts about her dear cousin? She was faintly disgusted by her derogatory thoughts about her Pakistani family. She loved and respected her grand-parents, and her aunts and uncles living on the other side of town. She blushed at the idea that one of them could have read her thoughts. And soon she'd be travelling with them to Pakistan to spend her annual six-week summer holiday there! The hot, sticky, dusty, overfilled city of Islamabad awaited them.

On further reflection Fatima hoped that her years of football training, her passion for swimming and her daily cycling would nevertheless hold her in good stead today in the gym. Compared to her poor cousin Sara, she could be classified as an all-round athlete! She thanked her Mother once again for her understanding of what counts in this neck of the woods.

Fatima strode across the school yard just as the bell was ringing. The babble of chit-chat in the PE changing rooms was a little louder this morning, no doubt on account of the nerves most of the girls were experiencing. She swung her rucksack down onto the bench next to Pia and, smiling at her good friend, asked, 'Are you ready?'

'Sure, this is nothing to get uptight about, Fats,' Pia reassured her. 'Can you come up to the lake this evening? We were just discussing getting a group together 'coz of the heatwave. It'd be fun, and Theodor might be there!' Sliding on her training tights, Fatima glanced up at Pia and replied, 'Sure, that's nothing to get uptight about. My Mum's on late shift again but, for once, Nasir can look after Rashid.'

Being assessed in 3C

Convinced that the entire class could hear his heart beat, Thomas planted his sweaty palms on the wooden floor, and knew instantaneously that his worst fears were about to be realized. His willing, muscular upper body could do nothing to compensate the dizziness he felt as his head was tilted down. Rather than bringing the spikes of a cartwheel to mind, his uncontrollable movements conjured up images of a car tyre blow-out on a highway. 'Thank you, Thomas. That'll be all for today. Next please!'

'Excellent, Kaya! Well done! That's the best cartwheel I've seen today!' exclaimed Miss Olsen. She resembled a Cheshire cat as she turned to face the involuntary audience. 'Did you all observe her rhythm, balance, body alignment? A definite start and finish; no ugly toes out of line here, oh no! Perfectly executed! You *all* have a lot to learn from this performance.'

Kaya wished the floor would open up and swallow her. For God's sake, it was simply a cartwheel! You'd think it was some sort of great achievement, the way she's ranting on. At the back of the group she could see some of the boys exchanging retching signs, fingers stuck down their throats. Others were beginning to whisper impatiently. Class 3C had had their fill of cartwheels, and morning break awaited them. Fatima felt a pang of sympathy for the wretched girl, although if the truth be known she'd always thought Kaya aloof and rather cold. Miss Olsen clearly didn't share her sentiments, 'coz there was no doubting who her pet pupil was! Mortifying, concluded Fatima.

'Now that's enough small chatter, thank you! Time to put the mats away, and then showers, please! Everyone! As usual, I'll give you your grades for this test next week. I'll be in my office prior to, and immediately after, the lesson. OK? This is the last grade for your individual sport, but you all … .' Boys and girls started dragging mats to the storeroom before she had a chance to finish her sentence. They'd had enough for one day, and Merete Olsen didn't protest at their impatience as she, too, felt desperately in need of a sit down. Assessing 27 pupils was no easy way to spend a morning, not least as she was still struggling to put faces to names. She'd inherited them from Ole following his resignation. She hoped she'd made the right decision when she'd lined them up one by one. How else was she to ensure that the grade matched the name? It's always a challenge to get to know these large groups and especially difficult taking on a final-year group.

As her office door clicked behind her, and she made room for her clipboard on the untidy, battered desk, she was convinced she'd made the right decision. 'To hell with those who rant on about keeping everyone active!' she said aloud, whilst musing about how unfair and difficult it would have been to allow several performances at the same time. She pushed the switch button down on her jug kettle and rummaged again on the messy desktop to locate the Nescafé jar. She was definitely in need of a cuppa. Usually she found the sound of the kettle frustratingly noisy, but today it's rattling and rumblings were drowned out by a raucous exchange from what seemed to be the boys' changing rooms. Just as she was mulling over whether or not she could be bothered to execute some discipline, she was interrupted by a knock on the door. Before she could answer, it burst open and before her stood a clearly agitated young man.

'It's customary to wait for an answer, Johan,' Merete reprimanded. 'What's all the racket in the changing rooms about? Something to do with you, perhaps?'

'No, Miss. Or rather, sort of. I just started a discussion, that's all. About our grades, the tests today.'

'I see.'

'Well, I don't know if you do see, Miss.' Johan replied cheekily. Glancing at the torn-off scrap of paper in his hand, he continued: 'We want to know what exactly it is you've been looking for today? How are you going to judge us? How are we meant to know what's a top mark or not? What do we have to do for an average grade, and where do you draw the line for a fail?'

'I don't think that's the way to address a teacher, is it Johan? I thought you knew better than that.' Stunned by the confrontation, this was all she could muster herself to say.

'We're not all active gymnasts like Kaya and Pia, you know. They might know your secret code, but we lads are still in the dark, if you get where I'm coming from? Where's it written down that we have to do a cartwheel, anyway? When have you ever taught us all this la-di-da toe-pointing stuff, eh? Or how to do a cartwheel, for that matter! I can't remember the last time you spoke to me in a PE lesson! How am I meant to *know* whether I'm improving or not? Why can't I be assessed in swimming, 'coz that's an individual sport? But then that's not your thing, is it Miss, so we're all forced to do gymnastics!' Although recognizing that he'd stepped over the line, Johan somehow couldn't halt the urge he felt to carry on. 'We're not poofters, you know! None of us are! I'm here on behalf of the lads to find out where in the National Curriculum it states that we have to point our toes at a certain angle! Please, Miss, can you tell me where? How's all this meant to help us keep fit and healthy? It seems totally unfair to us. That's the bottom line! My Dad says it's 'coz you teachers are afraid there are too many lawyers at this school so that's why you've gotten hung up on all this measurement stuff. Is he right, Miss?'

Research context

This ethnographic fiction is based upon in-depth interviews with a sample of young Norwegian people (young men and women from a range of social and ethnic backgrounds) and their parents/guardians about their experiences of physical education classes and their attitudes and practices with regard to physical culture. In particular, the research has been concerned with focusing upon the young people's 'narratives of location' (Anthias 2005) in school PE and in physical activity more generally. Assessment, and experiences of being evaluated in PE, is a theme which featured strongly in many of the interviews, which is perhaps not surprising given that grades in PE are part of pupils' formal learning assessment. Six is the highest grade and 1 is the lowest.

Reference

Anthias, F. (2005) 'Social stratification and social inequality: Models of intersectionality and identity', in F. Divine, M. Savage, J. Scott and R. Crompton (eds) *Rethinking Class. Culture, Identities and Lifestyle*, London: Palgrave/Macmillan, pp. 24–45.

Recommended reading

Evans, J. (2004) 'Making a difference? Education and "ability" in physical education', *European Physical Education Review*, 10(1): 95–108.

Evans, J. and Davies, B. (2006) 'Social class and physical education', in D. Kirk, D. Macdonald and M. O'Sullivan (eds) *The Handbook of Physical Education*, London: Sage Publications, pp. 796–808.

——(2008) 'The poverty of theory: Class configurations in the discourse of physical education and health', *Physical Education and Sport Pedagogy*, 13(2): 199–213.

Hay, P. and Macdonald, D. (2010) 'Evidence for the social construction of ability in physical education', *Sport, Education and Society*, 15(1): 1–18.

Kirk, D. (2010) 'Four relational issues and the bigger picture', in D. Kirk, *Physical Education Futures*, London: Routledge, pp. 97–120.

Dances with wolves

Kitrina Douglas

Mrs Rythkin, the School Sport Coordinator, was first into the hall. She stood, momentarily enjoying the peace in the dark, quiet hall which contrasted with the chaos of the playground. That was until Tania crashed through the heavy doors, allowing them to slam.

Glenna turned. 'Ah, Tania,' she smiled, welcoming the first dance teacher. 'How's it going?' Tania dropped her large bag on the floor and then placed her CD player beside it. Her red cheeks and glistening forehead gave Glenna an inkling of how she was, as did the dark patches on her T-shirt underneath each armpit.

'Well,' she said, standing up and mopping her brow with her now free hand, 'I have to tell you, it was hell getting out here.' She reached down and pulled a small bottle of water from her bag while continuing to describe her journey. 'There's no bus straight here from where I live, and Linda couldn't pick me up this week.' Mile High was a small rural primary school which, from where Tania lived, meant two buses and 90 minutes of travel, and that was only to go ten miles, a journey that took less than 20 minutes in a car. 'Ah – the joy of crowded buses,' Glenna thought as she watched Tania tip her head back and down the full bottle of water. Tania reminded Glenna of a galleon in full sail and, apart from when she was dancing, she would never have guessed Tania's profession. As she watched, Tania pulled off an amazing feat which saw her damp T-shirt fly over her head. It was then used to dry her armpits before each was doused with body spray. In another equally impressive move, a bright, crisp, clean yellow T-shirt with *let's dance with change4life*[1] emblazoned on the front was produced. She dived into its middle and came up like a synchronized swimmer, full of grace and poise. She was now ready.

The entrance doors crashed again and this time it was Linda, the lead choreographer, disrupting the peace. In contrast to Tania, Glenna thought Linda was everything she imagined a dancer would be, from the way she sat in the chair at steering group meetings to how she sipped her tea.

'Hi Tania, hi Glenna,' Linda said, smiling, before glancing round the empty, dark hall, 'So where are all the children?'

'Well,' Glenna replied walking over and flicking the light switches, 'I thought we could just have a final chat about which children we select for the video filming on Saturday before we invite them in.'

'Oh?' Linda replied, releasing her bag onto the wooden floor. Her eyes seemed detached from proceedings as she ran her fingers through her long hair. After taking a moment to ensure her long locks were under control, her fingers then knotted themselves together and rested on her head, and a small furrow appeared in her brow. Without making eye contact with Glenna, her short statement was partly a question and partly an answer, 'I thought we'd already decided?' Her eyes met Glenna's. Glenna looked down at the floor where she focused on Linda's bag, while her index finger began tracing the shape of her lips. It seemed like the motion of the circle was giving her time. 'I just had,' she said, still staring at the bag, 'a, um, a few concerns about one or two of the children we selected and … .' She paused again. 'Um,' and looking back at Linda finished with, 'I wanted to be fair.'

Linda didn't speak, but took a small book from her briefcase and began to look through a list on a bright yellow piece of paper. As her eyes traced each line, her lips formed their names silently. Lucy, Zoe, Daisy, Rupert, Zac … down the list she went until each name had been mimed, and each child pictured in her head. She knew their bodies, their limitations, their potentials. These were the ones who had been eager to sign up; some of them would never make a sports team; some had chronic forgetfulness when it came to their PE kit, but miraculously never forgot their dance kit. Linda glanced at Glenna, and then toward Tania, her dance shadow who was, at that moment, connecting the CD player to the speaker system.

'Tania', she called. Tania looked over, 'Have you any concerns?'

'Like what?' she asked, walking over.

Without speaking, Linda raised her eyebrows, shrugged her shoulders and turned her palms to the sky. There was silence as the two dancers waited. Glenna had their undivided attention.

'Well,' Glenna began selecting politically correct words, 'I don't think Daisy and Kimberly should be in the video, I don't really think they are up to it.' Linda and Tania exchanged glances as Glenna continued, 'They're out of synch with the group, they just … .'

'OK', Linda cut in with enough force to stop Glenna mid sentence, 'Let's get them all in, run the rehearsal and we'll make a final decision afterwards, shall we?'

The momentary stalemate signalled show time as 20 children burst into the echoey hall, screaming, full of life, laughter and joy. 'OK, OK everybody,' Glenna shouted, clapping her hands twice. Moments later the music was on and the children were in full swing.

In the front row, one little girl put her right leg forward when all the others put their right legs back, and then she clapped her hands low then high, when all the others in the group went high then low. She always seemed a step behind the group. In the third row, another little girl continually got her left foot and hand muddled up, occasionally bumped into the dancer next to her, but she carried on. Both children seemed absorbed by the music, their faces and bodies immersed, although their eyes glanced left and right to amend their moves to fit in with the others. At the point in the routine where the children were asked to improvise, the girl at the front became a bunny and hopped round in circles while the girl in row three became a crab, her body becoming a wave with first her shoulders, then trunk, then hips, knees and finally her feet slithering sideways. Linda loved it, *all* the children looked fabulous and were trying 100 per cent. They had understood what she had asked them to do.

While Tania led the group, Linda stood quietly next to Glenna, eyes fixed on shapes, curves, bodies, the orchestration of movement patterns, expressions and energy being unleashed, held back, channelled.

'You know,' she whispered, not taking her eyes off the children, 'those girls look fabulous, this is exactly what we want, they are expressing themselves, they're being creative, they are fully engaged, we *must* have *that* in the video, we need to capture that, especially for this project.' While she sounded authoritative, her cool exterior belied her concern: two eager little girls were about to be axed because they weren't technically skilful enough. Working with different schools meant working with different philosophies. What the two girls lacked in style and skill they made up for in other ways and, more than anything, they demonstrated you don't have to be technically proficient at dance to join in. But Mile High were partners in the project and, therefore, it wasn't just her decision; the others had their say, too, and one of them was Glenna Rythkin, the School Sport Coordinator. They both continued watching.

'But, they're not good enough,' Glenna replied very matter-of-factly, 'I wouldn't pick them if they were that far behind the others for the swimming team, or athletics team. There are other children who are much better.'

Linda tilted her head toward Glenna and continued in a whisper, 'I understand your concerns, but this project is about getting everyone dancing, not just those who can dance or who are skilled or who take to dance easily.' She continued watching the group and noted Tania's enthusiastic input at the front. Then she turned once again to look at Glenna, 'and dance is about being creative, and this is about participation, not excellence.'

'That's all well and good,' Glenna said, facing Linda, 'and I support that, but this is a video for teaching purposes, and it's our school's name that will be on it, and it's our kids that will be judged, and our school that will be evaluated! I want our best kids there, not ones that can't dance!'

Research context

The story is based on an evaluation of 'Let's Dance with Change4Life', a series of mass participation dance events commissioned by the Department of Health. The research team observed practices at schools, colleges and dance centres, attended planning meetings, partner meetings and rehearsals, and additionally attended four mass participation dance events in the South West of England during May to October 2010. We took field notes, carried out group and individual interviews and recorded photographic and video data. The story 'Dances with wolves' is an attempt to communicate some of the hidden tensions in project delivery. Through writing, it becomes possible to investigate the scene in a more complex way. For example, this story sheds light on some of the contrasting and at times competing agendas of organizations. The story plot then provokes consideration about how different agendas might influence particular individuals, their choices and what this might mean for children participating.

Note

1 Change4Life is a project developed by the Department of Health to encourage families to eat more healthily and increase their physical activity levels.

Recommended reading

Ball, S. J. (2003) 'The teacher's soul and the terrors of performativity', *Journal of Education Policy*, 18(2): 215–28.

Kirk, D. (2005) 'Physical education, youth sport and lifelong participation: The importance of early learning experiences', *European Physical Education Review*, 11(3): 239–55.

Marsden, E. and Weston, C. (2007) 'Locating quality physical education in early years pedagogy', *Sport Education and Society*, 12(4): 383–98.

Tinning, R. (1997) 'Performance and participation discourses in human movement: Toward a socially critical physical education', in J-M. Fernández-Balboa (ed.) *Critical Postmodernism in Human Movement, Physical Education and Sport*, New York: University of New York Press, pp. 99–119.

'You hurt me Fizz-Ed': The socially classed discursive practices of the PE lesson

lisahunter

A play (Act I of two)[1]

Cast of characters

Group B

Year 7 school students: SAM, EMILY, TALENTEDBORED, UNCOOR-DINATED, FATNUGLY, CHATTERBOX.

Group A

Year 7 school students: RUNFAST, SWIMFAST, JUMPHIGH, TRYHARD, WELLBEHAVED, SCORE; Teacher: MR GAMESANSPORT.

CURTAIN RISE: *All are sitting along the front of the stage, Group B stage left and Group A stage right, while a narrator speaks.*

NARRATOR (*hidden*): 'Of course, there are more ways to do a text then (*sic*) to just read it to an audience. The text can be performed … . The author can even bring the audience into the performance … hand out a script, give audience members speaking parts, make a communal performance out of the scholarly text.' So says Norman Denzin back in '95 (1995: 207). So here we are, ready to act out this play. You want to be teachers, hey? I wonder what it feels like for the kids who might be in your classes, as it was in my class? As an exercise, take on one of these positions, as a student who likes PE and participates in it in ways that work with the teacher, as a student who is either marginalized or marginalizes themselves from PE, or as a teacher who subscribes to a particular version of PE. Take up the position, embody it for later discussion with your colleagues. Imagine, we are on a playing field at the back of the Hamilton Primary School in Brisbane, just after lunch break. It is the PE lesson that we, as students, have once a week with a specialist teacher who is not our classroom teacher. The specialist PE teacher instructs the class to get into groups of 'like-minded' students. This proves to be a challenging task, because how indeed do we define like-mindedness? Two main groups emerge: Groups B and A. Each group goes on to present its members.

Subsequently some subgroups also emerge, as the students struggle to identify themselves in relation to their values and attitudes towards the subject.

SAM, EMILY, TALENTEDBORED, UNCOORDINATED, FATNUGLY, AND CHATTERBOX (*in chorus*): We value PE for a chance to talk with friends, have fun, and get good grades without too much effort or having to think about, or take into account, others.

RUNFAST, SWIMFAST, JUMPHIGH, TRYHARD, WELLBEHAVED, SCORE and MR GAMESANSPORT (*in chorus*): We value PE for working on social skills, such as cooperation and tolerance.

(*Spotlight narrows to subgroup of A.*)

JUMPHIGH, WELLBEHAVED, SCORE and MR GAMESANSPORT (*in chorus*): We are further separated by some of us highly valuing *being* with friends, agreeableness towards the teacher, and not having to work *too* hard.

(*Spotlight shifts to next group who stand to speak then hold position.*)

RUNFAST, SWIMFAST, TRYHARD (*in chorus*): And we might be described as the more 'serious' students who are very motivated towards working hard through skill acquisition, aiming for good skill outcomes and therefore good grades.

(*Both groups move across stage to stage right.*)

NARRATOR: We can also understand each of these individuals through common social grouping lenses that influence their overall social class positioning, of 'race' ...

(*A mix run to form group stage left, while another two form groups stage right and centre stage.*)

(*Stage left group*) SAM, EMILY, UNCOORDINATED, FATNUGLY, CHATTERBOX, RUNFAST, JUMPHIGH, WELLBEHAVED, MR GAMESANSPORT: White angloceltic born in Australia.

(*Stage right group*) SWIMFAST, SCORE: Mixed heritage born in Australia.

(*Centre stage group*) TALENTEDBORED, TRYHARD: Mixed heritage born out of Australia.

NARRATOR: Economic resources such as parental income.

(*Reshuffle to form left, centre and right group.*)

(*Stage left*) MR GAMESANSPORT, SCORE, TALENTEDBORED, JUMPHIGH: Middle class with mum and dad in professional jobs.

(*Stage right*) CHATTERBOX, RUNFAST, WELLBEHAVED, SWIM-FAST, TRYHARD: One-income working, one parent either professional or well-paid service work.

(*Centre stage*)

SAM, UNCOORDINATED, EMILY, FATNUGLY: We don't have much money.

NARRATOR: Age.

(*Five different groups clump across stage. Group 1 = FATNUGLY, SCORE; 2 = SAM, EMILY, UNCOORDINATED, CHATTERBOX; 3 = SWIMFAST, TALENTEDBORED, TRYHARD; 4 = RUNFAST, JUMPHIGH, WELL-BEHAVED; 5 = MR GAMESANSPORT.*)

NARRATOR: Ability.

(*Cluster into three groups.*)

(*Stage left*) RUNFAST, JUMPHIGH, SWIMFAST, TALENTED-BORED, SCORE, MR GAMESANSPORT: I'm good at sport and represent the school and district in my sport. I'm also in a club for … (*each names their own sport for last word, e.g. RUNFAST says soccer, SCORE says basketball*).

(*Centre stage*) EMILY, WELLBEHAVED, TRYHARD, CHATTERBOX: I do OK at PE and do lots of physical activity such as blading, swimming, drama and riding my bike with friends.

(*Stage right*) SAM, UNCOORDINATED, FATNUGLY: I'm not in a club and I'm not so good at PE.

(*Whole class keeps moving around and clustering as groups on teacher's whistle.*)

NARRATOR: And the list goes on around size, appearance, behaviour, talent, effort and the like. These all act as ways of grouping people, as does sex. (*Reshuffle to form left and right group with FATNUGLY teetering between the two.*)

(*Stage left*) SAM, UNCOORDINATED, MR GAMESANSPORT, SCORE, TALENTEDBORED, JUMPHIGH: Boys.

(*Stage right*) EMILY, CHATTERBOX, RUNFAST, WELLBEHAVED, SWIMFAST, TRYHARD: Girls.

(*All return to original group A and B where they started as Narrator talks.*)

NARRATOR: These labels and categories can all act strongly to socially position individuals relative to each other and within what is valued in PE. So you can see how complex it can be. Even at the individual level there is complexity. To illustrate, listen to how a few of them describe themselves …

(*When they finish talking they move stage right and sit as though waiting for a teacher.*)

SAM (*Standing up with spotlight on him*): I'm Sam and I'm ugly. I ride to school every day and I know how to use a computer. I only live with my mum and my bird, Jerry, and the fish that I have, in a tank. I don't know my dad. I have heard from him once. He sounds like a Country and Western guy sort of, so deep. I'm not in the teacher's good books 'coz I like to muck around a bit. You can't take PE too seriously, you know. (*Walks to stage right to take up position, freeze as EMILY begins speaking.*)

EMILY (*Standing up and addressing audience, acting out physical activities as she mentions them*): I'm Emily. I do tap-dancing, karate, jazz, um cricket, netball and softball. I live with my mum and sister, and my dad … is … whatever they are (*pause*), I don't think they're married. They split when I was in grade 4. I'm concerned about getting really, really fat. The teacher never listens to what some of us have got to say, so we do lots of the same old stuff. I want choice. (*Moves to stage right near SAM, freezing while TALENTEDBORED stands.*)

TALENTEDBORED: Yeah, well I was born in Bangladesh; I came here when I was 4. My dad's an accountant and my mum, she works at home. She does this sewing thing at home so she can look after us. I like school 'coz you get to be with your friends and learn new things and … well, you learn to like get along with each other and all that. I don't like all the schoolwork, it gets really boring. I have fun in PE but, because it's so easy and I'm good at sport, I get bored easily, muck around and then get in trouble. (*Moves to stage right near SAM while UNCOORDINATED stands.*)

FATNUGLY: When I was two days old I had to get this operation – a disease of the bowel. I want a good education and not turn out like my dad. I don't want to yell at people like he does, he always yells at the stupidist things. I try hard sometimes and not other times. The things I don't under-stand I don't really try. You can probably guess why my name is Fatnugly. It turns me off PE a bit, but I still have a go. (*Moves to stage right near SAM while CHATTERBOX stands.*)

RUNFAST: I enjoy doing athletics, sport, playing video games, reading; my family, my sporting ability, probably being able to play video games and have free choice of stuff is important. I like numbers, but English is boring – no challenge. I play for the club, soccer.

SWIMFAST: I like getting fit, hanging with my friends, watching TV, eating, um … reading, just like, having fun (laughs). I go to the pools, go shopping, go to the movies and go blading and play hit and run, when you knock on people's houses, on their door, then run away. My parents smoke and I'm concerned they're gonna, well, pass away any minute. I hate the war in Bosnia, that's where my parents come from.

JUMPHIGH: I'm school captain, I play soccer, cricket and I like riding my bike and walking the dog. My schoolwork and family are important because if I get a better education I could live a better life. With the wars I reckon that the government should crack down more on what happens and they should make the police more tougher with the crimes.

WELLBEHAVED: I'm school vice-captain and I play netball and softball and I play the violin. I have a Mum, of course, and she's at college doing accounting. My dad died when I was 7. I'm concerned about things like get-ting a job. I like the teachers, being with my friends and learning new things. I finish all the work before other people.

(*Moves to stage right; along with CHATTERBOX leaves stage right.*)

(*Spotlight on MR GAMESANSPORT at the front of the stage.*)

ALL STUDENTS IN UNISON: Mr Gamesansport is 30-something – a tall old teacher who looks pretty fit and sporty. He is our Year 7 PE teacher, who has been in the school as the only PE teacher since we came to PRIMARY SCHOOL.

(*MR GAMESANSPORT moves to position in front of the students, stage right, silently talking to the students whose eyes are on him, with the exception of SAM who is fidgeting. TALENTEDBORED looks bored, occasionally looking at the teacher. TALENTEDBORED is talking to WELLBEHAVED who has finger to lips trying to tell TALENTEDBORED to be quiet. EMILY is glaring at the teacher with hands on hips.*)

NARRATOR: While the scene unfolds, watch to see how these groupings, or social classes, play out. How do individuals position others or themselves, particularly in relation to their values towards PE? At the beginning of our PE lesson we are reminded by the teacher MR GAMESANSPORT of the skills we did in last week's lesson before being set into teams to do a warm-up relay run. The teacher is selecting the teams and instructs us to line up behind the white soccer field line. SAM is first in his team's line with TALENTED-BORED, UNCO and FATNUGLY behind him. (*Each of these moves into line as name is called by Narrator and teacher points.*)

EMILY is second in her line with RUNFAST in front of her and SWIMFAST and WELLBEHAVED behind. (*Each moves to place.*)

The next team over has SCORE, TRYHARD and JUMPHIGH in the team. (*Each moves to place.*)

MR GAMESANSPORT: OK boys and girls, line up behind the sideline. You run one at a time around the goal post and back to tag the next one in the team. OK boys and girls …

ALL STUDENTS: Why does he always say 'boys and girls' when he talks to us? And it's in that order, too. What work is the teacher doing on us here?

MR GAMESANSPORT: … you do this three times each and when you've finished the team sits down. Ready, set … (*raising hand but stops and turns to Sam*). Where's your hat, Sam? You know you have to wear a hat when you do PE so that you don't get sunburnt. It's school policy. That's another detention for you!

SAM (*dropping head looking to audience*): What's new … (*and mumbling*) I forgot, sir.

MR GAMESANSPORT: Look at me when you're speaking. Speak up.

SAM (*lifting head but not looking at teacher, speaking very loudly*): I *forgot, sir.*

MR GAMESANSPORT: You're always forgetting (*said with anger then returning to the whole class and raising hand again*). Seeeeeeeeet. 'Tweet.' (*He blows the whistle and SAM, RUNFAST and SCORE run stage left while those on stage start cheering for their teammate.*)

EMILY (*talks loudly in the direction of MR GAMESANSPORT who ignores her, instead watching the running students*): How come we have to do soccer again today? We always do soccer. Why don't we do netball for once? You go in front of me, you're faster than me (*pulling SWIMFAST ahead of her and stepping away from the white line*).

Ha, look at Sam winning the medal for funny runny – he could be in the Ministry of Silly Walks! (*EMILY calls this out talking to no one in particular, doing a straight leg walk in time with 'Ministry of Silly Walks'.*) Have you ever seen that on the Simpsons? (*She turns to WELLBEHAVED asking the question and swapping positions with him. At the same time TALENTEDBORED, UNCO and FATNUGLY point to stage left laughing at SAM's funny run.*) Go Sam, go … oh that's right, I'm going for RUNFAST (*behind her hand and in the direction of the audience, then sarcastically clapping in time with calling out*).

Goody, goody, aren't we good! We are winning like we should!

(*TALENTEDBORED, UNCO and FATNUGLY laugh at EMILY's statement.*)

UNCO (*yelling at the top of his voice*): Come on Sam, you goose (*laughing again and flapping his arms*).

(*RUNFAST and SCORE re-enter stage left puffing heavily and close to each other, running across the stage to tag the next person, SWIMFAST and TRYHARD, in their lines, shouting as they tag.*)

RUNFAST and SCORE: Go, go, go. (*They go to back of their line while SWIMFAST and TRYHARD take off stage left.*)

EMILY (*directed towards teacher*): Wouldn't we be better to be doing this with soccer balls if we're going to do soccer? Better still, let's do it with netballs. (*Turning to WELLBEHAVED and TALENTEDBORED she explains and demonstrates.*) Hey, Wellbehaved and Talentedbored. There's this good drill where you catch the ball and land then pass the ball before you do stepping. So you pass it between you and a partner. We do it all the time at netball. Wanna do it?

(*WELLBEHAVED shakes head and gets ready at the front of the line calling out to team runner SWIMFAST.*) WELLBEHAVED: Go Swimfast, you're doing really well.

(*EMILY shrugs shoulders and looks in direction of runners calling out in a mocking tone, clapping at the same time.*)

EMILY (*In a mocking tone, jumping up and down and punching fists to air in time with chant*): Go Swimfast, go; go swim fast, go!

TALENTEDBORED: Come on, I'll do it with you. (*They both pretend to do the drill across the stage front but behind MR GAMESANSPORT's back.*)

(*All start cheering for their runners as EMILY and TALENTEDBORED return to their lines laughing.*)

TALENTEDBORED (*laughing but calling to SAM*): Hurry up, you idiot! (*SAM runs on stage left and tags with TALENTEDBORED who runs across stage, stage left and off. SAM falls down and rolls around at the back of his line.*)

(*FATNUGLY kicks at SAM laughing, while others in team cheer for their runner.*)

EMILY (*pulling at RUNFAST then pushing him ahead of her in their line*): You're faster than me, so you go ahead of me.

RUNFAST: Yeah, there's no hope winning with you on our team. (*EMILY glares at him in anger and turns to the audience while everyone on stage freezes.*)

EMILY: They reckon I'm fat. We did some dumb tests the other day called *be your eye*, no (pause, thinking) BMI. The teacher put us on some scales and weighed us (*demonstrates*). Then we had to measure our height against the post (*demonstrates*). Then we did some maths (*scribbles on hand and makes a thinking gesture*). And bingo (*explodes upwards*):

I'm too fat. (*Said slowly and deliberately.*) Bastards! Everyone was going (*in silly voice*) 'what did you get, what did you get?' Runfast saw my numbers and the cross where I fit in the chart and called out –

RUNFAST: We've got a wiiiiiiiiiiiiiiiiiiiinner! We've got a fat one!

EMILY: I hate him, I hate the teacher and I think I might start hating PE. It's so dumb.

(*All return to moving scene. TALENTEDBORED and TRYHARD run back onto stage left with SWIMFAST just behind, each tagging the next person in the line and moving to the back of their lines. CHATTERBOX wanders in stage left and stands next to TALENTEDBORED and begins talking.*)

MR GAMESANSPORT: Get up, Sam. You need to get ready again. Where have you been, Chatterbox? Never mind, join a line. Come on everyone, cheer them along. How's your dad, Runfast? I saw him on the weekend at the athletics meet. He ran a good time. Behave yourself, Emily. (*He turns to look in the direction of the runners, calling.*) Keep it going, you're doing well.

RUNFAST: Good thanks sir, he is training for the state trials next week and Saturday's run was his PB.

EMILY: Hey, this isn't fair! Score's team only has three in it. They'll finish before the rest of us.

MR GAMESANSPORT: It's not really a race, it's just a warm-up and your turn's coming. How did your basketball game go at the weekend, Score? (*He turns to Score and has a quiet chat.*)

EMILY (*in a deep loud voice mocking the teacher's voice*): And how did your netball go, Emily? (*Addressing audience.*) He never asks me! (*Turning to face teacher.*) Well, we won the district finals this week, sir and I got a coaching award for the under 8s I help with.

(*In teacher voice.*) Oh did you Emily, well good on you (*glares at teacher and shuffles to the end of her line again*).

(*SAM picks at the grass and talks to UNCO.*) SAM: Hey Unco, you doing any sport?

UNCO: Nuh, mum and dad's gotta work. You?

SAM: Nuh, mum says it's too expensive and I've got lots of jobs to help her with. She reckons vacuuming is a good way to get exercise. When my step-dad comes over we play Playstation. I like that. I got this great game off him last week called 3D Fighting School.

UNCO: Oh that's cool, I've got that one on my iphone. We could play it at lunch tomorrow. Actually I'd rather play with Talentedbored, so you're not invited.

SAM: Yeah? (*excited then sad*) Nah, I've got detention anyway 'coz I didn't do my homework last night (*pause*) again. I keep forgetting and I had to cook tea 'coz mum wasn't home until late. Got to watch this cool movie though, Kill Bill 2.

(*Runners return to stage, tag next in line who begin to run off.*)

MR GAMESANSPORT: That'll do, everyone. You should all be pretty warm by now. Today we're going to play soccer. (*Chorus of cheers by all except Emily and Talentedbored.*)

EMILY (*front and centre stage*): Booooo, if anyone is asking.

TALENTEDBORED (*walking to front of stage addressing audience*): And it won't be *proper* soccer like we do at our club on weekend competition.

MR GAMESANSPORT (*turning to stare at Emily*): But only if you *behave*.

SAM, UNCO, FATNUGLY, CHATTERBOX (*running to front of stage to spread out and kneel*): Well that leaves us out because we don't behaaaaaave and are no good.

MR GAMESANSPORT: But first some drills.

TALENTEDBORED (*throwing arms in air, walks, rolling eyes as addresses audience*): And that leaves me out too. Booooring ...

EMILY (*walking to front stage but away from TALENTEDBORED. Hands on hips*): Soccer, soccer, soccer. That's a boys' sport. Why don't we ever get to do a girls' sport like netball?

MR GAMESANSPORT (*turning his back on Group B and addressing Group A*): Now get into your teams for a dribble relay like we did yesterday.

MR GAMESANSPORT, RUNFAST, SWIMFAST, SCORE, WELL-BEHAVED, JUMPHIGH, TRYHARD (*clustering closer together as Group A, to face the audience*): We like PE that is certain, structured, competitive, and where we can show how good we are. In PE we value working on social skills, such as cooperation and tolerance, being with friends, showing agree-ableness towards the teacher, and not having to work too hard, but we are motivated towards 'working hard' through 'skill acquisition' for 'good skill' outcomes and 'good grades' (*use two fingers each hand to indicate when saying words in quotation marks*).

EMILY, SAM, TALENTEDBORED, UNCO, FATNUGLY, CHATTER-BOX: We value different things differently in PE. Different things ... differently.

NARRATOR: And they don't cluster together around what they dislike about PE so are not united to challenge Group A who are united by what they like. They don't collectively challenge Group A. Group A works with the teacher as a social class to differentiate from Group B. But Group B does not unite in their marginalization or alienation. Each individually challenges Group A, and at times works *with* those in Group A, but are not strongly positioned to shift what is valued by Group A, as they are not united. Alone, Emily is not able to convince enough students to challenge the teacher to allow them some choice of activity in PE.

EMILY (*standing up and crossing arms*): But I value fun.

SAM (*standing up but looking downhearted*): Me too, but I don't like girls (*taking a step away from Emily*). And no one likes me.

TALENTEDBORED: I like to get good grades without too much effort.

UNCOORDINATED: I like having the chance to talk with friends.

FATNUGLY: I do OK when we do swimming as I'm the second fastest behind Swimfast, so sometimes I really like PE and the teacher likes me. But during athletics, cross-country and soccer they all tease me 'coz I'm fat and I don't know how to stop them … .

CHATTERBOX: I like having the chance to talk with friends without getting into trouble, but the trouble is I often get in trouble, as does the person I'm talking to. But I'm good friends with almost everyone.

RUNFAST, SWIMFAST, JUMPHIGH, TRYHARD, WELLBEHAVED, SCORE, MR GAMESANSPORT (*pointing to Group B*): You make us laugh and you annoy us, why can't you just fit in?

SAM (*stepping forward*): I can't wait to go to high school! I'm a bit scared about getting my head flushed down the toilet from the older kids but I can start all over again. I can get on the good side of the teacher. I'll try really hard.

EMILY: I can't wait to get to high school with so many more sports to do *including* netball and so many more friends to make, and hopefully not have a loser teacher.

CHORUS ALL: Who's in? (*All, including Group A, point to Group A with teacher in middle.*) Who's out? (*All point to anyone in Group B.*) What's PE about? (*Gesture questioning.*)

(*Continue gestures with chant that decreases to whisper as lights dim.*) Who's in, who's out, what's PE about? Who's in, who's out, what's PE about? Who's in, who's out, what's PE about? Who's in, who's out, what's PE about?

(*Lights fade … to black for last question by Narrator.*)

NARRATOR: How did the teacher meet the needs of the students? Which students? Why? How did which students meet the needs of the teacher? What discourses were operating to value certain people or certain ways of being? How might our classes' pedagogy change for a more engaged learning experience for all? What will you do when you are our teacher?

To be continued … .

Acknowledgements

Many thanks to the students and teachers who consented to the research that sits behind this performance, and to Doune Macdonald and Richard Tinning who advised the study.

Research context

This narrative originates in an 18-month ethnography of one class of (28) students in their final primary year, their classroom teacher and HPE teacher, and the students during their first year of secondary school. Field texts were constructed through student and teacher interviews, researcher class observations, photography and videography of lessons, student questionnaires and diaries. Questions orienting the study included, *What are the practices and processes experienced by young people, through physical education, during their middle years of schooling?* and *What is the nature of the field of physical education and how does this impact on young people and their experiences of it?* Theoretical perspectives included critical theory, feminism, border pedagogy and cultural studies with an emphasis on Pierre Bourdieu's conceptual tools of field, capital, habitus and practice. Methodology also included critical discourse analysis and grounded theory.

Note

1   lisahunter (2010) "'You hurt me Fizz-Ed" (Act II of two): Students' stories of exclusion and other forms of violence when playing Physical Education', paper presented at Australian Association for Research in Education, Melbourne, November.

Recommended reading

Hunter, L. (2004) 'Bourdieu and the social space of the PE class: Reproduction of doxa through practice', *Sport, Education and Society*, 9(2): 175–92.

lisahunter (2006) 'Pleasure or pain? Students' perspectives on physical education', in R. Tinning, L. McCuaig and lisahunter (eds) *Teaching Physical Education*, French's Forest, New South Wales: Pearson Education Australia, pp. 127–33.

——(2009) 'Should kids be seen and not heard?: Where are the students in HPE curriculum?', in M. T. Dinan-Thompson (ed.) *Health and Physical Education and Curriculum Study: Contemporary Issues in Australia and New Zealand*, Oxford: Oxford University Press, pp. 80–105.

lisahunter and Macdonald, D. (2010) 'Physicality and learning', in D. Pendergast and N. Bahr (eds) *Middle Years Reform: Rethinking Curriculum, Pedagogy and Assessment for the Middle Years*, East Melbourne: Allen and Unwin, pp. 175–87.

Mitra, D. (2004) 'The significance of students: Can increasing "student voice" in schools lead to gains in youth development?', *Teachers College Record*, 106(4): 651–88.

Part III
Engaging with narratives

3 Professional development and narrative inquiry

Fiona Dowling

In Parts I and II of the book we have explored theoretical perspectives of difference and narrative ways of knowing, and provided 15 stories about difference and (in)equality in a wide range of physical activity contexts. Here we aim to illuminate ways in which you might engage with the narratives by linking them to your personal experiences and to different theoretical lenses. We believe that by working with narratives in this way it is possible to examine our all-too-often taken-for-granted values and understandings of the social worlds we inhabit, and stimulate professional, critical reflection about educational practice.

Difference, (in)equality and critical reflection

First of all, let us refresh why we believe it is important to spend time on reflecting about difference in physical education (PE), youth sport and health. Why should professional educators grapple with social theory, you might ask? Our position is one which recognizes that education is a political act. Despite the fact that many public education systems are framed within rhetoric of *education for all*, we know that persistent social inequalities can prevent *all* young people from realizing educational achievement. Considerable numbers of young women and men are not afforded opportunities to become physically educated because social categories like class, gender, sexuality, ethnicity, religion or disability work in ways to exclude them. Their physical education and sports experiences take place within unequal relations of power in society at large and within 'relations of dominance and subordination – and the conflicts – which are generated by these relations' (Apple 2006: xi). As human beings we are born as equals, yet social structures (the ways in which our societies are organized) position us differently from birth. Some of these differences are perhaps inevitable, others are less discernible, but what we think is important is to recognize the fact that such differences are socially constructed and value laden, and are therefore always open to question and can be challenged. At the heart of our concern for a focus on difference in PE, youth sport and health is the need to ask questions about whether the positioning which takes place due to difference is just and fair, or whether it is in fact unjust and discriminatory.

In our view, to be a 'good' PE/health teacher or a sports coach entails more than having sound subject knowledge and the ability to teach it to others, although this, too, is of course important. Indeed, we believe that teachers need to be more than 'transmitters of given knowledge' in PE, health or in sports contexts, and need to ask questions about 'Why this particular set of knowledge?', 'Who benefits from this type of knowledge being legitimate?' and 'Who loses out?' (Apple 2004, 2006; Carr and Kemmis 1986; Evans and Davies, 1986; Kirk, 1992). To illustrate what we mean, let us take the example of competitive sport. Rather than taking its status in PE for granted, the reflective physical educator might ask questions like: Why is competitive sport dominant in the curriculum, what consequences does teaching competitive sport carry, for whom, and what might replace it if it were to be removed? Given that competitive sport has been an arena where men and so-called traditional masculine values have dominated, is this still the case today? Do children and young people from privileged backgrounds have greater access to out-of-school competitive sport and thereby have hidden advantages when they encounter sports in PE lessons? How do students with a disability fare in competitive sport? The questions are many. Similarly, we would argue that the professional teacher needs to interrogate matters like what do we *actually* mean when we talk about *inclusive* education, because this is a contested concept and embedded in competing socio-political value systems (Sikes *et al.* 2007). In the case of a student with disability, is s/he, for example, included in a PE lesson if s/he is set a different task, perhaps even in a different room, than non-disabled students? Are girls included in PE if they are taught in single-sex classes?

In other words, we believe that professional teachers or coaches ought to be concerned with a broad project of education for social justice and democracy (Hargreaves 2003; Hargreaves and Shirley 2009; Sachs 2003), rather than limiting themselves to what Friere (2006) termed becoming a depositor of knowledge (from PE, health and sport) in the banking system of education. Heeding Lingard's (2005, 2007) observation, this does not mean that teachers or coaches alone can make inroads into establishing more equitable learning environments, and we see the need for an unromantic approach to making a difference in the lives of young people, which is firmly grounded within an analysis of the current political structures of any given pedagogized society in the late modern, global age. Indeed, Hargreaves and Shirley (2009) argue that caring professionals who aim to educate young people for global democracy and social justice, or what they term 'resilient social democracy', depend upon having their vision supported by strong health services, housing systems and a good social service sector, which is a remit far beyond the confines of the sports hall. Thus, our critical pedagogical position can best be labelled as 'modest' (Tinning 2002). Central to this vision, however, is the belief that teachers and coaches are simultaneously teachers *and* students; they are viewed as caring, empathetic adults who enter reciprocal learning environments with their pupils (Friere 2006). They have a moral obligation to continue to wrestle with issues about what counts as legitimate knowledge in their respective subjects and in society beyond, and to continually strive to educate themselves as well as their students.

To this end, we believe that a narrative approach, including both autobiographical reflection and engagement with Others' stories in education, can contribute to, and enhance, such professional critical reflection and inquiry (Armour 2006; Butt *et al.* 1992; Clandinin and Connelly 2000; Cortazzi 1993; Day 1999a, 1999b; Fernandez-Balboa 1997; Garrett 2006; Goodson 1991; Handal and Lauvås 1987; McNiff 2007). By generating self-narratives, educators can examine their taken-for-granted values about learning and teaching, as well as other aspects of life, and they can reflect upon whether their espoused teaching theories (what they say about teaching) and their theories-in-action (the behavioural world of the classroom) are aligned (Argyris and Schön 1974 cited in Day 1999a). Similarly, by reading stories about colleagues' and students' varied experience in PE, youth sport and health education settings there is a potential to enter into the imagined worlds of those with whom we work, and not least those whose lives we wish to influence in a 'good' way (Arendt 1958). Students' stories can assist us in gaining a better understanding of the consequences of our pedagogical decisions (both of our conscious and subconscious didactic actions), and they can provide informative insights into youth cultures and identities. By using different theoretical lenses from social and educational theory, personal narrative experience can be contextualized and understood within broader socio-historical structures. Whilst teaching and learning are intensely personal, individual stories are inevitably intertwined with the available stories in a given culture, and the value of individual narratives is dependent upon them being located within a history or genealogy of context (Goodson 1991). Indeed, although it is possible and enriching to engage in such critical reflection on an individual basis, we concur with those who also see a value in establishing collaborative relations with 'critical friends', who can be supportive in the process of locating individual teaching/learning experience within local historical and social contexts (Carr and Kemmis 1986; Stenhouse 1975). Working in collaboration brings, however, a whole host of challenges concerning issues like equitable relations, mutual respect, trust, anonymity and, not least, the possibility of discomfort when exposing one's self and one's practice for 'public' scrutiny. It seems, therefore, paramount to establish a set of common 'ground rules' for collaborative work, and we would argue that genuinely collaborative relations can only be forged by voluntary participants.

Narrative analysis and critical reflection for professional development

In Chapter 2 a variety of ways to analyse narratives were outlined, and we will not repeat these here. On the other hand, in keeping with our belief in the importance of contextualizing lived experience within social and political contexts, we think it is useful to reiterate Gubrium and Holstein's (2009) view that stories need to be interpreted not only with regard to their internal organization but also with regard to the circumstances of the telling. Stories can simultaneously fulfil a number of functions, so when we read and reflect upon our readings of a tale, either alone or together with others, we ought to explore multiple interpretations. At the end of each narrative in Part II there are a number of recommended readings with regard to some possible theoretical perspectives which might inform your interpretations of the tales, but these, as indeed the discussion in Chapter 1 about understanding difference, are merely suggestions to aid your analysis. It is important to realize that theoretical lenses recommended by one scholar may, of course, be relevant for other tales. Due to individuals' multiple identities, and the intersubjective process of interpretation, multiple ways of knowing the social worlds of a single tale are possible. In keeping with our critical-interpretive paradigm there is no 'right' way to interpret a story. Whilst the researchers/tellers of tales offer you their informed and moral interpretations of the realities of PE, youth sport and health, they are undeniably offering *a* point of view among many possible interpretations. All of us are bound to interpret narratives of difference from our subjective, embodied locations. Indeed, in addition to seeking theoretical understandings of tales from the field, we believe that it is equally essential to reflect upon your embodied and emotional understandings of the stories of difference. How did you *feel* on reading and/or discussing a particular story – were you sad, moved, enraged, angry, amused or complacent, and in what ways did these feelings influence your interpretations? Caring and empathetic educators with a moral purpose aim to embrace rather than eschew emotional understanding (Hargreaves 2003).

Being acutely aware of the dangers of prescription and providing closure to a tale, we have therefore chosen to devote the remainder of this book to sharing some exemplars of how we, personally, have engaged with some of the narratives contained in Part II of the book. Our aim is to motivate critical reflection at a personal and a group level about the stories of difference and (in)equitable practices in PE, youth sport and health with the view to creating more equitable teaching/learning environments, rather than signpost any 'true reading' of a tale. To this end, we also provide a series of related exercises with the objective to facilitate storytelling and storysharing (Barone 1995) for the purpose of a professional development which celebrates difference and education for social justice. We suggest that it is useful to read, interpret and discuss several of the tales at the same time; often we gain new insights through the process of comparing and contrasting experiences. Similarly, when appropriate, it can be a useful learning strategy to read aloud or act out the narratives, not least with regard to the dramatic and poetic representations. We hope that these ideas will encourage you to pursue narrative inquiry in your everyday professional lives, and we think many of them lend themselves to working with young people.

We are, of course, not proclaiming that this engagement with narratives of difference is an easy task; it is demanding, both intellectually and emotionally. It is worth keeping in mind, too, that if a narrative's educative potential for change is to be realized in order to create more inclusive learning environments, the story-as-told needs to be relinquished to pave the way for imagining a different story. Stories of inequity and inequality need inevitably to be reworked and to be retold. Such transformation is undoubtedly difficult to achieve, not least in PE and sport cultures, where professionals who are attracted to them have, on the whole, had nothing but positive experiences of physical activity. Different ways of thinking can appear to be threatening to one's sense of self. We should not underestimate the risk of telling the 'unspeakable' in a seemingly hostile environment, and it is important to be vigilant about not dismissing less powerful voices in the analysis of narratives. Reflection about what is *not* narrated can be as important, or even more significant, than what is actually articulated.

References

Apple, M. (2004) *Ideology and the Curriculum*, 3rd edn, New York: Routledge.
——(2006) *Educating the 'Right' Way. Markets, Standards, God and Inequality*, 2nd edn, London: Routledge.
Arendt, H. (1958) *The Human Condition*, Chicago: University of Chicago Press.
Armour, K. (2006) 'The way to a teacher's heart: Narrative research in physical education', in D. Kirk, D. Macdonald and M. O'Sullivan (eds) *The Handbook of Physical Education*, London: Sage Publications, pp. 467–85.
Barone, T. (1995) 'Persuasive writings, vigilant readings, and reconstructed characters: The paradox of trust in educational storysharing', in J. Amos Hatch and R. Wisniewski (eds) *Life History and Narrative*, London: Falmer Press, pp. 63–74.
Butt, R., Raymond, D., McCue, G. and Yamagishi (1992) 'Collaborative autobiography and the teacher's voice', in I. Goodson (ed.) *Studying Teachers' Lives*, London: Routledge, pp. 51–98.
Carr, W. and Kemmis, S. (1986) *Becoming Critical: Education, Knowledge and Action Research*, London: Falmer Press.
Clandinin, D. J. and Connelly, F.M. (2000) *Narrative Inquiry. Experience and Story in Qualitative Research*, San Francisco, CA: Jossey-Bass.
Cortazzi, M. (1993) *Narrative Analysis*, London: Falmer Press.
Day, C. (1999a) *Developing Teachers. The Challenge of Lifelong Learning*, London: Routledge, Falmer.
——(1999b) 'Professional development and reflective practice: Purposes, processes and partnerships', *Pedagogy, Culture and Society*, 7(2): 221–33.
Evans, J. and Davies, B. (1986) 'Sociology, schooling and physical education', in J. Evans (ed.) *Physical Education, Sport and Schooling. Studies in the Sociology of Physical Education*, London: Falmer Press, pp. 11–37.
Fernandez-Balboa, J-M. (1997) 'Physical education teacher preparation in the postmodern era: Toward a critical pedagogy', in J-M. Fernandez-Balboa (ed.) *Critical Postmodernism in Human Movement, Physical Education and Sport*, New York: University of New York Press, pp. 121–38.

Friere, P. (2006) *Pedagogy of the Oppressed*. 30th Anniversary edn, New York: Continuum.

Garrett, R. (2006) 'Critical storytelling as a teaching strategy in physical education teacher education', *European Physical Education Review*, 12(3): 339–60.

Goodson, I. (1991) 'Studying teachers' lives. Problems and possibilities', in I. Goodson (ed.) *Studying Teachers' Lives*, London: Routledge, pp. 234–49.

Gubrium, J.F. and Holstein, J.A. (2009) *Analyzing Narrative Reality*, London: Sage Publications.

Handal, G. and Lauvås, P. (1987) *Promoting Reflective Teaching*, Milton Keynes: Open University Press.

Hargreaves, A. (2003) *Teaching in the Knowledge Society. Education in the Age of Insecurity*, Maidenhead: Open University Press.

Hargreaves, A. and Shirley, D. (2009) *The Fourth Way. The Inspiring Future for Educational Change*, Thousand Oaks, CA: Corwin.

Kirk, D. (1992) 'Physical education, discourse and ideology: Bringing the hidden Curriculum into view', *Quest*, 44(1): 33–55.

Lingard, B. (2005) 'Socially just pedagogies in changing times', *International Studies in Sociology of Education*, 15(2): 165–86.

——(2007) 'Pedagogies of indifference', *International Journal of Inclusive Education*, 11(3): 245–66.

McNiff, J. (2007) 'My story is my living educational theory', in D.J. Clandinin (ed.) *Handbook of Narrative Inquiry: Mapping A Methodology*, London: Sage Publications, pp. 308–29.

Sachs, J. (2003) *The Activist Teaching Profession*, Buckingham: Open University Press.

Sikes, P., Lawson, H. and Parker, M. (2007) 'Voices on: Teachers and teaching assistants talk about inclusion', *International Journal of Inclusive Education*, 11(3): 355–70.

Stenhouse, L. (1975) *An Introduction to Curriculum Research and Development*, London: Heinemann Educational Books.

Tinning, R. (2002) 'Toward a "modest pedagogy": Reflections on the problematics of critical pedagogy', *Quest*, 54(3): 224–40.

4 Exemplar One: Health, physical education, pupils, parents and teachers

Fiona Dowling

'Run rabbit, run' and 'It's not for the school to tell us, Charlie … after all, to us you are healthy big'

Before I share my reflections about the narratives crafted by scholars Lisette Burrows and Emma Rich, I want to articulate that my epistemological and ontological position as a critical-interpretive scholar purports that there is *no* single preferred reading of these narratives. The thoughts and reflections I share here represent therefore merely one, among many, possible interpretations of the stories about young people, teachers, parents, health and physical education (PE). This is not to say that the interpretations I offer are incidental and, even though they are subjective, they are nevertheless constructed within current theoretical understandings about health and PE, and I strive, in this sense, to present 'scientifically' valid interpretations. I expect the reader to make judgement calls about whether, or not, my interpretations cohere and are consistent with knowledge in the professional community, and whether they resonate with the reader's personal experience (see Chapter 2 for further explanation). Indeed, these interpretations of tales from the field are proffered as a contribution to the dialogical, hermeneutical process of trying to gain a deeper understanding about the way difference affects individual lives and the social spaces of health and PE. I hope that they can stimulate further dialogue about social justice in a range of educational contexts.

I will structure my analyses of the tales around the following themes and/or questions:

- What is this a narrative about? What's the plot (a comedy/tragedy/satire/romance)?
- Who are the main characters? (What are their main characteristics?)
- In what context(s)/setting(s) is the story played out?
- Are the stories that the characters tell easy and/or difficult to tell? Are they acceptable tales/challenging tales? Is it possible for the characters to tell alternative tales? Was it risky to tell the tales?
- Is the narrative about exclusion and/or inclusion?
- What function can the story(-ies) have in health and PE, and beyond?

- How can theory help me unpack the narrative?
- What lessons can I take away from the story as an educator in PE, health and sport?

First of all, I will reflect upon the narrative 'Run rabbit, run' (pp. 63–6) and, thereafter, share my interpretations of 'It's not for the school to tell us, Charlie ... after all, to us you are healthy big' (pp. 119–123). Finally, I will share some thoughts about both of the tales.

After my initial reading of the tale, 'Run rabbit, run', I found myself in a state of mixed emotions. I had warmed to the main characters, Tom and Casey, and the evocative description of huntsmen in fields of dried-out sheep dung had transported me back to my own childhood. Despite having grown up on the other side of the world, in England, I could connect to the frustrations of home-made catapults and the adept scurrying of the 'enemy' with long ears. Sure, the green and pleasant pastures of my nation contrasted with the burnt brown paddock, and we had had to contend with the challenge of squidgy cowpats rather than sheep droppings, but it was not difficult to get a sense of place or the excitement of the chase. I could smell the alluring aroma of a barbecued banger and imagine the airy texture of the white loaf wrapping. I connected, too, with the boys' contempt for Harold the Giraffe and the adult metaphor focusing upon toll and customs. What did the import of goods have to do with children's seemingly endless summer days of play, BBQs, ice-cream and sleep-overs? On the other hand, this 'feel-good factor' created by the tale metamorphosed into indignation and frustration as Mrs Tam carried out her lunch-box inspection and, clearly, Casey's suffering, as he gasped for air through constricted air passages in the cross-country race, was a less than amusing twist in the plot.

Rather than shunning these emotions, I used them as a starting point with which to reread the story and help me unpack it further. What was the story about? What was the plot? As with many narratives, it was possible to trace various interrelated storylines. At one level I interpreted the narrative to be a story about the friendship between two young boys from the rural countryside in New Zealand. As a reader, I became privy to glimpses from their forms of communication, their experiences of play, their preferences for particular food, and of their schooling. The description of their young lives was in many ways drawn from well-rehearsed cultural narratives about schooling and family life; spelling tests were spawned, homophobia was used to marginalize Harold the Giraffe, the boys taunted Tom's sister Sarah, and the cross-country race made a child sick with fear. Yet, as well as being a tale about the boys, at the same time it was a story about their families. In particular, I had gleaned a picture of Tom's parents and sibling, whilst Casey's mother remained a more elusive figure in the background. It was also, of course, a tale about the boys' health teacher, Mrs Tam. By turning my attention to the characters in the narrative and their roles in the plot, I found myself, however, faced with a whole host of new possible interpretations. With Tom and Casey cast as protagonists or heroes, it was possible, for example, to perceive Mrs Tam and Harold the Giraffe, within the discourse of this health education programme, as antagonists. The tale could accordingly be read as a story about forbidden foods, about naming and blaming, inclusion and exclusion, health or a lack of it, to name but a few parallel themes woven into its fabric.

Framed within a narrative about current health messages, and influenced by my understanding of relational and poststructural theories about identity and health, the innocent tale about 24 hours in the lives of a couple of lads in rural New Zealand became a somewhat more troublesome tale. It could be read as a tale about practices of surveillance and self-surveillance with regard to nutritional intake, a tale which objectifies bodies, and/or a story which illustrates the problematic nature of narrowly defined meanings of 'health'. Similarly, drawing upon theory about pedagogy and teacher professionalism, I found myself posing a series of questions about Mrs Tam's teaching strategies and her seemingly moralizing behaviour in the classroom. Was there, for example, room in the classroom for Casey to react in alternative ways than the painful reaction which ensued? What alternative learning strategies about nutrition exist than that of public scrutiny or shaming? Why do I think Mrs Tam chose the lunch-box inspection, and why might she think that Harold the Giraffe can be a useful pedagogical tool? How can I analyse the boys' evident ridicule of the Giraffe and its preaching?

Aware of the importance of contextualizing individual stories, I thus broadened my analytic gaze. No doubt the connection I felt to the boys' meanings was partially influenced by subconscious comparisons with my own intermittent desire for 'forbidden foods' such as sausages and ice-cream, and a sense of ambivalence towards the never-ending flow of health imperatives. 'Eat five fruit and veg a day!' 'Exercise more regularly!' I, too, had felt the frustration of being told what to do by the welfare state. Their story could not, I reflected, have been told by boys living in dire poverty or in a country where the so-called 'obesity epidemic' (Burrows and Wright 2007; Gard and Wright 2005) had not gained solid purchase. Indeed, the tale derived much of its authenticity from its resonance with health discourses in my own country of residence, Norway. Certainly children in Norway would not be acquainted with Harold, but similar health education campaigns are increasingly to be found in the Norwegian classroom (e.g. The Keyhole Campaign for Healthy Food, Norwegian Directorate of Health 2010), and one of the mandatory school subjects in compulsory schooling is 'Food and Health' (Norwegian Directorate for Education and Training n.d.). Casey's description of his mother's healthy 'lifestyle choices' (reading magazines about healthy food, going to the gym, buying the 'right' food, providing her child with healthy meals) are behaviours which are practised worldwide by many adults in rich nations and, indeed, with which I, in part, can identify. So why might I thus describe the tale as becoming troublesome, you might ask? Is it not positive that governments invest large sums of public money to combat the 'obesity epidemic', and that children learn about what types of food are best for their health?

My deeper reflections around the narrative concerned me as an educator for several reasons and, following Burrows and Wright (2007), stemmed from unease about the way in which the 'obesity epidemic' and its ensuing health imperatives allow social practices which previously would have been viewed as contrary to ideas of social justice and equality of education. Masked within rhetoric of 'for the good of the nation' and, not least, for the 'good of the individual subject', it could be argued that school subjects like health and PE are inadvertently contributing to overzealous bodily self-monitoring practices, the surveillance of others' bodies and the creation of 'fear' or repulsion of certain body types and practices. Lurking within the shadows of Tom and Casey's tale is the abhorrent fat, 'unhealthy' and morally defunct body (Burrows and Wright 2007). Harold the Giraffe's health messages and Mrs Tam's lunch-box inspection depend to a large degree upon the fear of not eating 'healthily', and the fear and risk associated with becoming a 'wrongly shaped' body. According to much government policy, ignoring today's health imperatives means that individuals run the risk of 'lifestyle diseases' such as coronary heart disease, obesity and diabetes. Simultaneously, the story is constructed relationally to Western society's current preoccupation with 'ideal' slender, fit, 'healthy' bodies which symbolize success and status (Bordo 2003; Featherstone *et al.* 1991; Shilling 1993, 2008; Tinning and Glasby 2002). Casey's mother's fitness and eating practices are, for example, typical of the late modern 'project' of self-identity, in which the outer appearance of the material body is seen by many as central in the pursuit of self-worth (Giddens 1991). 'Run rabbit, run' can, from this theoretical perspective, be interpreted as a tale about preferred and/or marginalized bodies, and a story about the ways in which young children's identities are inextricably affected by current health imperatives.

It is a story about becoming an embodied subject, in relation to other subjects, and it is a narrative about the positioning of the 'Other' in educational settings (Burrows 2010; Hunter 2004). Certain children become privileged in the school classroom on account of their bodies (read: thin, trim, self-disciplined, 'healthy' bodies), whilst others are marginalized due to being 'wrong' bodies (read: overweight, unfit, lazy, 'unhealthy' bodies). The practice of moral judgement lags seldom far behind judgement calls about body shape and size. The narrative does not, in fact, provide the reader with any indication about the body shape of any of the characters, and although I would like to think of myself as someone who aims to avoid the trap of classifying bodies in this way, I could not help but reflect upon the fact that I had searched for any tell-tale information about Tom's and Casey's body size. Recognizing this potential to 'Other' the bodies of these children is, I think, symptomatic of the all-pervasive nature of the discourse of 'the look', and of its inherent danger to distribute power (Burrows 2010). The public health messages which constitute the context for this tale saturate young people's lives across multiple sites, such as the family, government agencies, corporate bodies and the media in all its breadth. As a result, healthy eating mantras easily become taken-for-granted aspects of our lives and remain unchallenged or perceived as 'unproblematic'.

When I considered whether Tom and Casey could have told an alternative tale, I surmised that this would indeed have been difficult. Casey certainly attempted to challenge 'the Truth' about sausages being labelled as 'bad things', exclaiming that they taste good, and both the boys had a hearty laugh at the Giraffe, albeit in a homophobic, discriminatory way, but these fragmentary moments of resistance paled into the background against the dominant message of healthy eating within an 'obesity epidemic' discourse. Drawing upon the work of Leahy (2009), it is useful to conceptualize Casey's pounding heart, and evident discomfort at the realization that his lunch-box contained 'bad things to put in his body', as a so-called 'biopedagogical moment'. Even before Mrs Tam offered her expert nutritional knowledge to counteract the contents of the offending lunch-box, Casey demonstrated self-monitoring behaviour (heart racing) and, as she transmitted the 'truths' of healthy eating, his classmates joined in with her surveillance strategy via their muffled laughter. As Leahy (2009) claims, this is a very potent pedagogy, and we can only begin to imagine what it feels like for the child at whom it is directed. Evans *et al.* (2008) concur that humiliation is indeed a powerful technique of biopower (the way in which the body is regulated to fit the requirements of modern capitalist societies), where emotionally charged, visceral incidents in the classroom can be understood as affective bullying. The latter is all the more repugnant on account of the way in which normal-izing and moralizing about the 'healthy' body is legitimized in much current, neo-liberal health education and school policy. The indignation I felt the first time I had read the story became a more intense emotion as I reflected upon today's society's preoccupation with the pursuit of an 'ideal' body which, for the majority of people, remains elusive and, for some, can have life-threatening consequences (Evans *et al.* 2008). I wanted to be able to interpret Casey's indignant claim that sausages must be 'good' because they taste good, as a sign of resistance against the simplistic health imperatives with which he was bombarded, symbolizing instead the complexities and contradictions of 'good' health. I nevertheless concluded that his embodied discomfort probably outweighed the resistance to be found in his speech (Burrows 2010).

Dwelling further upon the context of the narrative, I continued to ponder over the seemingly unproblematic nature of the health messages which tea-chers, like Mrs Tam, convey to children. In particular, Casey's asthma proved to be an interesting example from which to pose the question, 'What counts as being "healthy"?' Even if Casey's body were to fit late modern society's 'ideal' body (and as we know, the tale does not make us privy to his body shape or size), whilst he suffers a bout of breathing difficulties, it would clearly be difficult to classify him, in categorical terms, as 'healthy' (free from illness). The oversimplification of messages like thin body = healthy, and fat = unhealthy, is plain for all to see. Such dichotomies and, indeed, the evasion of the uncertainties in, for example, the science of the so-called 'obesity epidemic' would appear to result in moral justifications for advocating 'healthy' behaviours, as opposed to knowledge-based reasoning (Burrows and Wright 2007; Evans *et al.* 2008; Rich 2010). Images of the body, like the metaphor of a country with customs staff, or the more commonly used metaphor of the machine (Tinning 1990, 2010), objectify the children's bodies and ignore the socio-cultural aspects of their subjectivities. 'Run rabbit, run' revealed how Casey's lunch-box contents are inextricably linked to his socio-economic context. I could only surmise that Casey probably did not usually feel the panic, which he clearly did when Tom's mother had been the provider of his nutrition, because his mother *knew* all about the 'right foods'. Tom, on the other hand, was more likely to frequently be subjected to the moralizing gaze and shaming pedagogy about the 'bad things' in his packed lunch because his mother did not seem to openly engage with the health discourse. The ideology of healthism, which tends to define health as essentially an individual responsibility about making the 'right' lifestyle choices, thus overlooks the dialectic between individual and structural control (Burrows and Wright 2007; Tinning 1990). Of course, I recognize that we all make some choices with regard to '(un)healthy' behaviours, but I believe it is paramount for educators like myself to acknowledge the reality that not all choices are open for everyone; structural constraints prevent some children from being able to make the 'right' choice. According to the British website, the Poverty Site (n.d.), 13.5 million people live, for example, on incomes below a low-income threshold in the UK, which represents approximately a fifth of the population. Identity markers such as social class, religion, age, gender and disability will influence, to a greater or lesser degree, the opportunity to exercise 'choice'. Despite some health and PE teachers' desire to help young people to become critical consumers of health messages, I concluded that in today's neo-liberal school environment it seems increasingly difficult (and in some cases, totally unimaginable) to offer a narrative in which health education is not framed in this way. The dominant narrative appears to suppress alternative storylines.

Turning my attention to the tale, 'It's not for the school to tell us, Charlie... after all, to us you are healthy big' (pp. 119–123), which is crafted from data in a UK research project, I discovered a number of overlapping themes with 'Run rabbit, run', despite the very different nature of the narrative. The narrative was, for example, constructed in relation to the global 'obesity epidemic', the 'ideal' of a slim, fit and 'healthy' body, and teachers who are cast by governments in the front line of the battle against fat. It also provided the reader with glimpses into the meanings that young people attach to health imperatives, and their experience of school and of family life. Yet, in addition to these interesting comparisons, the story about Charlie was at the same time a very different narrative to that of Casey and Tom, and I used these differences and similarities to help me reflect upon the tale.

With regard to the temporal framework for the tale, the story was played out within a short period of time from the end of a PE lesson and on the walk home from school. It was, I reflected, a fragmentary, messy tale about young people's experience of everyday school life, and it lacked closure compared to the dramatic ending in 'Run rabbit, run'. For me, the story could be characterized as a brave tale to tell, but clearly it was a very risky narrative which had to be confined to private audiences like Tom. I asked myself whether I could characterize Charlie's desire to be big and strong as symbolic resistance to the all-pervasive health imperatives in current UK school policy. I wondered, too, whether it was a narrative about 'queering' fat, and my thoughts grappled with the notion of 'fat' role models for young people, whose bodies could defy today's 'ideal' shape; bodies which could challenge the notion that only slim, trim people are deemed as successful and worthy of status. The British DJ Chris Moyles was perhaps one such role model and, for my generation, comedians like Dawn French and Victoria Wood have offered defiant messages about success. Yet, for many, their success has probably been constructed *in spite of* their body shape and size (and gender), and the media have tended to pathologize their bodies, too, as a swift internet search could quickly confirm. In relation to difference and social equity in PE, youth sport and health I mused that few such role models are or have been legitimated, and that the ideologies of mesomorphism (the pattern of beliefs and values which define preferred body shape as being mesomorph, with little body fat) and 'shapism' (desirable, gendered, body images) have perhaps never been more prevalent than today (Tinning 1990, 2010). What does all this mean for young people's self-identity work, and their sense of embodiment? Does it mean, for example, that proudly told tales about being big and physically active (and Charlie was evidently an active kick-boxer) will continue to be suppressed in public spheres?

Unravelling the interrelated storylines, the narrative could easily be interpreted as a tale about the hostile learning space of a PE lesson, in which bodies were hierarchically organized: skeletal, undersized bodies and flabby, uncontrollable, oversized bodies wielded seemingly little power in the course of the battery of fitness tests. There was evidence of peers exercising moral judgement when, for example, Lydia claimed that no one would wish to be friends with Charlie or Mark on account of their size, and when the boys themselves evaluated Marie's eating habits in a derogatory fashion. The evaluative gaze of Others was, in fact, everywhere: it was evident beyond the school gates, in the school's canteen and was a feature of the PE teacher's pedagogy. In this sense, the tale could be read as typical of the experienced pressures of negotiating 'totally pedagogized schools' (Evans *et al.* 2011) or illustrative of the rhizomatic character of obesity surveillance, which occurs not simply in a top-down model but across a series of interconnected sites (Rich 2010). In other words, I witnessed similarities with the surveillance practices which Casey and his classmates had experienced.

Indeed, I felt anger as I contemplated the realities of the monitoring techniques described in the school canteen, so similar to the lunch-box inspection in New Zealand. Although clearly the feedback on a print-off sheet may seem to be a more private affair, I could not however imagine that the potency of naming and blaming could be any less damaging for Charlie or his fellow pupils, not least on account of the expectation that Charlie's parents should join forces with the school and wave a moralizing finger at his nutritional 'choices' (Burrows and Wright 2007; Burrows 2009). Once again, I would like to reiterate that I do, of course, think it is preferable for young children to eat a nutritionally balanced diet, and the anger I express here centres upon the methods used to 'educate' young people, rather than the goal itself. Whilst the monitoring system in the canteen did not actually resonate with my experiences of the Norwegian school system, because canteens are a rare feature of school culture, I could more easily relate to the body-monitoring practices of weighing, the use of skin-fold calipers and the use of endurance tests. Mrs Oliver's PE lesson could well have taken place in a Norwegian school where categorical research about the 'objective' body receives considerable attention. Height and weight measurements, together with fitness scores, are recorded, collated and, in some cases, published as an integral part of learning in PE. How could body mass index (BMI) charts or Cooper test results evoke meaningful, pleasurable movement experiences for the likes of Charlie and his mates, I wondered? Why should these statistics incite them to be physically active? How could these pupils relate to the risk of lifestyle diseases, such as cancer of the colon or heart disease? How do disabled pupils fit 'the mould' of the discourse? Why does the PE community seemingly continue to ignore the complexities of pupils' health mediated via their classed, gendered and ethnic backgrounds, and to liken the body to a machine or reduce it to a measure like BMI? Why do we overlook the subjective and emotional aspects of health, and why do we not get beyond the mantra of 'you've only got yourself to blame'? How could the canteen print-out take account of Charlie's social background? The narrative resulted in a tidal wave of professional considerations.

I became wary of the danger of being judgemental about Mrs Oliver's practice; of the 'pot calling the kettle black'. After all, I, too, had contributed to, and contribute to, the 'obesity assemblages' (Rich 2010) described here as a teacher and teacher educator in PE. Treading the pathway between the long rows of red-brick, terraced housing, together with 'big' Charlie, brought back not simply memories of my home country but also flashbacks to the heady days of 'health-based physical education' in England in the late 1980s (Dowling 1987). I thought about how we are all party to our professional socialization and its preferred knowledge, which in this instance has meant the dominance of the biological sciences and their tendency to objectify the body. Similar to Jackie Oliver, I had experienced my professional status as being enhanced by the 'health and fitness boom'. The contextual background for 'It's not for the school to tell us, Charlie ... after all, to us you are healthy big' is such that it is currently difficult to envisage alternative ways of performing 'the PE teacher'. Recruitment to PE teacher education programmes tends to attract white, mesomorph, physically active, competitively successful sportswomen and men (Douglas and Halas 2011; Dowling 2011; Armour and Jones 1998; Tinning 1990, 2010), whose bodies inadvertently, yet so powerfully, underline the narrow definitions of what counts as the 'right' body, shape and size. PETE programmes tend to re-contextualize many of the 'truths' of risk and uncertainty associated with 'unhealthy' practices, and schools, as already mentioned, are caught in a web of multiple policy initiatives about health imperatives (Evans *et al.* 2008, 2011; Rich 2010). Many PE teachers are socialized into technical-rational ways of teaching motor skills within school programmes dominated by competitive sport, leaving little room for explorative pedagogies in which teacher and pupil negotiate what counts as knowledge (Dowling 2006, 2011; Kirk 2010; Tinning 2010). As Hunter (2004) observes, the *doxa* of PE limits multiple, legitimate ways of embodiment, and, within today's neo-liberal 'performative' culture of schooling, notions of teacher professionalism which accentuate performance pedagogies have gained currency at the cost of marginalizing the educational goals of social justice for democracy (Dowling 2011; Hargreaves 2003). Against this contextual backcloth it was easier for me to understand Mrs Oliver's moralizing pedagogy, in which 'fat' and 'overweight' so easily became associated with a lack of self-control, shame and being 'irresponsibly ill' (Evans *et al.* 2008). From the government's perspective, PE lessons like that of Mrs Oliver, and health education initiatives undertaken within 'The National Healthy Schools Programme', help to increase pupils' knowledge, skills and behaviour about health-related practices.

Despite this commendable objective, I could not help but continue to feel unease about Charlie's tale, which I concluded was a narrative about being excluded from the dominant discourses of current PE. Although I desperately wanted to envisage a day when Charlie would share his dream about being big, strong and powerful with all his classmates in the gym, I rather despondently realized that this was an unlikely turn of events, at least during his school days. What did this mean, I wondered, for his sense of self-worth? How could PE lessons motivate him to enjoy being physically active and to gain pleasure from moving? Somehow I could not imagine the emotional turmoil he must have felt in a learning environment in which his body appears to be alienated and his voice is not heard. In relation to education for social justice and democracy, this narrative seemed to pose considerable challenges.

Indeed, both 'It's not for the school to tell us, Charlie ... after all, to us you are healthy big' and 'Run rabbit, run' are narratives which raise important questions about the types of social spaces that health and PE classes represent, the consequences of the pedagogies used in lessons, and the social meanings which are inscribed upon children's and young people's bodies. Furthermore, they richly demonstrate the intricate web of pedagogical sites which 'educate' young people's bodies in the late modern age, as indeed that of the identities of PE and/or health teachers. From my perspective, it seems that we can learn much from Charlie, Casey and co., if the profession genuinely aims to reach its goal of 'physical activity for all'. Their tales beg us to revisit the social construction of our subject, imbued as it is with power, and to ask: How can we incorporate greater reflection about the social meaning of the body in PETE, and in PE and health lessons? How can we get beyond simplistic reasoning like physical activity = slim = healthy? How can we move beyond objectifying bodies? Acutely aware of PE's legitimate history of 'disciplining' the body in schools (Hunter 2004; Kirk 2010; Tinning 2010), how can the profession accept this responsibility without inadvertently bestowing unequal worth to different subjects? How can we nurture agentic subjects, who find pleasure in their embodiment?

Generating and analysing tales about health and fitness

Here are a number of exercises to activate biographical and institutional narratives, and storysharing. Remember to establish a set of ethical ground rules when you engage in storysharing, such as honouring the anonymity of the storyteller and listener, if requested, and respecting the anonymity of characters/institutions in the tales. You might, for example, wish to use pseudonyms for people and organizations. Remember that mutual respect is of utmost importance, too, particularly when you do not necessarily share the same points of view about the social world. Recounting, telling and listening to stories can be very emotional, so keep this at the back of your mind, too. Stories can do things to people; they are not necessarily innocent, and they can lead to unanticipated reactions.

Exercise one – tales about testing

Reflecting upon your own experiences as a student at school, can you recall any stories which were told and circulated about the PE department's fitness tests (for example, Cooper tests; skin-fold caliper tests; Sargent jumps)? If so, write down a short story.

Share your story with a fellow student. Are there similarities between the two tales? What do the stories say about fitness tests; what do they say about students? Use the questions on pp. 159–160 to help you unpack the stories, and to analyse the possible functions that stories about fitness tests can have had at your respective schools. In particular, reflect upon who the story 'includes' and/or 'excludes', and why this is the case. What theories of difference can inform your analyses?

Exercise two – stories about being fat

What stories circulate about fat people in your peer group? Write down a short narrative and share it with a fellow student.

What function do such stories have among your peers? What do you think it feels like to be the fat person in your stories? How is the fat person positioned in relation to other people? What other identity axes feature in the stories? Are there similarities between your narratives? If so, why do you think this is the case? Is there any sign of 'naming and shaming' going on? Would you characterize your stories as typical or atypical? Why? How do they relate to what's going on in society at large? How can the theories in the recommended reading be used to analyse your tales? Which theoretical lenses do you find most useful, and why is this so?

Exercise three – cultural stories about health and fitness

Choose a recent television programme about health and fitness (for example, the UK's 'Superfat versus Superskinny'), or a national campaign about 'healthy eating', and analyse the types of stories being told in the media about health and fitness. Use the questions on pp. 159–160 to assist you to see what types of bodies/identities are being constructed, and who is being 'included' and/or 'excluded' in the narratives. How can the theories in the recommended reading be used to analyse your tales? Which theoretical lenses do you find most useful, and why is this so? Are there other theories of difference which can help to broaden your analysis (for example, theories about gender or ethnicity)?

Exercise four – myths about students and teachers

Stories about teachers and students abound in schools and on professional training courses. Write a short narrative about each of the following 'mythical' teachers and students: 'teacher's pet'; the 'motor moron'; the caring teacher/coach; the unfair teacher/coach.

Share your stories with a fellow student. Reflect upon the similarities and differences in the stories. Discuss how your emerging professional identity/identities is/are developing in relation to the 'mythical' characters in your tales. How can theories of difference help you to interpret the different characters in the stories? What values, and ways of knowing, are represented in the different tales? Why do you think such stories tend to represent pairs of opposites (the talented/non-talented; unfair/just)? What tales can be told about the 'average' pupil or the 'average' teacher and coach?

Exercise five – PE teachers' and coaches' bodies

What stories are told about PE teachers' or coaches' bodies? Write down a narrative about a teacher or a coach you have known.

Exchange stories with a fellow student, and compare and contrast the descriptions of the characters. How can theories of difference help you to analyse the tales? Do the bodies tell a story about health and/or fitness? If so, what cultural stories do they draw upon? Reflect upon how students may react to these 'body stories'. How do these tales compare to the story you might tell about your own body? How can theories of difference be used to explain the stories?

References

Armour, K. and Jones, R. (1998) *Physical Education Teachers' Lives and Careers*, London: Falmer Press.

Bordo, S. (2003) *Unbearable Weight: Feminism, Western Culture and the Body*, 10th edn, Berkley, CA: University of California Press.

Burrows, L. (2009) 'Pedagogizing families through obesity discourse', in J. Wright and V. Harwood (eds) *Biopolitics and the 'Obesity Epidemic'. Governing Bodies*, London: Routledge, pp. 127–40.

——(2010) 'Kiwi kids are Weet-Bix kids', *Sport, Education and Society*, 15(2): 235–51.

Burrows, L. and Wright, J. (2007) 'Prescribing practices: Shaping healthy children in schools', *International Journal of Children's Rights*, 15(6): 83–98.

Douglas, D. and Halas, J. (2011) 'The wages of whiteness: Confronting the nature of ivory tower racism and the implications for physical education', *Sport, Education and Society*, 1–22, DOI: 10.1080/13573322.2011.602395.

Dowling, F. (1987) 'A health focus within physical education', in S. Biddle (ed.) *Foundations of Health-related Fitness in Physical Education*, London: Ling Publishing House, pp. 13–18.

——(2006) 'Physical education teacher educators' professional identities, continuing professional development and the issue of gender equality', *Physical Education and Sport Pedagogy*, 11(3): 247–63.

——(2011) 'Are PE teacher identities fit for post-modern schools or are they clinging to modernist notions of professionalism? A case study of some Norwegian PE student teachers' emerging professional identities', *Sport, Education and Society*, 16(2): 201–22.

Evans, J., Davies, B. and Rich, E. (2011) 'Bernstein, body pedagogies and the corporeal device', in G. Ivinson, B. Davies and J. Fitz (eds) *Knowledge and Identity. Concepts and Applications in Bernstein's Sociology*, London: Routledge, pp. 176–90.

Evans, J., Rich, E., Allwood, R. and Davies, B. (2008) 'Body pedagogies, P/policy, health and gender', *British Educational Research Journal*, 34(3): 387–402.

Featherstone, M. Hepworth, M. and Turner, B. (1991) *The Body: Social Process and Cultural Theory*, London: Sage Publications.

Gard, M. and Wright, J. (2005) *The Obesity Epidemic: Science, Morality and Ideology*, London: Routledge.

Giddens, A. (1991) *Modernity and Self-identity: Self and Society in the Late Modern Age*, Cambridge: Polity Press.

Hargreaves, A. (2003) *Teaching in the Knowledge Society. Education in the Age of Insecurity*, Maidenhead: Open University Press.

Hunter, L. (2004) 'Bourdieu and the social space of the PE class: Reproduction of doxa through practice', *Sport, Education and Society*, 9(2): 175–92.

Kirk, D. (2010) *Physical Education Futures*, London: Routledge.

Leahy, D. (2009) 'Disgusting pedagogies', in J. Wright and V. Harwood (eds) *Biopolitics and the 'Obesity Epidemic'. Governing Bodies*, London: Routledge, pp. 127–40.

Norwegian Directorate of Education and Training (n.d.) Available from: <www.udir.no/Lareplaner/Grep/Modul/?gmid=0&gmi=6350&v=6> (accessed 26 September 2011).

Norwegian Directorate of Health (2010) 'Nøkkelhullet' undervisningsopplegg (Keyhole teaching pack). Available from: <www.helsedirektoratet.no/vp/template/ver1–0/print.jsp?articleID=674934> (accessed 30 September 2011).

Poverty site (n.d.) Available from: <www.poverty.org.uk/summary/key%20facts.shtml> (accessed 26 September 2011).

Rich, E. (2010) 'Obesity assemblages and surveillance in schools', *International Journal of Qualitative Studies in Education*, 23(7): 803–21.

Shilling, C. (1993) *The Body and Social Theory*, London: Sage Publications.

——(2008) *Changing Bodies. Habit, Crisis and Creativity*, London. Sage Publications.

Tinning, R. (1990) *Ideology and Physical Education. Opening Pandora's Box*, Geelong: Deakin University Press.

——(2010) *Pedagogy and Human Movement: Theory, Practice, Research*, London: Routledge.

Tinning, R. and Glasby, T. (2002) 'Pedagogical work and the "cult of the body": Considering the role of HPE in the context of the "new public health"', *Sport, Education and Society*, 7(2): 109–19.

5 Exemplar Two: Disability and difference in schooling and home

Hayley Fitzgerald

The beginning of Chapter 1 captures a snapshot of James's, Anna's and Matt's diverse lives, and we briefly get a sense of the ways they experience difference and inequalities. As we read these short tales we are likely to interpret, empathize and relate to them in a variety of ways. Like the zoom of a camera lens, each of us will be attracted to, and focus on, a particular aspect of the tales. For example, were any of these tales familiar stories which you might tell yourself? Did you relate to a specific character, plot or situation? And, if so, did this result in you feeling more empathetic and understanding, or evoke bad memories that you would rather leave well alone? Or did hearing about James's, Anna's and Matt's lives make you feel uncomfortable – as if you were treading on unfamiliar territory to which you have not previously been exposed? If this is the case, it perhaps reminds us that our own experiences will not always be the same as those of the young people we teach or coach. An ongoing challenge for practitioners is to get to know young people within, and beyond, the classroom and the gym in ways which can usefully help to support positive and stimulating health and physical education (HPE) and community sport experiences. This is a challenge that practitioners and researchers in HPE and community sport have been perhaps, to a certain degree, loath to embrace (O'Sullivan and MacPhail 2010). I would argue it is a challenge that we need to attend to, if we are serious about offering fulfilling and enabling HPE and community sport to all young people.

In this exemplar I focus on a few of the young people featured in the narratives of Part II and aim to stimulate conversations and reflections on how the practices, attitudes and values of practitioners, young people and family can contribute to maintaining, or challenging, difference and inequalities experienced by young, disabled people in HPE and community sport. In the same way that I invited you to zoom your camera lens and reflect on your interpretations of James's, Anna's and Matt's short tales, I will offer my reading of two tales, 'Them special needs kids and their waiters' (pp. 124–9), and the auto-ethnographically inspired tale, 'Second toe syndrome' (pp. 90–3). I crafted 'Them special needs kids and their waiters' on the basis of my researcher analyses, what Polkinghorne (1995) terms a 'narrative analysis'. As

Chapter 2 discusses, my narrative story is a synthesis of the incidents and episodes reflected through the various sources of data generated, and aims to be *explanatory*. My theoretical and experiential lenses are implicitly present in the narrative, but they have *explicitly* guided the structuring of the tale. As such, I have a more intimate and different relationship with this tale than with the others in Part II. For example, in my role as a researcher, I walked the corridors, had many lunches in the school canteen, witnessed onslaughts of abuse directed at the disabled pupils and talked at length with the various characters featured in this tale. I feel a physical and emotional closeness to this tale, because I was there, the narrative analysis is mine.

More broadly, my professional experiences of working in sports development mean I have been exposed to these kinds of school environments for many years. As the memories of some schools, teachers and pupils have faded, others stay with me and are a reminder of the work that still needs to be done to ensure disabled pupils have positive and fulfilling school experiences. These sediments of experience have also affected the way I tell this particular story; they form a part of my researcher/writer identity. For example, I remember at one school I was the sport development officer to which the disabled pupils were dismissively dispatched by the so-called 'trained' HPE teachers, as if my subject knowledge or skills were any better than theirs. These HPE teachers didn't want to have the disabled pupils in their class. At another school I was the person asking tricky questions of HPE staff when I saw disabled pupils not taking part. I made it my business to seek out these pupils; they were usually hidden away in the library or 'quiet room', but I made sure I got their side of the story. I was the one who spent weeks on end sitting with Sam, a disabled pupil, who had been 'allowed' to take part in HPE for the first time. She had been told for years that she shouldn't, and couldn't, do HPE, so it wasn't surprising to me that it took some persuasion to convince her that she should have a go. Because of these kinds of experiences and my closeness to 'Them special needs kids and their waiters' you may find your reading(s) of this tale, and indeed 'Second toe syndrome', differs from mine – but this provides a starting point for conversations and critical dialogue beyond what is written in this text. What is interesting to note is the way in which I can continue to reflect upon, and engage in the hermeneutical process of understanding the story I authored, because I can use new theoretical lenses with which to revisit the young people's experiences and my interpretations of them.

Before I focus on 'Them special needs kids and their waiters' and 'Second toe syndrome' I first want to reflect more generally on a striking feature I was drawn to when initially reading all the narratives found in Part II, the *talk* about young people. As I was drawn to this talk, a number of questions came to mind. How are young people talked about in these tales? Where does this talk come from? How does this talk influence these young people and others around them? Take, for example, Kirsty, a HPE teacher featured in Rossi's tale who talks about 'the fat kids' and 'the uncos' (uncoordinated pupils). The young people in lisahunter's play are distinguished according to assumptions made about performance ('Runfast', 'Jumphigh'), behaviour ('Wellbehaved', 'Chatterbox') and body shape ('Fatnugly'). A number of characters in Morrison's and Fitzgerald's tales talk of 'retards' when referring to disabled young people. As I initially read the narratives this assortment of 'talk' jumped from the pages and it illustrates how the naming and labelling of young people is commonplace in many schools and community contexts. I was reminded of my own schooling and some of the derogatory nicknames that circulated – 'Lardy Arse', 'Bugs Bunny', 'Ray the Gay' and 'Pizza Face'. Reading the tales in Part II provided an uncomfortable reminder of the role I played in helping to maintain this kind of talk. But I also remembered the occasion when I attempted to challenge others and the backlash I encountered as a result; I, too, then became the butt of mean and unfriendly whispers and gossiping. Whether it is the nickname that one pupil calls another, a name used in the privacy of the staffroom or something unspoken that is evoked in the mind of a practitioner, it is the repeated use of these labels, and their associated discourses, that contributes to shaping the ways in which young people 'become known' and 'make themselves known' (Priestley 1999). Whilst this talk may seem rather innocent it is, in fact, laden with value. As Wright (2004: 20) observes: 'Questions can, therefore, be asked about how language works to position speakers (and listeners) in relation to particular discourses and with what effects.' Who is perceived as 'sporty', 'fitting in', 'successful', 'odd' or a 'wimp' will be governed by the talk and choices in language circulating in the gym, corridors, classes and staffrooms. Of course, much of this talk also seeps into other social spheres (such as the family, sport and popular culture), and this continues the ebb and flow of meanings and values afforded through discourse to different young people (Holt 2011). Consider for a moment these questions: What talk (names and labels) about different young people circulates in the contexts you have worked? How is this talk reproduced? What kinds of meanings and values are associated with this talk? What may the consequences be for the young people who are talked about? By reflecting on these questions you may be better positioned to begin to understand the role you, and your colleagues, play in supporting discourses that legitimize and celebrate some young people's identities, whilst marginalizing others.

Next, I turn to one group of people who often experience marginalization and feelings of otherness – disabled people. Historically, disabled people have been institutionalized, segregated from society and deemed to have no meaningful purpose in life (Miller and Gwynne 1972). Examining the meaning of the words used to describe disability also reinforces this kind of negative outlook. For example, the term 'handicap' (hand-in-cap) originates from the begging many disabled people were forced, and continue, to endure in order to survive (Eide and Ingstad 2011). Moreover, the prefix 'dis' in the word disability provides a constant reminder of the perceived inferior and negative relationship between disability and an 'able-bodied' person. More broadly, non-conforming disabled bodies have been perceived as 'spoilt' (Goffman 1968), 'flawed' (Hevey 1992) and in need of care (Hunt 1966). To a large extent, international changes associated with legislation and policy developments promoting inclusion and equity have gone some way to redressing the position and the place that disabled people hold within contemporary society (Slee 2009). Whilst these changes may be positive, sediments from the powerful discourses of the past continue, however, to influence society's view of disability and perceptions of disabled people. By reflecting on 'Them special needs kids and their waiters' and 'Second toe syndrome', I want to 'home in' on these sediments and offer an interpretation of the ways in which the characters featured in these tales navigate, and (re)articulate, contemporary understandings of disability. Whilst not disregarding other identity markers such as gender, social class and ethnicity, I draw what Archer *et al.* (2001) describe as a 'provisional boundary' around disability. In doing this, I seek to illuminate disability within the wider contemporary debates and political agendas focusing on difference and inequality. As Chapter 1 outlines, there is good reason for doing this, not least because of the lack of concern that scholars in HPE have afforded to issues of disability in relation to difference and inequality. By foregrounding disability and talking of 'disabled people'[1] I am aware of the ways in which these discussions may contribute to an essentialist discourse of disability that assumes commonality, rather than difference, between disabled people; I talk more about this later in the chapter in relation to the narratives.

The first narrative I will consider is 'Them special needs kids and their waiters'. As I revisit this tale that I constructed, and reflect on the 'provisional boundary' of disability within the school, I am immediately drawn to the talk circulating about the disabled pupils. For example, Josh (a non-disabled pupil) calls some disabled pupils 'fuckin' retards' and then goes on to give examples of activities he believes they cannot engage in properly: 'can't even eat properly', 'can't do lessons like us' and in PE 'everyone has to pretend they have scored'. These comments are not expressed in a friendly or complimentary manner, but rather emerge out of a series of frustrations that Josh experiences as he attempts to get some lunch at school. When further reflecting on the bustling and tussles that dominate the beginning of this narrative I began to wonder if there was more to be considered about where Josh was actually directing his anger. His words seemed to be pointed and filled with venom, as if his anger had been stored up in readiness for an attack on the disabled pupils ('the retards'). And, although Josh has unfinished business with those who caused his late arrival to the school canteen – Michael pulling his backpack and the sixth-form boys laughing at him – it is not these boys he decides to focus his energies and retaliation upon. So, why did Josh target the disabled pupils for his subsequent outburst? Were they just in the wrong place at the wrong time? Could it really be that simple? Or was there something else, something about the pupils having a disability? Did Josh use them in order to position himself in a more favourable light? For Slee (2004), Josh's reaction can be rooted in society's understanding(s) of disability, and on this matter he asks: 'How do we come to know disability?' and 'What do we know about disability?' He argues that the answer for most of us is likely to be 'from a distance and through the powerful discourses and ideological frameworks of others' (Slee 2004: 50). Building on Slee's questions, we could ask why Josh draws the conclusions he does about the disabled pupils.

To some extent it could be argued that Josh is measuring the disabled pupils through a normative non-disabled ideal: after all, as Josh puts it, he attends 'a normal school, not one of them special schools'. This begs the question what is a 'normal' school or, in fact, what is a 'normal' person? Josh's observations are perhaps not surprising when you consider broader educational discourses and practices that operate in ways that maintain the position of disabled pupils as contrary to the norm (Ashby 2010; Slee 2011). For example, the distinction Josh makes between mainstream/regular ('norm') and special schools situates the mainstream/regular as places for 'normal' pupils like himself, as opposed to special schools where disabled pupils would be better positioned. This kind of thinking raises a number of fundamental questions about schooling. Why is it that a separate system of mainstream/regular and special schools exists? Who benefits from this system? What are the costs of this system? Who are its advocates and what arguments are put forward to support it? What are the alternatives? (For further discussion of these issues see: Barton and Armstrong 2007; Gabel and Danforth 2008; Higgins *et al.* 2009.) A number of scholars have highlighted specific mechanisms which exist in mainstream schools that reinforce differences between disabled and non-disabled pupils (Davis and Watson 2001; Shah 2007). Indeed, within his school, Josh distinguishes the disabled pupils by the adult support they receive and the different rules that operate for them (particularly around queuing for lunch in the school canteen). On this latter issue he perceives this arrangement as grossly unfair and is particularly annoyed with the situation. Again, a series of questions could be asked about these arrangements. Who benefits from these 'special' arrangements? What are the costs of the arrangements? What arguments are presented as a rationale for them? What are the alternatives?

The question of costs is one that could be considered in a number of ways. What came to your mind – financial cost, or perhaps resources and training? From my reading of this narrative, costs could also be considered in relation to Josh's understandings of disability. Josh frames disability as something that is undesirable and deficient relative to the 'norm'. By focusing on what the disabled pupils cannot do, a medical model view of disability is emphasized (Barnes *et al.* 1999). In this way, attention is drawn to the individual 'deficiencies' of disabled pupils, and Josh perceives these pupils as not meeting the normative characteristics of other non-disabled pupils at the school. The cost then becomes one of perpetuating stereotypes and maintaining a value system that affords superiority and legitimacy to a non-disabled status. By reinforcing such stereotypes, I am reminded of Brisenden's observation: 'The word "disabled" is used as a blanket term to cover a large number of people who have nothing in common with each other, except that they do not function in exactly the same way as those people who are called "normal"' (Brisenden 1986, cited in Shakespeare 1998: 22–23). Here, Brisenden alerts us to the differences that exist between disabled people – something Josh seems unable to acknowledge. Recognizing such differences challenges the theoretical explanation of difference underpinned by categorical thinking that essentializes disability. Chapter 1 offers an extended discussion around categorical theorizing and also draws attention to how social theory underpinned by an intersectional lens may be useful for moving beyond this reductionalism and offers possibilities for seeing the pupils whom Josh talks about as gendered, classed and ethnically diverse (Björnsdóttir and Traustadóttir 2010; Connor 2008).

Conceptually, the social model of disability also offers an alternative explanation of disability (Connors and Stalker 2007; Goodley 2011). Take, for example, the remarks Josh makes about the disabled pupils not being able to 'do lessons like us'. The relational nature of the social model of disability would not seek to question individual inabilities but, instead, would centralize the role that school structures, curriculum and pedagogy play in disabling these pupils. So, in response to the claim that the disabled pupils are not able to 'do lessons like us', this alternative view of disability would question why the lessons have not been planned and delivered in ways that enable the disabled pupils to participate more fully. In this instance, adopting such a perspective shifts the attention from the individual 'deficiencies' of the disabled pupils to the preparations and pedagogy of the class teacher. In relation to the school subject HPE, Josh observes that the disabled pupils 'can't kick a fuckin' ball if it's lined up for them'. I can only imagine that the recipients of this gaze are likely to feel frustrated and humiliated, rather than positive and fulfilled by this kind of HPE experience. Is it simply a matter that these pupils need to improve and fit in better with an activity? If this is the conclusion you arrive at, you may want to reflect on the values guiding such an outlook. For example, are you more concerned to ensure pupils experience the activities you enjoyed in HPE as a youngster? Do you want pupils to experience a 'popular' sport? Are you thinking about the school sports teams and wanting to ensure these sports remain part of the curriculum? Of course, each of these responses also triggers a series of counter-questions underpinned by social model thinking. These help to shed light on why the constitution and practices of HPE continue to be exclusionary for disabled pupils and, indeed, many other young people. For example, is the traditional nature of HPE, with an emphasis on competitive team sports, the most appropriate path for HPE to take if it is striving to be inclusive of disabled pupils? Is competition for the minority more important than participation of all? How is HPE supporting lifelong active lifestyles when the curriculum and pedagogy often alienates, rather than stimulates, positive dispositions to HPE? By adopting a social model view of HPE, the conclusion that might be drawn is that disability is magnified because of the exclusionary, socially constructed, activities, pedagogies and spaces that penalize people with impairments.

I want next to briefly focus on the concept of 'inclusion', as it is closely related to the social model of disability. Indeed, both place the onus on change within the education system (policy, curriculum and pedagogy) rather than expecting (disabled) pupils merely to fit into existing practices and arrangements which may be exclusionary (Fitzgerald 2011). It is claimed that 'inclusion has become the mantra of education systems worldwide' (Rioux and Pinto 2010: 622) and, within HPE and community sport, inclusion is increasingly advocated in policy and practice (Thomas and Smith 2009). A few of the comments made by Josh provide an initial indication that discourses around inclusion are also beginning to seep into the vocabulary of pupils. 'Inclusion? That's a fuckin' joke, it's us that end up being excluded.' For me this comment raises key questions about what inclusion is, and whom it seeks to benefit, which are both questions that continue to be debated by academics (Gabel and Danforth 2008; Slee 2009, 2011). I have found Armstrong *et al.*'s (2011: 30) questions particularly useful when contemplating the meaning and purpose of inclusion. They ask: 'What does it really mean to have an education system that is "inclusive"? Who is thought to be in need of inclusion and why? If education should be inclusive, then what practices is it contesting, what common values is it advocating and by what criteria should its successes be judged?'

Did any episodes from the tale prompt you to think more deeply about your understandings or experiences of inclusion? I was drawn to the various gatherings of the disabled pupils – sitting having lunch together and waiting inside the main entrance ready to be transported somewhere. These gatherings made me ponder if inclusion can be promoted when there is intermittent separation of the disabled pupils from other pupils. Does this kind of arrangement, in fact, reinforce differences that are perceived as contrary to the norm? Or can separation work and, if so, what needs to be in place to support pupils like Josh to recognize these practices in more positive ways? I could not help but wonder if these arrangements were initiated by the disabled pupils or simply regulatory mechanisms put in place by the school. This difference is important and, by utilizing the social theory offered by Foucault, an analysis could be made of the nature of power, agency, resistance and knowledge operating in this school context (Foucault 1977).

Research in education in general (Curtin and Clarke 2005; Díez 2010; Mortier *et al.* 2011), and more specifically in HPE (Fitzgerald 2011; Haegele and Kozub 2010), has highlighted the impact that support workers have on the lives of disabled pupils at school. In this tale, I found the role of the support workers, or, as Josh describes them, the 'waiters', intriguing. I wondered how these staff help to promote inclusion and in what ways do they reinforce exclusion and difference? How would you envisage working with a support worker and what kind of inclusion would this promote? Or, indeed, do you think support workers have a useful role at all in schools? You may want to consider the costs and benefits before you draw your conclusions. My final thoughts about this tale and inclusion focus on HPE and, to some extent, I have already rehearsed some of my thoughts when discussing the social model of disability. However, it is perhaps worth rearticulating the possibilities that could open up for critically reviewing the constitution and practices of HPE if a standpoint of inclusion is foregrounded. For example, a number of the questions outlined earlier could be considered in relation to HPE and inclusion. 'Who is thought to be in need of inclusion *in HPE* and why? If *HPE* should be inclusive, then what practices is it contesting, what common values is it advocating and by what criteria should *HPE* successes be judged?' (Armstrong *et al.* 2011: 30). These are questions I am sure you will spend time reflecting upon yourself – questions which are likely to stimulate a set of further questions, rather than simply answers.

'Them special needs kids and their waiters' is a narrative organized around a linear time-line – there is a beginning, middle and end to this tale. In contrast, I would describe 'Second toe syndrome' as a thematic narrative which is time bound, but not in a linear way. It features three key characters, Leo, Leo's Mum and Leo's Dad, who reflect on their childhood and specific incidences important to them. Leo's reflection is a more recent one, whereas Leo's Mum and Leo's Dad have to think back a little further – although they seem to remember with precise detail their stories, as if they are well-rehearsed and talked of, or thought about, often. Unlike 'Them special needs kids and their waiters', the setting for 'Second toe syndrome' shifts from a school to non-school contexts and what might be described as 'leisure spaces'. Each of the characters' narratives could be read separately and, when I did this, I gleaned momentary glimpses into their childhood. Leo's obsession with diggers and scaffolding made me wonder if this would continue to influence his life and future career. I felt sorry for Leo's Dad playing One Man Rugby on his own; it was a shame he had no one else to practise with. I wonder whether he got to wear the All Blacks jersey of his dreams. I didn't envy Leo's Mum having to dodge the sheep droppings and scotch thistles as she refined her sprint starts. I wondered if I would have had the appetite to train under such conditions, but then remembered Leo's Mum wouldn't have known any different. The descriptions of the paddocks and sheep droppings and reference to 'townies' gave me a sense that Leo's Mum and Dad had a rural upbringing and, whilst this may seem idyllic, they had to 'make do' with what was around them in order to enjoy sport. Their experiences are not too dissimilar to Matt's life sketched out at the beginning of Chapter 1 – whilst he lives in an urban area, he, too, seems adept at improvising so that he can play the sport he loves. The descriptions of improvisation and creativity remind me that material resources and opportunities do make a difference to the kinds of lives (including leisure and sport) that young people navigate (McDonald *et al.* 2011).

Whilst considering each character's tale separately was useful, by reading them in combination I began to get a better sense of how these characters' storylines are interrelated. By considering the stories in this way, my reflections focused on issues relating to family and, in particular, sporting 'habitus' within the family. I drew on the thinking of the social theorist Bourdieu to understand habitus as 'a product of history' (Bourdieu 1990: 54) that, over time, produces an individual's life history of social experiences, unique to the individual but also comparable with the habitus of others around them, such as family. In social life we can observe the habitus through choices, preferences and lifestyles (Shilling 2003). For example, Leo, Leo's Mum and Leo's Dad all have something to say about their preferences and outlook towards sport. From my reading, Leo's Mum and Dad offer a performative narrative – they loved sport and were successful (Tinning 1997). We got to hear about Leo's Mum being a 'fabulous starter' and 'always winning', and Leo's Dad 'playing all over the province' and getting 'picked for a rep team'. Sport seemed to be an important part of their childhood passed onto them through their upbringing via the sporting 'habitus' of their parents. Like Kay (2009) has found, it is interesting to note that both characters mention only their fathers as significant influences on their sporting attitudes. As adults, Leo's Mum and Dad seemed keen to instil this sense in their children or, as Leo put it, Saturday was 'team sport' day. On the other hand, for me, Leo's tale evoked a sense that he derived little pleasure from playing soccer or rugby – apart from the occasion when he got a cake for accidentally scoring a try! This sporting achievement was important to Leo and he seemed acutely aware of the impact that this had on his Dad, who, according to Leo, was 'chuffed'. Whilst Leo has little desire to participate in sport, he seems well aware of his parents' enthusiasm and investment in sport. So, which of these characters do you most closely relate to in terms of your experiences and views of sport? You might also want to think about your family and how they supported your socialization into sport. As I read the tale, I am reminded of my own childhood and, just like Leo's Mum and Dad, would have recalled those important wins, individual successes and representative honours I achieved. If your reflection is like mine, you might want to think about how well these experiences equip you to teach, or coach, young people like Leo.

As well as being a tale about family and sport, I read this narrative as also offering some insights into disability and family. At one level it is a reminder that disability is an all-encompassing term which includes a diverse range of people with impairments. The media unhelpfully heighten a perception that disability predominantly concerns wheelchair users. This is not the case. Take, for example, Leo, who has 'dyspraxia'. Are you wondering what this is? Well, if you reviewed a few medical texts or searched the internet you would quickly be able to establish the symptoms and types of behaviour associated with this condition. Words like 'the individual has limited', 'the individual has difficulty' and 'the individual lacks' will feature in the descriptions you find. This approach to understanding disability is underpinned by a medical model view, similar to that articulated by Josh in 'Them special needs kids and their waiters'. Whilst this kind of understanding of disability dominates societal views and perceptions, it is interesting to note that Leo's Mum attempts to downplay the significance of dyspraxia by offering an alternative label for Leo: 'Expert Scaffolder and Digger'. This label emphasizes positive qualities and presents Leo as more than just an individual with deficiencies or a disability.

Whilst supporting the idea that Leo is not defined solely by his dyspraxia, there seems to be a tension between this outlook and his parents' commitment to sport. Following Fitzgerald and Kirk (2009), the tale offers a glimpse into how Leo's parents reconcile his disability with their sporting 'habitus'. For example, Leo is aware of his parents' views towards sport but is unable to reciprocate their passion, desire or success. The pervasive nature of the sporting habitus within Leo's family is exemplified by the various attempts his parents make to 'find' a team sport he could play; first soccer and then rugby. Leo has a strong sense that rugby is valued highly by his father; this game had to be played in a particular way, with hegemonic traditional masculine values dominating (Pringle and Markula 2005). The consequences of not achieving this benchmark are clear to Leo, and the onslaught of verbal abuse, being heckled from the sidelines, remains vivid in this mind – 'Stop playing like a girl's blouse' and 'You're playing like a pack of pansies'. From my reading of these remarks, I felt convinced that Leo's Dad was helping Leo to develop, rather than disrupt, what Evans *et al.* (1996) describe as a 'fragile physical identity'. Leo also experiences the unforgiving way in which team sports, such as rugby, can marginalize players who do not match up to the skills expected of that sport; he stopped receiving ball passes. Would you want Leo on your team? Well, the brutal truth is likely to be 'no' because you, like the players that feature in the tale, would want to win the game. By focusing on such a competitive goal, team sports such as rugby and soccer become exclusionary, particularly for many young disabled people (Fitzgerald 2005). Within community sport and physical education, if the game does become more important than the people playing, then, I would argue, any aspirations about working towards inclusion are likely to be compromised.

In reading this tale one can only speculate about how Leo may have fared with individual sports, aesthetic activities or martial arts, activities that have repeatedly been cited as offering activity possibilities for a broader range of young people (Kirk 2010). It was, in fact, martial arts that Leo eventually took up – a sporting transition that Leo's parents had to reconcile themselves with, not least in relation to their own sporting biographies as well as broader cultural expectations of the 'Kiwi male' (Morrison 2009). His parents eventually found an 'alternative' kind of sport for Leo, and this situation prompted me to question more broadly, 'Why aren't these kinds of activities more prominent in HPE?'

The sporting habitus within Leo's family was disrupted still further when he joined the Cadets. Like martial arts, this was an activity unfamiliar to his parents but one that Leo seems to enjoy and value in the same way his parents do sport. The narrative does not include any commentary from Leo's Mum and Dad about his involvement in the Cadets. I am, therefore, left with a series of unanswered questions about the ways in which they value Cadets: How do they perceive Leo's achievements at Cadets? How are these acknowledged and celebrated? How do Cadets measure up to their sporting achievements and those of Leo's brothers? The answers to these questions are important as they would offer insights about the ways in which Leo is able to generate and convert what Bourdieu (1998) describes as capital (for example, social, physical and cultural) within his family.

I found an intriguing aspect of the tale to be the various references to 'second toe syndrome'. What did this mean and where did it come from? According to the tale, Leo's family believe having a longer second toe increases the likelihood of sporting success. This was something Catherine's Dad had instilled into his family and she passed this thinking onto her children. It was evident from the tale that Leo wished he had a longer second toe and he contemplated if this would have helped him to play rugby better. I do wonder if this family folklore may have inadvertently contributed to limiting Leo's sporting prospects. After all, why would Leo bother to even try to do well in sport when he knew his shorter second toe would always restrict the possibilities for sporting success?

In searching the internet for 'second toe syndrome' I found out that this condition is also known as 'Morton's Foot' or 'Greek Foot', and can lead to instability and musculoskeletal pain. Discovering this made me wonder if the folklore within Leo's family had botched this possible outcome of 'second toe syndrome'. Would Leo be as keen about wanting a longer second toe if he knew the disabling effects this may have on his body? From my reading of 'Second toe syndrome', the dominant discourse seems not to have reflected this alternative account and instead emphasizes an individual weakness that positions Leo less favourably than his parents or siblings. As I thought further about this issue, I also pondered about at what point do such disabling effects become a disability – who decides this, why is the line drawn at a particular point, and who benefits? And why is it that some disabilities matter and mark individuals out more than others? I felt there were contradictory messages within Leo's family about his identity. On the one hand, Leo is presented positively; he is an 'Expert Scaffolder and Digger'. In contrast, the family folklore about the consequences of his shorter second toe seems to reinforce the deficit model that Leo's Mum is attempting to dispel by disregarding the label, dyspraxia. My final thoughts about this narrative, family and disability moved me beyond the storyline found in this particular tale, and I contemplated how, with a change of characters, the tale may have played out. What could we expect if Leo was an only child, a girl, living with one parent, with same-sex parents or had a different kind of disability?

When reflecting upon the tales, 'Them special needs kids and their waiters' and 'Second toe syndrome', I have gleaned insights about how some young disabled people negotiate their everyday lives. Of course, each tale is inextricably connected with broader social structures within society: 'Them special needs kids and their waiters' offers the vantage point of schooling and 'Second toe syndrome', the family. They both reveal how the identity work of these young disabled people is actively played out in these settings and influenced, in part, by interactions with others around them. Their self-narratives reflect the cultural narratives which are available to them in their local contexts. The contested nature of disability and inclusion is reflected in both tales, as are the inequalities experienced by young disabled people. In my view, these understandings should serve as a prompt for you to continually reflect upon your understandings and practices when supporting young disabled people in HPE.

Evans and Davies (2006: 111) remind us that all practice is 'theory-laden', rather than 'theory-free', and the different social theories discussed in Chapter 1 offer a range of possible explanations about the inequalities experienced by young disabled people in HPE and social life more broadly. That is, explanations about the *disabling* effects that much HPE and community sport can have on young disabled people. More specifically, social theory helps to make sense of the way(s) you, and others around you, conceptualize disability. So, if the first question you contemplate when working with a young disabled person is 'What disability has he/she got?', then you might want to reflect upon why this is the first question you ask. What does this question mean? What kind of response are you expecting, and from whom? And how will the response you receive influence your practice? Of course, you may not get the answer you are expecting, particularly if it's from Leo's Mum; remember she argues he is an 'Expert Scaffolder and Digger'. By reflecting on these questions of disability, social theory helps to make sense of the way(s) you understand, and work with, young people (with a disability): for better, or for worse.

In finally reflecting upon the two narratives, I recognize I have paid particular attention to certain characters and also focused theoretically on the social model of disability, notions of inclusion and the thinking of the social theorist Pierre Bourdieu. There are, of course, other characters and sub-plots I could have considered. Take, for example, 'Them special needs kids and their waiters' and the characters Nathan, Anthony, Jane and Helen, all eating their lunch at the special needs table. Their conversations offer possibilities for exploring gendered dynamics operating in schools, and resistance and agency of young disabled people. How do you interpret this part of the tale and what social theory would help you to engage in this process?

Generating and analysing tales about disability, HPE and community sport

Here are some exercises that will help you to explore a number of biographical and institutional narratives focusing on disability, HPE and community sport. As suggested in Chapter 4, when engaging in these exercises, you should establish some supportive ethical ground rules. Also, remember, these exercises can be adapted to stimulate reflection and storytelling about other issues concerning difference and inequality.

Exercise one – searching for 'the facts' about disability

As Chapter 1 outlines, politicians and policy makers often draw on quantitative, survey methodologies, to establish patterns of inequality and from these data feel better positioned to develop policy and programmes that seek to address inequalities. Search the internet to see what quantitative data you can find about disabled people and participation in HPE and community sport. Your search could begin by focusing on data available from national population statistics, government education or sports departments and national (disability) sports organizations. What key facts did you find and what does this tell you about disabled people and participation in HPE and community sport? Next, consider your work context: How would you and your colleagues respond practically to these data?

Whilst this descriptive review is useful, there is another approach that can be taken to reviewing these data that centres on the nature and meaning of the questions asked. By drawing on the survey data you have found, consider: What kinds of categories of disability are identified? How is disability defined? What categories relating to class, ethnicity, gender, sexuality and age are identified? How are different categories grouped together? How are comparisons made between, and within, categories? What categories are absent? How are respondents accounted for who do not identify with the categories adopted? What are the implications of these answers for the meaning and value of these data and broader understandings of disability? With these additional insights in mind, consider again the work context you reflected upon earlier; how would you practically respond now?

Exercise two – stories about HPE, sport and disability

Find a story about a disabled person and HPE or sport. Your search could begin by reviewing school or sports club newsletters, reading the biographies of disabled people, searching blogs, YouTube and discussion forums found on the internet, or searching in some of the academic journals referenced throughout this book. What do the stories tell you about the experiences of the disabled people featured in the tales? And what do they tell you about the practices found in HPE and sport (use Armstrong *et al.*'s (2011) questions on p. 178 to help you to reflect on this issue)? In a small group, share your stories and consider the similarities and differences between the tales. How can these be explained?

Exercise three – knowing disability

Reflect on your HPE experiences as a pupil or practitioner, and see whether you can you recall any stories that circulated about disabled pupils. Write a short story that captures some of these insights. Use the questions on p. 174 to help you to reflect upon your story. In a small group, share your stories and consider the ways in which disabled pupils are understood in these tales. Are these understandings similar or different, and why might this be the case? How would you feel if you were the young person featured in these stories?

Exercise four – working with young disabled people

Can you remember the first time you worked with a young disabled person? What were your thoughts about this young person and your practice? Write a short story that reflects this experience. In a small group, share your stories and consider how disability and inclusion is understood. How can social theory associated with intersectionality help to develop understandings of the young people in these tales?

Note

1 I acknowledge that the international audience of this text will have different expectations regarding the way in which disability and disabled people are referred to. Given that this chapter is influenced by British Disability Studies I believe it is important to adopt the understanding of disability found within this field. This includes referring to 'disabled people' rather than 'people with disabilities'. See, for example, Barnes *et al.* (1999: 7): 'We will avoid the phrase "people with disabilities" because it implies that the impairment defines the identity of the individual, blurs the crucial conceptual distinction between impairment and disability and avoids the question of causality.' This understanding of disability is also accepted and used by the British Council for Disabled People (BCDP) and the Disabled Peoples' International (DPI).

References

Archer, L., Hutchings, M. and Leathwood, C. (2001) 'Engaging in commonality and difference: Theoretical tensions in the analysis of working class women's education discourses', *International Journal of Sociology of Education*, 11(1): 41–62.

Armstrong, D., Armstrong, A. C. and Spandagou, I. (2011) 'Inclusion: By choice or by chance?', *International Journal of Inclusive Education*, 15(1): 29–39.

Ashby, C. (2010) 'The trouble with normal: The struggle for meaningful access for middle school students with developmental disability labels', *Disability and Society*, 25(3): 345–58.

Barnes, C., Mercer, G. and Shakespeare, T. (1999) *Exploring Disability: A Sociological Introduction*, Cambridge: Polity Press.

Barton, L. and Armstrong, F. (eds) (2007) *Policy, Experience and Change: Cross Cultural Reflections on Inclusive Education*, Dordrecht: Springer.

Björnsdóttir, K. and Traustadóttir, R. (2010) 'Stuck in the land of disability? The intersection of learning difficulties, class, gender and religion', *Disability and Society*, 25(1): 49–62.

Bourdieu, P. (1990) *The Login of Practice*, Cambridge: Polity Press.

——(1998) *Practical Reason: On the Theory of Action*, Cambridge: Polity Press.

Connor, D. J. (2008) *Urban Narratives: Portraits in Progress, Life at the Intersections of Learning Disability, Race and Social Class*, New York: Peter Lang.

Connors, C. and Stalker, K. (2007) 'Children's experiences of disability: Pointers to a social model of childhood disability', *Disability and Society*, 22(1): 19–33.

Curtin, M. and Clarke, G. (2005) 'Listening to young people with physical disabilities' experiences of education', *International Journal of Disability, Development and Education*, 52(3): 195–214.

Davis, J. and Watson, N. (2001) 'Where are the children's experiences? Analysing social and cultural exclusion in "special" and "mainstream" schools', *Disability and Society*, 16(5): 671–87.

Díez, A. M. (2010) 'School memories of young people with disabilities: An analysis of barriers and aids to inclusion', *Disability and Society*, 25(2): 163–75.

Eide, A. H. and Ingstad, B. (eds) (2011) *Disability and Poverty. A Global Challenge*, Bristol: The Policy Press.

Evans, J. and Davies, B. (2006) 'The sociology of physical education', in D. Kirk, D. Macdonald and M. O'Sullivan (eds) *The Handbook of Physical Education*, London: Sage Publications, pp. 109–22.

Evans, J., Davies, B. and Penney, D. (1996) 'Teachers, teaching and the social construction of gender relations', *Sport, Education and Society*, 1(2): 165–83.

Fitzgerald, H. (2005) 'Still feeling like a spare piece of luggage? Embodied experiences of (dis)ability in physical education and school sport', *Physical Education and Sport Pedagogy*, 10(1): 41–59.

——(2011) '"Drawing"' on disabled students' experiences of physical education and stakeholder responses', *Sport, Education and Society*, DOI: 10.1080/13573322.2011.609290.

Fitzgerald, H. and Kirk, D. (2009) 'Identity work: Young disabled people, family and sport', *Leisure Studies*, 28(4): 469–88.

Foucault, M. (1977) *Discipline and Punish: The Birth of the Prison*, trans. Alan Sheridan, New York: Vintage Books.

Gabel, S. L. and Danforth, S. (eds) (2008) *Disability and the Politics of Education. An International Reader*, Oxford: Peter Lang.

Goffman, E. (1968) *Stigma*, Harmondsworth: Pelican.

Goodley, D. (2011) *Disability Studies. An Interdisciplinary Introduction*, London: Sage Publications.

Haegele, J. A. and Kozub, F. M. (2010) 'A continuum of paraeducator support for utilization in adapted physical education', *TEACHING Exceptional Children Plus*, 6, Article 2. Online. Available from: <http://escholarship.bc.edu/education/tecplus/vol6/iss5/art2> (accessed 27 January 2011).

Hevey, D. (1992) *The Creatures that Time Forgot: Photography and Disability Imagery*, London: Routledge.

Higgins, N., MacArthur, J. and Kelly, B. (2009) 'Including disabled children at school: Is it really as simple as "a, b, c"?', *International Journal of Inclusive Education*, 13(5): 471–87.

Holt, L. (ed.) (2011) *Geographies of Children, Youth and Families. An International Perspective*, London: Routledge.

Hunt, P. (1966) 'A critical condition', in P. Hunt (ed.) *Stigma: The Experience of Disability*, London: The Catholic Book Club, pp. 145–59.

Kay, T. (ed.) (2009) *Fathering through Sport and Leisure*, London: Routledge.

Kirk, D. (2010) *Physical Education Futures*, London: Routledge.

McDonald, P., Pini, B., Bailey, J. and Price, R. (2011) 'Young people's aspirations for education, work, family and leisure', *Work, Employment and Society*, 25(1): 68–84.

Miller, E. J. and Gwynne, G. V. (1972) *A Life Apart. A Pilot Study of Residential Institutions for the Physically Handicapped and the Young Chronic Sick*, London: Tavistock Publications.

Morrison, C. (2009) 'Deconstructing a narrative of physical culture', in H. Fitzgerald (ed.) *Disability and Youth Sport*, London: Routledge, pp. 132–44.

Mortier, K., Desimpel, L., De Schauwer, E. and Van Hove, G. (2011) '"I want support, not comments": Children's perspectives on supports in their life', *Disability & Society*, 26(2): 207–21.

O'Sullivan, M. and MacPhail, A. (eds) (2010) *Young People's Voices in Physical Education and Youth Sport*, London: Routledge.

Polkinghorne, D. (1995) 'Narrative configuration in qualitative analysis', in J. Amos Hatch and R. Wisniewski (eds) *Life History and Narrative*, London: The Falmer Press, pp. 5–23.

Priestley, M. (1999) 'Discourse and identity: Disabled children in mainstream high schools', in M. Corker and S. French (eds) *Disability Discourse*, Buckingham: Open University Press, pp. 92–102.

Pringle, R. and Markula, P. (2005) 'No pain is sane after all: A Foucauldian analysis of masculinities and men's experiences in rugby', *Sociology of Sport Journal*, 22(4): 472–97.

Rioux, M. H. and Pinto, P. C. (2010) 'A time for the universal right to education: Back to basics', *British Journal of Sociology of Education*, 31(5): 621–42.

Shah, S. (2007) 'Special or mainstream? – The views of disabled students', *Research Papers in Education*, 22(4): 425–42.

Shakespeare, T. (ed.) (1998) *The Disability Reader: Social Science Perspectives*, London: Cassell.

Shilling, C. (2003) *The Body and Social Theory*, London: Sage Publications.

Slee, R. (2004) 'Meaning in the service of power', in L. Ware (ed.) *Ideology and the Politics of (In)Exclusion*, Oxford: Peter Lang.

——(2009) 'The inclusion paradox: The cultural politics of difference', in M. W. Apple, W. Au and L. A. Gandin (eds) *The Routledge International Handbook of Critical Education*, London: Routledge, pp. 177–89.

——(2011) *The Irregular School. Exclusion, Schooling and Inclusive Education*, London: Routledge.

Thomas, N. and Smith, A. (2009) *Disability Sport and Society*, London: Routledge.

Tinning, R. (1997) 'Performance and participation discourses in human movement: Toward a socially critical physical education', in J-M. Fernández-Balboa (ed.) *Critical Postmodernism in Human Movement, Physical Education and Sport*, New York: State University of New York Press, pp. 99–119.

Wright, J. (2004) 'Post-structural methodologies: the body, schooling and health', in J. Evans, B. Davies and J. Wright (eds) *Body Knowledge and Control. Studies in the Sociology of Physical Education and Health*, London: Routledge, pp. 19–31.

Index